RAYLYNN VAN OORT

From Sh*t to Sunshine

A MEMOIR

RAYLYNN VAN OORT

From Sh*t to Sunshine

A MEMOIR

From Sh*t to Sunshine
Published by Raylynn Van Oort
Helena, Montana, U.S.A.

Copyright ©2024, RAYLYNN VAN OORT. All rights reserved.

No part of this book may be reproduced in any form or by any mechanical means, including information storage and retrieval systems without permission in writing from the publisher/author, except by a reviewer who may quote passages in a review. All images, logos, quotes, and trademarks included in this book are subject to use according to trademark and copyright laws of the United States of America.

VAN OORT, RAYLYNN, Author
SH*T TO SUNSHINE
RAYLYNN VAN OORT

Library of Congress Control Number: 2024918797

ISBN: 979-8-9913623-0-6 (paperback)
ISBN: 979-8-9913623-1-3 (hardcover)
ISBN: 979-8-9913623-2-0 (ebook)

BIOGRAPHY & AUTOBIOGRAPHY / Memoirs
BIOGRAPHY & AUTOBIOGRAPHY / Survival
TRUE CRIME / General

Editorial and Art Direction: Pique Publishing, Inc.

Cover image © Tamara Gore, August 28, 2019, Unsplash

QUANTITY PURCHASES: Schools, companies, professional groups, clubs, and other organizations may qualify for special terms when ordering quantities of this title.

For more information, visit ASprigofHope.com or email RaylynnVanOort@gmail.com

All rights reserved by RAYLYNN VAN OORT
This book is printed in the United States of America.

I dedicate this book to YOU.
You who are reading this.
You who are in need of hope.
Every word written is dedicated to YOU.

DISCLAIMER

This book is a memoir based on true events. It reflects my recollections of experiences over time and as recounted from my journals. Some of the names of people mentioned in my story have been changed, some events have been compressed, and dialogue has been recreated.

CONTENT WARNING

My story is a way to shed light on my journey of survival.

My experiences include, but are not limited to physical, verbal, mental, sexual, and emotional abuse; loss and grief; brainwashing, manipulation, and coercion; religious or spiritual abuse; abandonment; mental health issues; eating disorders and body image; loss of autonomy; harsh conditions; incarceration and reintegration challenges; and controlling relationships. My intent is to offer hope if you, too, have had any of these experiences.

Please prioritize your well-being and seek support if needed.

August 26, 1996—Havre, Montana

"LET HER GO!" I hollered as the cop handcuffed Jill. "She had nothing to do with this!" I was already handcuffed and stood by the side of the cop car with its lights flashing. My heart was pounding. Breathing heavy and sharp, I looked around frantically trying to find my daughter, Sunny.

"Oh God! Where is she?!" I couldn't find her or the younger kids in my care. Nowhere. Fear and worry gripped my heart. *Dear God, please keep her safe. Keep all of them safe.*

Cop cars were scattered haphazardly around the motel parking lot located on the outskirts of Havre, Montana, where we had spent the night. The sting came in the early morning, hours before we could check out of the motel. We, the check-writing criminals, had been captured. But *I* was the one who was writing checks. They rounded us up, handcuffed, and ready for transport. Five women. Four kids. Two men had already escaped capture. They ran out the back door. They fled. Ran across the open field. No concern for the rest of us. According to Curly, they'd pay a price. For their freedom.

I stood beside the cop car, hands behind my back, staring at the official emblem on its side. Reading the word below focusing on each letter. One at a time. Slowly. P-O-L-I-C-E. I tried to decrease the intensity of my breathing, but this visual only heightened the panic. I looked up as the stern-faced cop opened the back door.

"Get in," he said without emotion.

A gentleman. Opening the door for me, I thought, sarcastically attempting to inject a bit of jovial junk in my veins. *I'm a jacked-up jolly junkie,* I silently self-proclaimed. My internal dialogue was meant to diminish the dread of what's ahead. Cushion the blow.

Yet, apprehension created a cascade of sweat down my back.

Seeping from my perspiring armpits. Plunging down my neckline. Between my breasts. My imprisoned hands. Clammy.

Bending slightly at the waist, I backed my butt in and plopped it on the seat. Twisting forward, I put one foot in at a time and pushed myself back as far as I could go. The cop car door slammed shut. The force made me jump. With my hands cuffed tightly behind my back, it was difficult to sit straight in the seat. The more I twisted to try to get comfortable, the more the hastily snapped shackles dug into my wrists. I'd never been in a cop car before.

It. Was. Terrifying.

As the siren began wailing, lights continued whirling, twirling, and emitting their standard red and blue strobe stream. We left the motel parking lot and headed to God-only-knew where. I squeezed my eyes tightly shut and said a silent prayer. *Please Jesus, help.*

I stared at the cage-like partition separating us from our captor. Claustrophobia flooded my brain. A rancid sweat smell from the seat filled my nostrils. Panic robbed my lungs of sufficient oxygen. My eyes flew to the door handle. *I've got to get out!*

Self-talk soothing did little good. I looked out the window as the buildings flew by. Counting them one by one. Self-regulation by simple thinking tasks I've learned over the years can help. *1-2-3-4-5-6.* I continued watching. Counting. Detaching from the situation. My breathing slowed.

As a bit of sanity was restored, my thoughts turned to Sunny. Horrified at our situation, I prayed, *Lord, please let her be okay.* But my next thought. Terror.

Curly was going to be furious. And I'd be the scapegoat. For the screwup.

* * * *

Single file into the jailhouse. Literally a house converted for criminals. A convict castle. Across the drawbridge we went. Armed guards in the front. Armed guards in the rear. For the big, bad, check-bouncing babes. Clothes stripped. Convict coveralls donned. Fingerprints filed.

Click. Unlocked. We marched in single file through an entry door made of bars, then up a set of stairs. Ten steps. A landing. Ten more steps. A landing. There were doors on each side of a short hallway. A door straight ahead.

Which would we get? Door one? Door two? Or door three? Which one holds the grand prize? The prisoner prize.

Sharon and I were escorted through the door on the left. Jill, Loretta, and Lisa were taken through the door on the right. Our handcuffs were removed. We looked around at our new accommodations. A television sat on a stand in the corner of the small entry room with two stiff chairs facing it. In the dim light, we could see a connecting bathroom next to a doorless room with a bunk bed. Bare. Cold. Confining.

This was because I had written bad checks as commanded by Curly. His authorization was the key to the cash box. The credit cards. The checks on my account. Used for a holy purpose. Green light. Go for grub. Money for motel.

"It will be covered by the blood of atonement," he had explained. "We're cleansing the financial system." Checks. Banks. Credit cards. Stores. Motels. Any place requiring payment was a target. For Curly. Ironically, it was always places that provided our "needs." But most of all, his needs. His wants. His wishes. All bought with a price. And the price was us. No bank account or credit card ever displayed the name of Curly Thornton. We were the patsies. The pawns in his quest for the kingdom that he believed already belonged to him. And now we were prisoners.

Now what, Lord? I prayed. Dread overtook my thoughts. Panic set in. *What will Curly do?* He's going to be spitting angry. It was the hitting angry I feared most. I slumped down in one of the TV chairs and put my head in my hands. As tears welled up in my eyes, I swallowed hard. I couldn't fall apart now. Not here. Not in this place.

Maybe this is part of the plan. Atonement for the prison system? *After all, we must be here for a purpose.* Curly's purpose. Which means it's God's purpose, according to Curly. *What do we do now?*

Sharon and I laid on the bunk beds. Exhausted. The key turned in the lock. As we sat up, the guard brought in trays of food.

"Dinner time," he announced as he set them on the table. "I'll be back shortly for the trays," he said over his shoulder as he headed out the door. Click. Lock secured. I stared down at the bowl of unappetizing creamy-looking soup with gray chunks swimming in it. A hard-white dinner roll. A bowl of green Jell-O. A carton of two-percent milk.

I might as well eat. There's nothing else to do.

When the guard returned to collect the trays, he counted the silverware before he left. Silverware, we found out later, could be used as weapons in the hands of these "dangerous" check writers.

Click. Room secured. Once again. Night one in the Hill County Jail.

The day before was such a relief to leave Curly in Minot, North Dakota, for a short while. Less stress. Less intensity. Less beatings. I liked the separation. The split. The freedom.

This freedom, however, would last several years. No hits. No punches. No bruises. There was safety. Behind these bars.

Substitute Father—1960

I wanted a dad. One to love me. After all, that's what I thought dads did. Love. Nurture. Care. Mine had done so before he died when I was two. At least I got a new one. A replacement dad. Of course, he'll do the same.

Nope. Not even close. Jeff's object of love was himself. He, my adoptive dad, was the taker. We were the expected givers. And love to him meant doing his bidding. Running when he called. Obeying his every command. My adoptive dad.

His charisma was seductive. He'd seduced my mom and I'm not talking sexually. At this point, anyway. He had wanted her and us. So, he set the trap. Snapped it closed at the right time. We were all caught in the snare. A noose. Pulling. At his every command.

Jeff demanded that Brenda and I call him dad. "He's not our dad," Brenda would adamantly scowl, desperately loyal to our birth father, Raymond. She complied, eventually. Jeff was determined to erase our real dad from existence. His photographs didn't exist. His name couldn't escape our mouths. He wasn't even a ghost—he just never *was*.

My life was filled with attempts to achieve perfection. For him. Jeff. The Dad King. Plan A executed to do what he commanded. Failed. Figure out a Plan B to succeed…still…no matter what. It failed, too? Plan C. *For SURE I'll do it…this time. This way. Crap! It's a mess. Now what?* Plan D commence.

You see, we were pawns in his plan. His game to elude the draft. A family. A working ranch. So he used us. Me. My mom. My sister. A ready-made family. We needed him for support. So the good ol' USA said no. He dodged the draft. We got the shaft. In more ways than one.

I wanted attention. Dad hugs. Proud-father accolades. Those were few and far between. I figured it was my lack of perfection. My failures. My not-good-enough behaviors. Be perfect, get a pat on the head. Be not-so perfect, get scolded. Ridiculed. Berated. Spanked.

My ability to anticipate unexpected problems came from striving to be perfect during my childhood years. After all, that's what Jeff had expected. He saw himself as the king of the hill. The cream of the crop. Not just on the ranch where we lived in Waterloo, Montana, but anywhere he went. Couldn't displease him. He'd roar. I bowed. I was his subject. I was born to serve. As were my mom and sister, his parents and brother, too. Anyone who came under his spell.

Perfection became my goal each and every day. If I didn't achieve it, I lied. If I missed the high mark of excellence, I lied. If I didn't meet his expectations, I lied. I feared not being perfect, worse than the punishment for lying. At least he noticed me. Punishment was still attention.

I matured into a shy, insecure high schooler pushing to be perfect. After all, I had to prove my worth. My excellence. My equal status to my high-achieving sister, Brenda. Music came easy to her. I busted my butt practicing hour after hour on the piano. She excelled in sports. Queen of the cheerleaders. A state track-meet-going hurdler. I spent hours practicing just to keep up. But didn't. Instead, I quit as a senior when an underclassman showed me up. Faster with better form than me on the hurdles. I couldn't take the chance at being second best. Even to a better athlete than me. It made me less than. Less than perfect. In Jeff's eyes. Quitting was the only answer to not humiliate him.

Brenda spent minimal hours studying yet was chosen to give the valedictory address with her almost-perfect grades. I couldn't disappoint. She was my best friend. My hero. I followed in her footsteps four years later. Hours of studying earned me a 4.0 GPA. I received my high school diploma wearing the coveted valedictorian gold ropes around my neck. My valedictorian address filled with adoration for my fabulous teacher, Mr. Jeff Lauderdale—my adoptive dad, my self-appointed Dad King.

The king who marched around our house like a proud peacock, strutting his stuff as he opened the door to the bathroom and marched in. Naked.

I tried to avert my eyes as I sat nude in the tub. I could tell he was relieving himself in the toilet not even a foot away from where I sat horrified as I covered my sixteen-year-old breasts with my wet washrag. Humiliated. Shamefaced at my curiosity, I wanted to take a peek. I squeezed my eyes tightly shut holding my breath until he flushed the toilet. He laughed at my embarrassment and shut the door behind him as he left.

Other sexually charged encounters still burn in my mind. Painful memories I'd locked in a mental prison and thrown away the key. The hiding place secure in the deep recesses of my brain.

Betrayal of a young girl still missing her dad. Her real dad. The one who would never have hurt her. Who loved her. Who would have protected her. Who would never have done these un-fatherly things to his maturing, innocent young daughter. The one who never came home to his daughters and wife. Instead fell asleep at the wheel, overturned his panel truck, and crashed at the exit. Dead.

No, this dad would never have done these unspeakable things. But Jeff did. My substitute dad did.

Total Assholes—1964

"Is he dead?" my mom asked, standing with the .22 rifle still warm from recent firing gripped tightly in her hands. She lowered the gun as I climbed over the fence searching for the blasted victim. I stopped to pick up a bird leg with the rest of him dangling dead. Shot to shreds. *Poor bird,* my 8-year-old self thought.

"I think so," I replied to her question of his viability.

Early summer had been spent faithfully covering her precious plants with light, gauzy cheesecloth. A sure-fire way, she thought, to keep the birds from nosediving into the delicious strawberry dessert bar. Windy days didn't always cooperate with concealment. Blown-away gauze cloth lay useless, exposing juicy, red fruit seen by the watchful eyes of food-scouting robins.

They'd dine to their red-breasted heart's content, leaving half-pecked parts and pieces unfit for human consumption. Frustrated at the inconsiderate hole-pecking birds destroying the ripe fruit of her gardening labor, she went and got Jeff's small rifle. I didn't even know she could shoot. Her anger at the destructive red pilfering pests created a bird-murdering monster out of my mama.

She enlisted my help to determine the deceased-ness of the target of her temper. As I held up the stringy carcass of the condemned, my mom turned a bit green.

"I can't believe I hit it! I killed it!" Her anger evaporated as she looked down at the gun in her hand. "Damn it!" she muttered as she turned on her heel and headed inside the house.

I wasn't sure what that meant. Regret at assassinating our fair-feathered friend? No clue. My mom was kind-hearted and cared for animals. As long as they weren't destroying her garden. Or had four legs and was called a horse. She hated horses. I mean she

HATED horses. I think it was more fear than hate.

The working part of the ranch had numerous buildings. A large shop to fix the tractors, balers, and other necessary equipment. Up the road sat a small barn with three hay-filled feeding areas to entice each cow to shove her head through the narrow opening. Once each munched her meal, we'd close the loosely fitting stanchion around her neck. It made milking much easier.

Nearby stood a massive old rock barn with horse stalls lining the walls on both sides. The double-wide doors opened to a large corral. Sitting on the far side of the corral was a cement watering trough. At least ten feet long, four feet wide, and a good three feet deep. The edge measured about six inches on every side. A hot summer dip would have been fun, but it was strictly a watering hole for the horses.

On one particular day, after returning from a quick trip to Whitehall with Mom, I was heading to milk our cow, Bonnie. A gentle old soul who didn't act like she had a care in the world. Milking her was easy. I'd scoot the stool next to her side, grease up my hands with Bag Balm, and start milking. The barn cats sat within squirting distance, anticipating a stream of milk hitting their face. They wiped and licked as quickly as they could. Giggling each time, I went back to the chore of filling the bucket to take home.

After opening the stanchion, I shooed Bonnie out of the barn and headed out the door, bucket in hand.

I saw my mom heading to the hired hand's house with a bag of recently purchased groceries. Still dressed in her go-to-town clothes. Elbow-length sleeves and ankle-reaching pants. She'd shed her Jeff-deemed inappropriate town-going attire…sleeveless shirt and knee-length shorts…before we left the ranch. An important peace-keeping wardrobe change.

Her destination sat on the other side of the corral—cutting through made the walk much shorter. I saw her glance around, checking for the dreaded evil horses. The coast clear, she opened the gate and headed across.

Her movement was noticed by Cherry, Jeff's Appaloosa horse that was lounging in the barn. She loved attention. Out she trotted toward my mom, a bit of petting in her horse mind. Totally terrified, I watched my mom run lickety split with Cherry in pursuit. The horse did a double-time trot to intercept Mom's gate goal. Horrified, Mom diverted to the water trough straight ahead, catapulted from ground to ledge while grocery bag contents took flight. Her balance-beam edge walking triggered a bit of horse play. Cherry trotted beside her and round and round they went.

"Git away!" my mom yelled at the top of her lungs, bringing Jeff running from the nearby shop and Brenda from the calf barn. We all stood frozen in place.

The laughter started with my sister's giggle, making its way to me and, finally, Jeff. Hysterical hoots and hollers could be heard a mile away. We watched waiting for her beam-routine dismount, but none came.

"You ASSHOLES! Get this horse away from me!" she screamed at her audience of three as the horse, her playmate, continued their game of cat and mouse—or mom and horse.

We stood mesmerized watching Mom fast stepping, airplane arms flying, attempting to stay upright. The frantic pitch of her plea set Jeff in motion. Jumping the fence, he shooed Cherry back into the barn and shut the door. He headed back to the trough to lend Mom a hand, but she was on the verge of spitting nails and refused his help. A determined dismount finally ended her beam routine.

Irate and furious, she spat her frustration at us. "Thanks for the help, you assholes!" She marched off heading back to the house in a huff.

Brenda and I exchanged glances, swallowing the giggles rising to the surface. "Oh boy!" Brenda said, anticipating our unwelcome homecoming for not helping.

Playing in the yard with our big gentle dog, Bob, we delayed coming face-to-face with Mom. We were sure we'd get scolded for not rescuing her. Instead, we played tag with each other while Bob chased us both. A sweet Border Collie/St. Bernard mix with a short, little bobbed tail—the reason we called him Bob.

As we rounded the corner of the house, we heard the normal call to supper. "Come set the table!" It was our job to set out plates and silverware for four. We started shoving each other to see who'd go first into the house. Being older and taller, Brenda won. I slowly opened the screen door and tiptoed in followed by the foot-taller, four-year-older sister.

"Go wash your hands."

We ran—not walked—to the bathroom to avoid a motherly encounter. We washed, rinsed, and dried as slowly as possible. Cleansing could only last so long before she'd get suspicious.

Silently, we performed the assigned table-setting task as Mom stood stirring her homemade beef stew on the stove. Jeff arrived, and after washing up, sat down at the head of the table.

Not a word was spoken. Mom set the large pot in the center of the table and dished up our bowls with the steaming soup.

Still. Not a word.

We bowed our heads, pressed our hands together prayer style. And said "Grace," as was tradition in our Catholic household. "Amen," we all said in unison. Hoping it meant not only the end of the prayer but the end of the knife-cutting tension.

After taking a few bites, Mom said quietly, "You know you're all total assholes."

Spoons stopped in midair. Swallowing hard, I held my breath. *Oh no.*

Calmly Mom kept eating. Spoonful by spoonful. We stared. Wondering, *What now?!*

Nothing more was said. Such was life on the White Rock Ranch. Milk cows. Evil horses. Assholes. And beef stew.

Not-So-Lovable Daughter—1966

In late spring, we put cattle up on the Bureau of Land Management Forest land to graze. By we, I mean my Grandpa and Jeff. They were the cowpunchers. The expert horsemen. The flat-out professional cattlemen. They knew this work like the back of their hands. A solid seat in the saddle. Reins in their weather-beaten hands. Guiding their horses like puppet masters. A slight move of the hand to the left or right steered the horse right where they wanted it to go. Well trained. Well behaved. Perfect for ranch work. On the White Rock Ranch located eleven miles outside of Whitehall, Montana.

A small railroad town of about a thousand people, Whitehall sat nestled in the Jefferson Valley, named for the river traversing around its outlying borders. Railway workers and ranchers. Fishermen and hunters. Businessmen and bar regulars. All made up the diversity of this little town I called home. The gossip train ran trackless from house to house, unrestrained, sharing its insider secrets amassed at every stop. Typical small-town Montana.

I was the chosen sidekick that spring. At ten years old, I must have finally passed the horsemanship course directed by the unspoken approval or disapproval of Jeff. *Phew!* I sat a bit higher in my small saddle on my beloved old horse named Hillbilly. We called him Billy for short. The gentlest animal who did his job well making any inexperienced rider look fabulous. And fabulous we looked. All decked out in my cowboy boots and hat. *Ride 'em cowgirl! Let's go!*

I followed Grandpa and Jeff to the pasture where the cows and calves were held awaiting their move to higher ground. Forest land filled with edible grass. Any cow's summer dream resort. The jagged mountain horizon setting into a hilly sea of golden brush. Their euphoria. All that stood between them and their awaited feast was a rusty barbed-wire fence with a gate.

Jeff and Grandpa began separating out the healthiest cows and calves. Chosen to go. Picked for the pasture. And I was their gate opener. The keeper of the passage to cow dreamland. So I began practicing. I nudged Billy slightly with the heel of my boot to get him to inch closer to the gate. I reached down with one hand to grab the gate closure while holding tight to the saddle horn with the other. Keeping steady, I began maneuvering my horse Billy sideways and pulled it open.

Bingo! Success! I can do it! This was going to be an amazing day. Jeff would see how skilled I became. How valuable I could be to him. Finally. Today. Maybe he'd even say he was proud of me. The anticipation of receiving praise from him was thrilling. Positive strokes were few and far between. *This* would be the day. I'd show him how worthwhile I could be to him. *I'm going to be the best gatekeeper EVER!*

Jeff began herding a chosen cow–calf pair toward the gate. I'd been watching carefully so I knew when to spring into action. *Now!* Billy and I opened the gate and watched as the cow cantered through with her calf following close behind. Pair after pair were chosen and sent through the gate. My gate to praise was opening and closing time after time. I smiled secretly to myself.

The day was going so well…until that moment. Jeff's angry eyes were spitting nails. All directed at me.

The day that began with such exhilaration turned to utter despair with just one simple question from Jeff. "How many pairs is that?"

I swallowed hard. My 10-year-old heart was pounding out of my chest in fear. I looked at him wide-eyed and whispered in bewilderment, "I don't know."

His response thundered in my ears, "How stupid are you? Aren't you smart enough to count? I need to know how many pairs we put out to pasture so I know how many to bring down. How stupid are you?" He stared at me in anger. I crumbled in failure as tears slowly rolled down my cheeks.

My thoughts raced back to the early morning hour when I had saddled my horse and prepared for our ride. I didn't remember him telling me to count. Not a word. Not even a mention. Maybe I was supposed to just know that. Maybe I was just that stupid. Maybe he needed a different daughter. Maybe he needed my smart sister. Not stupid Raylynn. I hung my head in shame as he went racing through the gate to try to count the ones we had already put through. One more time I had proved worthless. A huge mistake that cost me his trust. Just a failure. As always.

Would I ever get it right? Would I ever do anything he would be proud of? Nope! I was the stupid one. Good-for-nothing. Just plain dumb. Again.

I sat in fear waiting for him to return. Waiting for his next tirade of criticism and berating to rip holes in my heart. I saw him come trotting around the bend on Cherry. His face beet red with anger, he glared at me in total hatred.

Is this truly how a loving dad looks at his daughter? Even if she screws up? Shaking with fear, I hung my head in shame. Couldn't even look at him. I knew what was coming. My dressing-down. Tongue-lashing. Raking over the coals. Hot coals of contempt.

"How in the hell am I supposed to keep track if you don't count them? What kind of intelligence does it take to know that? We can't afford to lose any! Thanks to you, who knows how many we'll lose? How stupid," he said through gritted teeth.

My heart was broken. A total mess-up. As always. I snuck a sideways peek at my Grandpa who sat stoic-faced. I silently begged him to defend me. He wouldn't even glance my way. But I could see the set of his jaw. His disagreement with Jeff's treatment of me was apparent. His silence said everything. Jeff was in charge. Now. And always.

Jeff spat his estimated number in my direction. Back to work. More pairs. More gate openings. I counted each and every pair, terrified that I would mess up again. The last pair trotted through. Gate closed for the last time. We finally headed home. I rode behind him and Grandpa hoping he'd forget I was there. My head ached. My heart hurt. Bad. I guess I deserved it. Because I was bad. Just a screwup.

As we neared the barn, I vowed to myself that I'd work harder.

Get smarter. Somehow. I'd have to be. If I wanted this dad to love his not-so-lovable daughter. *I can change. I will change. I can. Really, I can.* I vowed...*I will. Somehow. Someday. Soon.*

A beautiful day turned ugly. Dark. Depressing. High to low. Smart to stupid. Lovable to unloved. Once again. Deep breath. Sigh. Cry.

Egg-Cellence — 1971

"It's too HARD!" Jeff said, scowling at me. The harshness radiating from his glaring eyes made me cower. "I told you to cook it over-easy," he said, eyeballing the non-runny egg yolk as he poked it with his fork.

Yep, and it's SO easy to get it just perfect for you! Silently, I spat the sarcastic words I wished I could say. Instead, I stood shamefaced at my lack of perfectionism. Internal sarcasm was a cork stopper for the "bladder behind my eyeballs," as my mom so often referred to my lack of tear control.

He slammed down the fork. "Fry me another one. And do it right this time."

And I did. As he poked the second-round attempt, he looked up with a satisfied smirk. "Perfect. Good job."

My heart leapt on the springboard of his superior rating. I craved his approval, which I didn't get often. Perfection was expected. To Jeff, there was no lower standard that would be acceptable. At least for me and my sister, Brenda.

As a teacher and principal of Whitehall High School, he was strict but fair. And cared for the underdogs. The misfits. The kids whose family life wasn't the best. He spotted greatness in the depth of their personal depravity. He'd be the barber for kids whose parents couldn't afford to pay, or chose not to pay, for haircuts. At the insistence of the football coach for a bit of a snip of their locks, they'd come to Mr. Lauderdale for help. Because he cared. A desperate cry for help on the verge of suicide. Mr. Lauderdale was the hero that helped. Because he cared. He called me out of class to help a frightened freshman girl. Not warned of her soon-to-start womanly menarche, the unexpected experience terrified her. And she'd gone to the trustworthy and compassionate Mr. Lauderdale for help. Because he cared.

And although Jeff's compassion was very rarely focused on me, I saw the beautiful fruit born of the compassion he extended to students at school. He modeled it well.

These charismatic, compassionate characteristics were part of his professional persona. As soon as his foot crossed the home threshold, a switch flipped. The public pretense mask was peeled off. The real Jeff emerged. Like a hornet masquerading as a beautiful butterfly who creeps back into a dark cocoon each night, dragging his underbee-ings with him into the darkness. A Jekyll and Hyde narcissistic personality. As far as he was concerned, he was the bee's knees. The best of the best. A cut above any and all the rest. And we should be eternally blest. To belong to him.

He was a master at finesse, using a romance ruse as a ploy to pounce. On a grieving widow and her two dadless children. What a grand gesture of love to take us in. The hero to the helpless. A home builder for the bereaved. Yet his deep-seated need for power and control was disguised as the head-of-household rule enforcer given a daddy-duty obligation. Our vulnerability allowed him to become a manic manipulation master. He tugged and jerked our strings as he saw fit. He said jump. We asked how high.

Although Jeff required excellence at home, public perfection was of utmost importance. Our behavior reflected on him. We were spit-polished trophies displayed in his personal showoff case as proof of his superiority. His importance. His worth. Disgraceful behavior might tarnish his trophies, taint his reputation.

His disgraceful definition didn't mean a D grade. It meant less than all A's. Being a four-year straight-A student wasn't a goal to reach. It was the expected accession to the peak of perfection. Anything less was unacceptable. No accolades for accomplishment.

Valedictorian was not an honor bestowed. It was a family tradition upheld by every graduating senior with the last name of Lauderdale. Jeff and his brother. My sister. Now me. Bring no shame to the name was the game. For his reputation was at stake.

Our days were filled with expectations. And control. He demanded that "What happens at home, stays at home." Home was sacred according to Jeff. His sanctuary where secrecy was imposed no matter what happened. This was my normal. But all that took place during my growing up years. Wasn't normal.

Despite his controlling, haughty attitude, valuable lessons were learned. He and my mom worked exceptionally hard, modeling a strong work ethic. The clock didn't dictate when work was done. Especially living on a ranch. Calves were born at midnight or later. Chores were required after school. Cows still had to be milked. Eggs still had to be collected. Gardens still needed weeding and water. Animals still had to be fed. In the pouring rain, in the blowing blizzard, cattle still needed hay. Newborn calves still needed protection from the harsh elements. Ranch work was never done.

Although my need to achieve perfection at all costs was a mental detriment for many years, it taught me to drive for excellence. It taught me that I could do more. I could excel and exceed my own expectations. Limitations were only for those who are weak, is what Jeff had said. I learned to never show weakness, which served me well and helped me survive in many experiences later in life. It was mind over matter. If it mattered, you better set your mind to it.

And that's what I did.

September 2, 1996—Hill County Jail, Havre, Montana

I WANT TO TALK TO SOMEBODY!! I yelled half in tears, half in anger as I pounded on the locked cell door in the Hill County Jail. The makeshift cell was a remodeled upstairs bedroom in the house where once a family resided but had been fashioned into a jail. A lockdown. For lawbreakers.

The stairs creaked as the guard climbed step by step to see what the commotion was all about. He inserted the key and the door swung open. He looked at my defiant look and asked calmly, "What's going on?"

"I want to talk to somebody! NOW!" I demanded sternly.

He searched my face for a brief moment trying to figure out my intent. But he didn't ask. He just nodded and said, "Just wait. I'll be back."

Finally! I'll find out what happened to Sunny. Where they took her. Was she okay? My mama's heart was dying to know. Fear. Shame. Pain. All washed over me. Where was she? My heart cried.

Once again. Key inserted. Latch turned. Door slowly opened. Handcuffs ready, the guard snapped them shut over my extended wrists, making sure I behaved. He nodded his head, motioning me forward. I walked in front of him down the stairs in my too-large, dark-green jumpsuit jail fashion wear. We descended to the first floor. Once again, he motioned me onward through a door. A large rectangular table dominated the center of the small conference room. Around it sat and stood at least ten authoritative-looking people. I stared flabbergasted at their badges. At their jackets broadcasting official connections. Deputies. FBI. Border Patrol. Cops. Secret Service.

Are you kidding me? What in the world? Fear stuck in my throat almost choking me. It intensified, dislodged, and ran unchecked from my throat to my heart. From heart to head. From head to toes. Have you ever had your toes curl? From fear? Mine did just that. The guard ushered me forward and pulled out a chair, indicating I should plop my backside in it. I gratefully sat before I fell from fright.

The booming voice said, "What do you want to tell us?"

My head jerked up. I caught a glimpse of each stern face. *What do I WHAT?? Want to tell YOU?* I screamed inside. My mind was befuddled. My thoughts in disarray. Every eye was focused on me. Intense. Staring. Dead silence. I could barely breathe. All the anger and intensity I'd had in my mama-bear state dissipated.

I lowered my gaze and quietly explained, "I just want to find out where my daughter is."

I glanced back up hoping, begging for an answer. An explanation. A clue. My statement garnered sideways, eyebrow-raised glances as they looked questioningly at each other.

"You don't have anything to tell us?"

That same stupid question again. *What do they want from me? What do I have to tell them?* I shook my head in disbelief. This is not going like I'd planned. A standoff. Mama vs mob. Minute by minute elapsed in silence.

"We're done. She's not going to talk. Take her back," the in-charge official commanded my jailer. The guard dog. Guarding the big, bad prisoner.

As directed, I clumsily stood with handcuffs in place. My head hung in resignation. Back to the upper-level cell we trudged. Me in front. Guard behind. Up the stairs. Handcuffs off. I slumped against the now-locked door. Baffled and brokenhearted.

I lay on my back staring at the ceiling. Tears wet the flat pillow beneath my head. *Lord, where are you? Where is Sunny? Is she in a cell? Is she alone? Who is taking care of her?* Tears gave way to exhaustion. A fitful night. I replayed the meeting over in my head. Perplexed at their assumption of confession. To expose what? My mind searched for clues.

****

"Yes, I will," the worried voice of my mom answered in response to the operator's question about accepting a collect call. From a correctional facility. From her daughter. Imprisoned. Behind bars.

This was a call I'd been reluctant to make. I didn't want to worry my mom. A bit ironic when I'd spent the last few years emotionally and physically distanced from her. My so-called divinely appointed position dictated the daily duties commanded by Curly. Disobedience would lead to eternal damnation for me. For her. For Sunny. For all my family. Said Curly. Sadly, I believed him.

"Hi Mom," I said softly. Embarrassment for my prisoner predicament wrapped each word with shame as it came forth from my lips.

"Honey, are you okay?" I could hear the near-tears in her question.

"I'll be okay," I reassured her yet doubting the truth of my own statement. I was terrified. "Have you heard anything about Sunny? I don't know where they took her. Mom, I'm so worried about her," I blurted out.

"She's fine. She's with Brenda," she replied.

I was flabbergasted. "She's where?! How did she get there?"

My mom briefly shared Sunny's trek from Havre where we were arrested, to Superior, where my sister Brenda lived. "It was Mori," she said referring to my cousin who was the Chief of Police in Columbus. "Since she's a cop she heard about what happened and pulled some strings. She was really concerned about Sunny having to stay in that detention center, so she headed straight to Havre to pick her up. Then brought her to Whitehall to me. After your sister found out, she decided it would be best for Sunny to be with her, Bob, Bobbi, and Roni. She thought the kids would help keep her company until all this is figured out."

The thought of Sunny being in a detention center devastated me. My gut twisted in gnarled knots. Tortured. Tormented. *Oh Lord! My baby!* Days of held-back terror tears let loose and trailed down my cheeks, wetting the green collar of my jumpsuit. In that moment, gratefulness for my cousin, Mori, and my sister overwhelmed me. My sister was right. Sunny belonged with her cousins.

They grew up like three mischievous musketeers. Stair steps in age with Sunny in the middle. Always self-appointed as the boss even after being scolded by my mom.

"You're not in charge, Sunny. I am. So quit bossing your cousins around."

It didn't stop her from exercising her budding boss skills. She was a natural leader, and her cousins were an attentive audience to lead. Or at least attempt to lead. Oftentimes her direction involved persuaded fun and playful activities. Other times it was triple trouble.

Before Curly had come into the picture, Sunny and I had spent most every Christmas, Thanksgiving, and Easter at my mom's and Jeff's, at least before they divorced. It was our Polack family gathering place. Delicious dinners, drinking, laughter, and games for quarters. Throwing dice, cussing at opponent moves, and cards flying in playful disgust when you lost your last quarter. *You're out!* I could still hear the joyful jab of the winner.

"I'll come up to see you," my mom said as her worry-laced words came out hesitantly.

My heart leapt at the possibility of seeing my mom. Then the vision of her mortified eyes as she witnessed the jail jumpsuit and took in the shameful appearance of her daughter became a roadblock to expressing my need for her nurturing.

"Mom, I don't want you to see me like this."

I heard the conflicted emotions in her sigh. Dread of what might lie ahead for me. Her need to save me from myself. From Curly. Yet reluctance to see the sorrowful, shameful state of her jailbird daughter.

"Okay honey. I'll wait."

I breathed my own sigh of saving shame-faced relief. "I love you so much, Mom."

"I love you too, honey."

I carefully replaced the handset in the cradle, disconnecting the call. And sobbed.

****

Hmm. Nightly calls. *Boy, Curly must really have some pull.* Each night, the guards would bring me down to a small round table with an old black phone sitting in the middle.

"Pick it up," they'd say.

I'd answer tentatively, knowing it had to be Curly. Again. Hoping it wasn't. Wishing they'd say no. But they always said yes. Just the sound of his voice brought fear. Why here? *He can't get to me. Can he? Then why am I seated at this table talking on the phone with him?* Night after night. Starting day two. His voice encouraged me to stay strong. He'd take care of everything making sure I was okay. He'd be the almighty holy jail breaker. He'd get me out. He was the puppet master. I was the jailed slave. Cryptic messages to not disclose. Not tell. Not fail. Stand firm. Be a good soldier in God's chosen army.

Nightly calls. No one else was allowed this privilege. I probed the purpose. The plan. *Why me?* Understanding dawned slowly. The blood drained from my face. Was it about the drugs? The credit cards? After all he'd been a candidate for governor, senator, and president. Definitely high profile. Or was it the death threat letters? All I knew... It was a trap. A trick. A way to detect. A slip of the tongue. To disclose the place. The state. The city. They wanted me to spill the beans. Puke out the place. Be the patsy. No how. No way. I was loyal. Wasn't I? But I was afraid. I was hoping for help to get out. Somehow. Someway. Soon.

It was time to call in the calvary.

"This is a collect call from Raylynn at a correctional facility. Will you accept the charges?" said the operator matter of factly. My adoptive dad, Jeff, immediately said yes.

His less-than-perfect daughter had landed herself in jail. I explained the circumstances. An arrest for bad checks. I assured him Curly was taking care of it. Down deep I hoped he'd be my knight in shining armor and come rescue me. *Take me home.* My real home. Not Billings. To Whitehall. Conflicting emotions started a boxing match in my brain. *Do it! Beg for help to escape, and I don't mean jail.* Escape Curly's clutches. Escape fear of the threatened eternal damnation. Not just for me but for all my family. Their eternity rested in my hands. Browbeaten into my brain when Curly sensed unrest. Disobedience. Disloyalty. And it's not just browbeating I feared. Body beating. Bruising. Battering. This is what I feared.

Fear factors engaged. Shut mouth. Do not speak truth. My thoughts beat feet to mind-reading manipulation. Jeff's professed talent. *Use it now! Please! Summon your sixth sense, Daddy!* I silently pleaded for mental telepathic pathways to sprint through the phone line. *Please let him feel my fear,* I begged God. *Can you feel it, Daddy? Can you hear my heart? My fear? My desire to be free?*

His words broke through my concentration, "Is Curly helping you?" Jeff asked.

"Yes. He said he's working on ways to get me out," I said.

Hope crushing words traveled through the phone as he said, "Since he's helping you, I know you'll be fine."

His words devastated my heart. Shattered my faith. My dream of deliverance. Doomed.

Rise up, Raylynn. Be brave. He believes Curly's a good guy. Obviously, I'm wrong again. As always. Didn't trust myself. I was a wuss who couldn't take the heat. The hits or the hurts. Just a coward.

I barely heard his goodbye. The dial tone reverberated in my ear. I hung up the phone. The calvary is not coming. The knight has retired his armor. No help at hand. Now or ever. Eternally trapped in the snare of the snake. I'm sunk. Stuck. Screwed.

Save me, Lord, please?

Grief and Glut—1974

Over the years, ranch work, sports, and a young body had kept me in shape. I'd graduated from high school at 130 pounds and thought I was fat. Really? Well, my adoptive dad Jeff told me, "If you're fat, you're ugly." So, I believed I was fat. And ugly. Hoping so, anyway. Then maybe weird sexual encounters wouldn't happen. With him.

Then Grandma died. Jeff's mom. I was her sidekick since moving to the ranch when I was six months shy of four years old. Grandma was my superhero. A petite woman wearing worn-out jeans with a long-sleeved, front-snapped, western-style blouse tucked in. An old cowboy hat and boots added to her everyday wardrobe. Her kind eyes visible from behind her wire-rimmed glasses below the brim of her hat.

Animals were her world. Newly born calves were saved from a frozen demise under a heat lamp in her bathroom. When warmed and ready to try out their new legs, they'd run from the bathroom to the kitchen, then to the living room, with me scampering after them. *New pets,* I thought. Grandma sat drinking her coffee, eyes twinkling as she watched kid and calf play. Many animals lived because Grandma was gentle. Caring. Nurturing. But don't let this softness fool you. She was rough and tough as any rancher, even getting her face bashed in by a pissed-off cow trying to free herself from the stanchion didn't slow her down.

But her stroke did. At the age of 67. And she died two weeks later.

A month before she died, I had headed to the ranch to visit her and Grandpa. In a few weeks I'd be moving to Bozeman to attend Montana State University. She wanted me to drive her to Butte to cash her Social Security check. Traveling the back winding roads, it was about a 15-minute drive over the mountains.

I treasured this one-on-one time with her. We'd moved to town when I was in junior high, limiting my grandma time. Today was special. Grandmother and grownup granddaughter time. We chatted as we reached the summit and headed down, marveling, as we always did, at the curved switchback traversing down the steep slope, giving us an amazing mountaintop view of our destination. She gave me directions to the frequently visited liquor store where she cashed her check and bought a couple of bottles of whiskey.

Alcohol was her friend. Her comforter. Her ache easer. Her brain-numbing booze. Easier to down a drink than to tell the tales. No sharing the shit, so to speak, of a hard life lived. That was Grandma. Private. No one privy to her pain.

She opened the car door, brown bag of booze in hand. A white envelope in the other. She slid in and handed the envelope to me. Questioningly, I opened it and saw some tens and twenties inside. Instantly I knew it was the remainder of her check.

"Grandma, I can't take your money!"

Her kind eyes looked deeply into mine and she quietly said, "Honey, I don't need it where I'm going." She faced forward, letting me know that the conversation was over. Ended. No questions to be asked. Or answered. Now or ever. A month later she was dead.

"I want you to sing at the funeral. Grandma loved to hear you sing," Jeff dictated. It wasn't up for discussion. He called the shots.

A gut-wrenching day. Singing the Tom Jones song "Green Green Grass of Home" about did me in, especially when I literally whispered the last stanza of the song.

I choked back the tears. Be strong. Hadn't Jeff told me that it was him and me together? The strong ones. The nerves-made-of-steel ones. The locked-down-emotion ones. They won't cry. Shouldn't cry. Absolutely don't cry ones. Girded guards holding grief captive. With tear ducts plugged with prideful perception...of Jeff's. The don't embrace the emotion. Be strong. Be brave. It's a matter of principle. A matter of image. A matter of strength.

"Your mom and Brenda aren't as strong," he'd said. "It's just us. And you need to be strong for me, too."

What a burden to lay on a seventeen, almost eighteen, year old who was grieving herself. And that's exactly what I had to do. Be strong.

After her burial in the purchased plot at the Whitehall Cemetery, we headed back to St. Theresa's Catholic Church for the obligatory luncheon. A delicious spread of all sorts made by the caring women of the Ladies Auxiliary. I was devastated. My best friend and grandma. Dead. I stood on the sidelines not knowing how to act. *What do I do?* I was numb. Another devastating blow. Another traumatic loss. Another don't feel it. Don't emotionally acknowledge it loss. Just like my dad, Ray, when I was two.

My thoughts turned back to my toddler time. Jeff's first dad-decree demand, one of many to come.

"No longer are you to refer to Raymond as your dad. Do not even let his name cross your lips. He's dead. I'm your dad now. Don't be looking at his pictures. All it will do is confuse you. I'm your dad. I'm in charge now. You are to do what I say."

My almost 4-year-old mind had been confused. And not for the reason Jeff said. The romance between my mom and this nice-looking, take-charge man had resulted in marriage, whatever that was. I remember them walking out of the church hand-in-hand. My mom was all dressed up with a form-fitting dress and new fashion-statement hat. She ducked her head as people began throwing rice at the new couple. It was a fun game, I'd thought. Maybe this marriage thing would make my mom happy. She hadn't been happy since the day my dad hadn't come home. The day we were told he died. Since we had moved from San Diego to Montana. I'd peek around the door of her bedroom and see her crying alone many times. Never in front of me and my sister. Now her face was lit up with a smile showing off her adorable dimples. Glowing. Beautiful. I loved to see her smile.

Now this take-charge man did just that. Took charge. Took control. Dictated demands. Confusion set in. *Why didn't this new man like my daddy? Why didn't he want us to say his name? Look at his pictures?* I missed him. Grief was perplexing.

Where had he gone? Why hadn't he ever come home that day? I recalled the angry yelling, the fierce fighting right before he, my dad Ray, left to go to the grocery store. Maybe he didn't come home because of the fight. Maybe I did something wrong. *Didn't he want to be my daddy anymore?*

After the guy who wore a Navy uniform just like my dad had come to the door, my mom cried for hours. My mom's best friend, who we called Aunt Merle, had come rushing in the door. She almost ran me over. I'd been standing by the screen door watching. Waiting. For him to return. Aunt Merle knelt and hugged me and said she was so sorry. I wondered why she was sorry. *For what?* Confusion and chaos swirled in my little brain. I went running to Brenda, my comforter, my best friend. My little heart was pounding. Panic caught in my throat. "Why is mama crying? Why is Aunt Merle so upset?"

Brenda looked at me wide-eyed. Stricken. Stressed. Scared. My protective big sister enveloped me in a comforting hug, laid her cheek on the top of my head, and patted me on the back. "It'll be okay," she said reassuringly.

But it wasn't. We waited. We watched. We wished for understanding. Then the bomb dropped. Direct hit to the heart. And exploded. Sitting stiffly on our couch, my sister gripping my hand so hard it hurt. We sat anticipating. Fearing. Trembling. The untold horrible news. Mom knelt down in front of us her face streaked with tears.

"Your dad won't be coming home anymore. He died earlier today," she sobbed.

My tender, innocent heart could not contain the pain. *Never coming home? Whatever does that mean? Absolutely never?* Not ever. No. Never. Two children. Fatherless. One wife. Widowed.

Barely a year later. Sitting on a different couch. In an unfamiliar house. Together. Side by side. Brenda and me. We stared up at this demanding pretending-to-be dad, Jeff. We're never supposed to look at photos of our dad. Of him and my mom. Of him and us. His kids. Silently I screamed, *I want my daddy! My REAL daddy!"* All I have left are pictures. Why are you taking them away?

Numb, I accepted the command. After all, this is the man who made my mom happy and wanted to be my new daddy. The bubble burst. No fairy tale life. The longed for now lost. What if I'm left behind? I squeezed my eyes shut in an attempt to fend off the fear.

Thinking maybe my real daddy didn't love me enough to stay. Maybe that's why he left. Maybe this new daddy would love me. Would stay and not leave. As long as I'm good. As long as I do what he says. And demands. As long as Brenda is good. As long as she does what he says. And demands. I made a promise to myself. I'll be the best I can be for this new daddy. I longed so desperately to be loved. And never left behind.

In deference to Jeff, my mom had hidden the pictures, but Brenda and I found her secret place. The forbidden stash. When she wasn't aware, we'd sneak the envelope packed with pictures into our room and gaze longingly at the kind, handsome face of our father. Our dad. After all, Ray was our dad. Dead but still our dad. Replaced by marriage. And dictatorship. Over the years, the remembrance of my dad's love grew dimmer. Jeff's idealistic influence grew stronger. And stronger. Choking out the nurturing love embedded in my heart by my dad. Raymond. My namesake.

Now, I felt like I was choking on unspoken grief. Again. No outward grief to be displayed. Yet again. Today. At my beloved Grandma's final tribute. My heart grieved deeply. Internally. Would he hide Grandma's pictures, too? Forbid the photos? She died and was never coming back. Just like my dad. Would we be able to talk about her? Remember her? Without recourse? I feared the future. Without her. With Jeff.

My thoughts were abruptly interrupted when I heard my sister begin crying. It wasn't just a cry. It was a wail. A sorrowful wail. Family and friends raced to her side. Comforted her. Loved on her. I stood afar. Why is it okay for her to cry and not me? She was four years older and hadn't fallen under Jeff's spell as much.

She'd been eight when he married my mom. More independent. More outspoken. I remember her glaring at him. Fists clenched. Seething at her perceived injustice of his demand. "I WON'T call you dad. You're NOT my dad!" Then punishment would ensue but not enough to change her mind. Eventually he'd worn her down. But she never allowed him total control over her actions. Her thoughts. Her heart. And now she was able to openly grieve. With no repercussion from Jeff. I felt jealous. I felt left out. I felt alone. I felt abandoned...by my dad, Ray. By my Grandma. And now set apart from my sister, my mom, and my family. Choking on unspoken grief.

From my self-isolating corner, I wondered what I should do. All the attention was on my sister. I felt like a bystander. An outsider. My eyes fell on Jeff. Chatting with funeral goers. Suave as usual. No tears. I must follow suit. As I felt my resolve begin to crumble, I looked across the room at the large table displaying every kind of dessert you can imagine. All homemade. All delicious, I was sure. I stumbled toward it, not really understanding the draw. I grabbed a plate. Filled it full. Turned and walked back to the corner and ate. Stuffed myself. Satiated my grief. Put the fire out in my sorrow-filled heart. Over and over I filled my plate. And ate. And ate. It brought solace for my sorrow. My pain. It didn't put me down. It didn't demand I do anything. I was in charge and I ate what I wanted. No one noticed. No one cared. At that moment I began my destructive journey of emotionally eating. Food became my friend. My drug. It was one thing I could do that Jeff couldn't control. Especially since I was heading back to college at Montana State University in Bozeman. He'd never see. I felt smug. In my own little world. Of addiction.

Prince Charming—1982

MEN! All they want is a piece of ass. I stomped on the gas as painful emotions erupted as I drove down Main Street in West Yellowstone, Montana. I had just left work at the gift shop and gas station on the corner of the intersection heading into Yellowstone National Park. As I passed by the Best Western Hotel located on the right, I glanced in its large plate-glass windows to see my soon-to-be-ex-husband, Jerry, playing kissy face at the front desk.

Real professional, you two. Merry friggin' Christmas to me… *Get a room!* It'd be cheap. Just grab a key and head down the hall to a bed. I was angry. Hurt. Miffed. Even though I was the one who left, Jerry's proclamation of eternal love was nullified by the window display of coziness connection with the clerk. No surprise. But still just flat-out hurt.

Our relationship had been kindled in a local honkytonk in El Paso, Texas. It was July 1974, the summer after my high school graduation. I'd asked everyone for money as a gift. I wanted a senior trip, Texas-style adventure with my Grandma Lauderdale. My Grandma, mom, and Brenda had driven the 1,400 miles to spend Christmas with her cousins a few years prior. I loved it there. Bright Lone Star State sunshine, even in winter. The absence of snow in the 60-degree weather. The Southwestern landscapes with adobe brick homes. The big-city thrill for a small-town Montana girl. An opportunity to feel grown up. Untethered. And free.

Excitedly, we headed to the Bert Mooney Airport in Butte for our early morning flight. Grandma was a bit nervous about the flight so downed a few shots of whiskey regardless of the early morning hour. Her tonic to temper the fear. A bit tipsy, she slept all the way to Salt Lake City.

A businessman sitting next to me struck up a conversation. I happily shared our destination and plans. He politely inquired about the length of our SLC layover, almost 3 hours. I glanced at Grandma, a bit worried about how she'd make it. She was tough, though. The gentleman offered to take us to a club in the airport to pass the time. Having traveled very little, I was totally naive to airport clubs. What they were. Who they were for. I figured it was a public airport. So, a public club.

My grandma roused; we followed the man to an unmarked door. He took a key from his pocket, opened the door, and motioned us in. *What have I gotten us into?* I thought in panic. I stopped. And stared. At a reception desk ten feet in front of us sat a well-dressed woman, her brunette hair swept up in a regal French roll.

Smiling, she greeted the man by name. "What can I do for you today? Are these your guests?" she asked as she glanced our way.

He nodded and grinned. "I have a connecting flight so I won't be able to stay. Please take care of these two ladies. Whatever they want, please add to my tab."

My mouth flew open. "What in the world *is* this place?" I turned to thank the man, for what I wasn't sure yet, but he'd already disappeared out the door.

With eyes twinkling, the receptionist motioned for us to follow her. "If you'd like to lie down, ma'am, you can rest here." She opened the door to a beautifully decorated bedroom. My grandma walked in still feeling the effects of her tonic. She crawled into the high bed, curled up, and was almost instantly asleep. Our hostess quietly closed the door. "Let me show you around and you can choose whatever you'd like to do."

We toured rooms with expensive televisions. Cushiony recliners. Fluffy couches. Magazines galore. I sat down stiffly on the closest couch, really not knowing what to do. The hostess left the room and returned with an abundance of snacks and an assortment of drinks on a silver serving tray, assuring us that she will make sure we don't miss our flight. Never in my life had I been treated this way. I felt like royalty. The belle of the ball.

I sat back and finally relaxed, reveling in amazement. *Who WAS that guy?* I sure wish I knew so I could thank him. I grinned to myself. Maybe he was an angel. Our flying fairy godfather.

****

Safe and sound, we arrived later that day. Ready for our Texas tranquility. In my mind, sun and fun. Fun was soon to be had. I was still underage at seventeen, but no one carded back then. Who cares? Come on in. Dance. Drink. And drink.

It was the local hangout for the Vietnam vets who had served their time in the war and were stationed at Fort Bliss. After returning from the brutality of war, life wasn't the same for them. Downing drinks and dirty dancing gave them a reprieve from horrific war-event recall. New to the bar scene, I watched in fascination. A bit envious of their laughter and frolicking fun. However, I was blind to the tragedies, the destruction, the anguish, the guilt that many of them carried deep in their soul. These nights at the bar served as a cushion for coping. For sanity survival. For soul saving.

A young, good-looking man sauntered to the table where I was sitting with my cousin's single friend, who had dragged me to the club to introduce me to the El Paso Friday nightlife. And now I'm being approached and asked to dance by a charming stranger. A bit naive, I let him take my hand and lead me into the crowd of jitterbuggers, two-steppers, and tipsy dancers. My Grandpa Lauderdale had taught me to jitterbug at the Waterloo Community Hall Saturday night dances attended by the local farmers and ranchers taking a respite from working the fields.

But this night, dancing, I was transformed. I knew the steps well. Back and forth springing steps. Two steps in. Two steps out. Swing around. Hand over head. Now slide. This dancing stranger slid his hand across my lower back to grab my hand, a typical jitterbug move. Shivers ran down my spine. I looked at him embarrassingly. But he felt like the promise of adventure. Life being lived.

The music stopped and he walked me back to my table. He pulled out my chair and I sat down. And so did he.

"I'm Jerry," he drawled. Totally Texan through and through.

My cousin's friend winked at me as a new partner pulled her to her feet and hustled her to the dance floor, leaving me to chat with this attractive Texan. Army man back from Vietnam finishing up his tour at home base in El Paso.

We spent my remaining weeks dancing at the club until bar closing time, then making out in the back seat of his car. We would spend the days at local parks, seated on a bench, chatting, and watching kids play. It was at one such park that I first encountered a bit of the horror he'd experienced in 'Nam. We'd been watching a kids' football game, our spectator sport. Talking and watching. He grew silent. I glanced sideways at him, wondering if I'd offended him. He offered no answer or response in the conversation. He was still. Silent. And far, far away.

A bit frightened, I asked, "Are you okay?"

I sat waiting. Waiting. Wondering why the silent treatment. Then he spoke.

"We played football in 'Nam."

I breathed a sigh of relief that he finally acknowledged my presence. "You did?" I probed hoping to prompt him to continue. He did. Then I wished he hadn't. I wasn't prepared for the dialogue that followed.

"We didn't have a football. We used a head." His eyes were glazed over in pain. His words. Slow. Steady. Monotone. Haunting. My thoughts cartwheeled, trying to process his admission. The reality of war. Wounds. Not always physical. Visible. Healable. Oh. So. Horrible. I sat statue still. What could I say? I wanted to reach out and hold him to soothe the pain.

After what seemed like hours, yet was only minutes, he turned his face toward me. Sorrow-filled eyes bore deep into my soul. Heartstrings tied tightly to his tears. Hooked. Line and sinker locked on. Secured. Fastened. Creating my fixation on his pain. My rescuer role sparked. Ignited. Not 'til years later did I realize that it was this moment that hitched my heart to his. In sympathy. In, "I'll save you. I'll soothe your sadness. Patch up your pain." I failed. But I tried.

Grandma and I flew home in mid-August so I could pack and prepare for college. I ditched my first infatuation in the West Texas town of El Paso. Bound for book learning in Bozeman, Montana. Jerry wasn't happy I had to leave. Vowing we'd be together, he promised to be in touch.

College began with us dorm-dwelling newbies attending freshman orientation. A week of adjustment. Education game planning, consulting with academic advisors, and campus tours to prevent directional disasters. Bewildered wanderers. Readied for our intellectual relay.

College courses began. Information cramming. Data drilling. University professors. Pushing the pens. Handing out the hard homework. Freshman freakouts began.

Jerry did keep in touch as he promised. Letters. Phone calls. And a planned Thanksgiving holiday trip north. My romance heart strings he played well. He knew how to strum a guitar. And he'd learned how to strum my heart. I was living a romantic adventure much like I read in countless books. I devoured romance novel after romance novel, immersing myself in each heroine's fantasy life being pursued by the handsome stranger from afar. Pinching myself, I felt I was being pursued by the same. Prince Charming seeking out the maiden who fits the glass slipper. Any young woman's heart would be jumping with joy, a bit coy, not thinking she'd be jilted. Call after call, my heart palpitations increased. The day drew closer and closer. One last call before his car was Bozeman bound.

"You know what I expect when I get there. I'm not driving all that way for nothing," he drawled sexily.

A typical guy. Talking to an atypical girl. One who had been conditioned to never say no. To a man. Jeff's stern voice echoed in my head. *You NEVER say no to me!* I'd been told this enough. Not specifically directed at an amorous association. Just an overarching order to all actions associated with Jeff. A man. My supposed-to-be role model. Bully behavior builder. Brick by brick, mortared in my mind. Do his bidding. His every command. And I did.

This do-bidding behavior lodged subconsciously in my brain. For men. Not just Jeff. High-pressured pursuit resulted in my submission. "No" was omitted from my vocabulary. And Jerry was a pursuer. His implied expectation wasn't heard as a wish. A want. It was a directive. Reverberating beliefs bored into my brainwaves. Jeff style. Do-it style. As directed. And I did. No afterglow following the erotic encounter. Only shame remained. After he left.

Then, at least.

Time passed. Distance divided. A breakup inevitable. Jerry wouldn't wait. Heartbroken. Virginity no longer intact. Shame was my constant companion. I felt used. Abandoned. Alone. Bar hookups dulled the pain. Don't say no. And I didn't.

These liaisons created an out-of-control feeling. With each one, my hopes heightened. For more than a hookup. Maybe he'll care. Maybe this one will stay. Maybe he'll like me. Love me. Not reject me. But college is a playground for players. Looking for put-out partners. I put out…begrudgingly. Over. And over.

My college years. Studied some. Drank a lot. Me, the hookup whore attempting to fit in. A college coed carousing continually. Learning to outfox. Outmaneuver men. I couldn't say no but I could manipulate their manhood. Be good at sex. Then they'd want me. Then they wouldn't leave me. Then maybe, maybe, they'd love me. If I put out. If I masqueraded as the master mate. It didn't feel good. It didn't match my heart. Who I am inside. I hated the whore in me. How could I learn to say no? No clue. "Don't say no" was deeply imbedded in my brain. Held me prisoner. Degrading my soul. My spirit. My sanity.

It interrupted my studies. The high school valedictorian, voted most-likely-to-succeed, was failing. Not F's, mind you. The expectation of perfection was deeply ingrained. Less than A's, or even B's, equaled imperfection. Flat-out failure. Defeat. A disappointment to Jeff. I'd mar his reputation. So, I quit.

In December 1977, my senior year. I quit. Afraid of facing the repercussion—the failure fallout on the home front—I headed to El Paso, Texas. To stay with relatives on my Grandma Lauderdale's side of the family. My after-high-school adventure location. Where I had been Cinderella at the ball. Back to a place I felt loved. Accepted. No expectations of perfection. I fled to gain freedom. Distance from a disappointed domineering dad. Physically free. Mentally. Majorly. Mixed up.

****

I slipped into Texas life well. A relative recommendation landed me a job at the El Paso Natural Gas Company, my first post-college-quitting employment. Navigating the downtown traffic was a feat for this country bumpkin. Five lanes of traffic heading in one direction didn't exist anywhere in Montana. I purchased a little yellow Datsun B210 Honey Bee. Small size and small sticker price were the selling points. Easier to maneuver through the bumper-to-bumper rush-hour traffic.

My confidence was building with such freedom. It was 1,271 miles from Whitehall to El Paso. Enough mileage to break the bondage of dad control, or so I thought. Dodging dad from a distance felt fabulous. Weekend bar hopping with work friends. Bed hopping with potential suitors falling back into my I-hope-they'll-care carousing. But no. Just out-for-a-good-time guys hanging out with a won't-say-no girl. No ring givers. Just sex takers. And heartbreakers.

A sick day. I decided to stay home, curl up on the couch, and binge-watch television. I vacillated between semi-sleep and semi-watching game shows.

Brrrriing. Brrrriing. The sound blaring from the phone hanging on the wall right above my head jarred me awake. Being the only one home, I sat up and reached for the phone. "Hello?" I said sleepily.

The return "hello" literally jerked me up right. Heart-stopping jolt. The familiar Texas drawl from years before was heard on the other end of the phone. "This here's Jerry Holland and I'm looking for Raylynn Lauderdale. Do y'all happen to have her number? I met her back in '70 and I'm trying to get in touch with her."

Shock. Shivers. *Oh shit.* Pitter-patter palpitations played ping-pong in my heart. *Oh. My. God.* "Uhhh...this is Raylynn."

Jerry's response indicted he was equally surprised to find me at the same place I'd been visiting when we'd met. "What in tarnation are you doing in El Paso?"

We chatted back and forth for over an hour as if no time had passed. Finally, I got the guts up to ask, "Why were you wanting to get in touch with me?"

His response floored me. "I never quit thinking of you, and I realized I still love you."

Wow. The fairytale pixie must have just flown over the house and sprinkled magic relationship-mending dust. My heart melted. Our connection rekindled. Over the next month, the rush to restore the former love link led to my job resignation. My packed yellow car headed from El Paso to the east Texas town of Tyler to be with my kinda-tall Texan. Swoon fest at its best. The whirlwind romance. Caught up in his courtship pursuit. I'm in love. I thought. Falling into the tall tale. I was living a love story. The fairy fable fascination.

How far we can fall from bliss to broken in such a short time? The relationship turned rough and rocky. Heavyhearted, I returned to Montana, hoping to leave the hurt behind. But it doesn't end there. After his parents' persuasion, Jerry flew to Montana with an apology and a ring. Fairytale material, right? I thought so. After my mom and Jeff did everything they could to convince me this was a "really dumb idea," Jerry and I headed back to Tyler, Texas, via Las Vegas to tie the knot. A cheap chapel coupling made official by a few bucks for a license and a simple "I do."

Ours was no Cinderella storybook ending. No glass slipper slipped on by the charming prince when he finally found me. Reconnection didn't mean recommitment. Neither of us were marriage material. Both broken. Both needy. Both romance seekers. Neither of us truly understood the undertaking of holy matrimony. The talking, listening, compromising, and sacrificing that wedded bliss requires were unlearned skills. Their absence eroded the crumbling wall of amorous attachment and love entanglement, the only foundation we had for our Sin City certifying union.

After two years of navigating rough relationship waters, we decided to have a baby. Maybe a child will solidify our ties. Fix our family. Tie us together eternally. Nine months later a God-given gift arrived. Our beautiful bright-eyed, red-haired daughter, Sunny.

But babies don't fix anything. They are wee little humans who symbolize the magnificence of creation. Who bash the sight blinders and penetrate the hardened hearts to enable us to experience the wonderment of their new discoveries each and every day. Whose dimpled smile can charm the twisted pants off a pathetic pair of parents in constant callused contention. But child charm is no match for wedlock war. Nor should be used as a crutch for an already crushed couple.

Our years together were an ongoing saga of disagreements and bickering, widening the chasm and building an unscalable mountain. Harshness. Heartache. Deception. Unforgiveness. Selfish motives split the two, who became one, back into two. The end result? Ruptured promises ripped in pieces. Mangled marriage vows tattered and torn. Bleeding hearts experiencing throbbing, pulsing pain. Divorce. Exponentially repulsive. Ugliness personified.

My fairytale ended but it didn't have a happily-ever-after final chapter. Valentine's Day 1983. D-day for divorce. Our marriage ended. Finally free. It hurt. But I had an ache antidote and soul salve: my sweet little 2-year-old Sunny. She brought her brightness to each day. After all, she was my sunshine girl.

My Sunshine — 1980

We'd relocated from Athens, Texas, to West Yellowstone, Montana, the small tourist-trap town located at the West Entrance to the famous Yellowstone National Park. Having been offered a joint management job overseeing a gift store and gas station, we headed back to my home state.

A week before our Texas departure, Sunny had finally made her debut on November 30. Her final pre-travel checkup was at five days old. The pediatrician checked her over. Top to toe. Then stuck his finger in her face and said, "Never forget you're a Texan. You were born on Texas soil." He looked up at me and grinned. "Good luck in Montana."

Sunny was my sunshine. Jerry and I had begun our managing couple job, with baby Sunny sleeping behind the counter in the gift shop. A little more than two years later, the managing team of two reduced to one. Divorcing her dad when she was barely two left me raising her alone. Jerry left for Texas, his home state. Sunny and I remained in West Yellowstone. I'd taken on the task of managing both the gift store and gas station until the owners could find a couple to manage the property. Slower winter season duty demands made solo management possible. Visiting snowmobilers buying gas and gifts were easily handled with just a few part-time employees. However, as the busy summer season approached, it was necessary for a new management couple team to be in place by early spring. It was vital to learn the ropes before thousands upon thousands of tourists descended on this little town of 735 residents.

All the responsibilities were now on my shoulders. Selling clothes, jewelry, trinkets to the tourists. Gas to the snowmobilers. Even plowing snow by the gas pumps and the store. I'd watched it done numerous times. Just drop the plow and push or pull depending on the location.

No problem. A piece of cake. I've got this! Confidently I told the owners I could do it. I laughingly promised I wouldn't run over any gas pumps.

The time of reckoning was at hand when two feet of snow fell overnight. After dropping Sunny off at the daycare, I arrived at the store. The entrance was blocked by a large drift of snow. Shoveling and plowing first on the agenda. I jumped in the old GMC truck. Plowing performance commence. I slowly inched forward to the small storage shed behind the store. I pulled the lever—plop dropped the plow. I started to put the old truck in reverse. Distracted by a movement, my gear-shifting motion stopped. Frozen. In seemingly slow motion, I saw the door of the shed fall inward. White fluffy powder flew everywhere. And not from the plow . . . I'd just demolished the door.

I slammed the gear shift to park and flung open the truck door. Scrambling through the snow reaching to my knees, I inspected the damage. The hinges detached. The right side of the old wooden door was set free. Sent flying inward. Hanging by only the key latch and lock on the left. *Dang door!* Now swinging free. By the drop of my plow.

Horrified I tugged. I pulled. "Please close," I begged the plowed-in door.

The hardship of being alone in this two-person management job hit full force. I felt tears of frustration rise to the surface. Choking me. *I WON'T give in. I WON'T give up.* A self-lecture ensued. *Quit whining! You wanted out of the never-should-have happened marriage. Now pull up your dang bootstraps and do the work.*

Taking a deep breath, I pulled. I tugged. Again and again. 'Til the door fell into proper position, poised to do its duty once more. An injured door and a wounded soul. A tenacious will. A divorcee determined to survive. To rise. To raise her Sunny girl. Her sunshine. Her world.

****

Having been raised Catholic, I felt my responsibility extended to a religious upbringing for Sunny. I began attending Our Lady of the Pines Catholic Church. In the winter, heating costs and limited attendance meant that Mass was held in the basement. When Father John, the small church priest, learned that I played the piano and sang, I became the Cantor, leading the few members of the congregation in song responses. Sundays were fun. Sunny and I would show up early to visit with Father John about the music.

I'd open the basement door and hear, "Hey Sunny! Ya want some cookies?"

Sunny would go running to Father John's small living quarters to collect her plate of Sunday treats. Kind parishioners would drop off goodies throughout the week for their local priest, and he didn't eat sweets. So, the sweets belonged to Sunny. Each Sunday you could see a cute little girl with strawberry-blonde pigtails sitting in the front row of chairs. Sitting cross-legged. Plate on her lap. Eating cookies. This was her normal. Cookies and church. Every Sunday.

"Will you play and sing for our wedding?" I was asked by a young local lady. Father John had given the soon-to-be married young couple my name. The bride-to-be was calling to arrange music for their small upcoming wedding. Of course I would.

The program was set. The music picked. Practice done. Wedding day arrived. Nervously I sat at the organ located at the front of the basement room facing the door. From this view, I knew when to begin the entrance hymn. The bride appeared. It's go time. I saw her pause and wait for my start. My fingers began playing. My voice started singing. The wedding was beginning. I ended on time as she arrived at the altar. Handed off to the groom, they stood facing Father John. Eager for marriage. Ready for their vows. The union of their love finalized by matrimony.

Father John glanced around, surveyed the room, and said, "Since many of you here are not Catholic, I'll tell you when to stand and shit."

Oh. My. God! He didn't just say that! Did he?

The bride and groom's eyes widened. A giggle stifled. A grin here. A snicker there. I ducked behind the organ and put a hand over my mouth, smothering the laughter ready to explode. I saw the entire back row of the church vacate. Out the door. Bent over. Hysterically laughing. Finally, I could breathe. I looked at Father John. His face was expressionless. And he moved on. The marriage commenced. Vows were said. Mr. and Mrs. announced.

After the reception goers finally emptied the church, I looked at Father John and grinned, "Do you know what you said?"

He shrugged his shoulders and said chuckling, "Yes, but after it came out, what could I say? I couldn't take it back, so I moved on."

We sat and chatted. And laughed. Him, the man of the cloth. Me, the divorcee striving for sanity. Struggling to survive.

And the cookie-eating Sunny.

****

In April of 1983, Sunny and I left this quaint little town that we'd called home since she was a mere two weeks old. On to a new life with just the two of us. Starting in Whitehall living with her Grammy and Poppy 'til I could find a new job.

We stood in the kitchen of my mom's home one particular morning. Sunny was perturbed with her Grammy. And me. "O-un-ees!! I want o-un-ees!!" Mom and I looked at each other and shrugged. Neither of us had a clue. "I want o-un-ees!!" she declared for the third time.

The two-year-old tiny tot stood indignant looking back and forth between me and my mom, squeezing her hands in and out of little fists. It was her response to excitement or distress, and today it was the latter. A bit annoyed at our adult ignorance. For goodness sakes, she knew exactly what she wanted, and our lack of understanding caused her toddler hackles to rise.

Mom started taking food items out of the cupboard where Sunny's little finger was pointing. Graham crackers, Cheerios, animal crackers, Oreo cookies. All her favorite snacks. Sunny stood shaking her head emphatically no.

Finally, my mom pulled out a single snack-size box of Sun-Maid Raisins. Sunny clapped her hands in glee!!

"O-un-ees!!"

We laughed. "Those are raisins," my mom clarified for her.

"No! O-un-ees!!" she said as she shoved them in her mouth, selecting carefully one by one. Off she skipped as happy as a high-tide feeding clam.

My mom started chuckling. "I know where she got it. She was shoving a fist full of raisins in her mouth the other day, so I told her to eat *only one!*"

I doubled over in laughter, barely able to breathe. Curious as to the uproar of laughter in the kitchen, Sunny walked in. Still eating one raisin at a time. Her o-un-ees box clutched tightly in her hand. Oh, the vocabulary of my Sunny girl.

****

Single-parent survival meant providing a roof over our heads. Putting sufficient food on the table. And the responsibility was mine, not my mom and Jeff's. I'd snagged a great job as administrative assistant to the director of the Department of Agriculture in Helena, yet lived paycheck to paycheck. The hourly pay didn't always meet our needs. Sporadic child support payments did little to ease the burden. So I made up for it in fun. In our relationship. Sunny was my world outside of my state job.

Summer Saturdays were spent driving crisscross around Helena's garage sale circuit. Before we left home, I'd give Sunny five nickels to shop. Not understanding coins and cost, she figured that everything could be bought with a "nico." In her mind, this meant she'd come home with five items of her choosing. And she did. Her sweet smile. Her innocent face. Her cute little nico offer charmed even the toughest garage sale workers. An item marked three dollars meant nothing to her. It surely could be bought for a nico. And it most often was.

"Will you take a nico?" Sunny asked the money collector. I grinned as I watched her garage sale shopping tactics at work. The woman stared down at the innocent face of the red-haired, pigtailed 3-year-old little girl. Tucked tightly under her arm was a worn brown teddy bear with a 50-cent price tag dangling from its ear. Hanging onto it fiercely. Ownership was established. Sunny opened her little fist offering her only remaining nickel from our Saturday shopping excursion. I stifled a laugh as I watched the transaction.

"Of course, honey," the kind woman said with a huge smile as she glanced up at me and winked. "You enjoy that special bear. It was my granddaughter's, but she's all grown up and doesn't play with it anymore."

A look of triumph spread across Sunny's face as she came running toward me. "Look what I got, mama! For only a nico!"

As a single mom with limited income, this was our weekend entertainment. And my way of providing clothes and household items on a shoestring budget. Sunny loved it. She grew up laughing at my announcement each time I'd see a sign for the next one.

"GARAAAAGE SALE," I'd say with long emphasis on garage. I loved our Saturdays. I loved this Sunny girl that I'd been gifted. Mother and daughter. Heart to heart. Having fun.

My Sunny girl truly captured my heart from the very first day I laid eyes on her. A little over eight and a half pounds, twenty-two inches long, and long auburn hair at birth. A cowlick of red hair at the crown of her head stood straight up. Quite a sight on a cute little newborn.

My mom had flown to Texas on November 5 since my due date was the next day. Sunny had a different plan. I'd visited the doctor mid-November knowing full well he'd tell me I was in labor. I called that morning, telling him I think my water broke and headed to his office. After all, I'd had some kind of irregular contractions off and on for a week. I jumped up on the exam table, as gracefully as a 9-month pregnant woman can do, eager to hear the great news. A having-my-baby-day smile spread across my face. We'd even brought my packed birthing bag ready for hospital admittance.

The doctor finished his exam. Stood up and took off his gloves. I held my breath waiting to hear how far along I'd progressed. I looked at him expectantly. He shook his head slightly side to side.

Wait! Why is he shaking his head no?

"You're not in labor, Raylynn. I did, however, strip the membranes to help speed the process a bit. It's all I can do."

What? Not in labor? I was dumbfounded. "But my water broke," I fired back.

He looked at the nurse trying not to chuckle. "No. I'm sorry it didn't."

My mind went back to the wet sheets I'd felt after turning on my side that morning. Worriedly I asked, "Then why were my sheets wet? Why did water come leaking out?"

He kindly looked at me and said simply, "Urine. It was urine."

My eyes widened in humiliation! "You mean I peed the bed?"

He didn't answer, just nodded his head affirmatively. Oh. My. God. Just pee. A member of the Wetter's League. Beginning birthers enrolled in the Amateur Association. He reassured me this happens frequently with first-time mothers. No consoling the way-overdue massive mama. The desperate mess. The wannabe water breaker exposed as a bed wetter.

HU-MIL-I-A-TION.

I begged the doctor to do something. Back then, inducing labor was only done in emergency situations. He explained, "The guy upstairs knows much more about delivering babies than I do. Let's leave it up to Him when she comes."

I went home from my appointment exasperated. This baby has to arrive soon. But November dragged on and on. Day after day, home labor-inducing measures were taken. Long walks. Rides over bumpy back roads. Consuming fire-breathing, spicy foods. I stopped at my mom's suggestion to drink cod liver oil. *Ugh. Just no way. The baby may just have to stay.*

We discussed names. "If it's a girl, I want to name her Sunshine and call her Sunny," I excitedly told my mom.

"That's ridiculous," she retorted. "A hair-brained idea! If you're going to call her Sunny, name her Sunny."

I did. And my mom called her Sunshine.

****

Extra money for bills and necessities was needed. Enter an opportunity to become a Mary Kay Cosmetics consultant. Any additional income would help. Sunny loved being involved. What little girl wouldn't want to have birthday parties with a personal Mary Kay makeup consultant—a.k.a. Mom—as the entertainment? I had the supplies, so it was cheaper than buying party favors. Four little girls gathered around our small kitchen table. Infamous personal pink standup makeup mirrors propped up on the table in front of them.

Grinning from ear to ear, they listened attentively as I gave them my adult-geared spiel of makeup application tips and tricks. The girls leaned forward, laughing, wide-eyed for a closeup mirrored look. Concentrating to achieve correct eye shadow application. They sat back, admiring their work. Lipstick samples distributed, each choosing their favorite color. Lips puckered as they applied it carefully with the tiny lip brushes. Coloring in carefully as if their lips were an art masterpiece. Smeared, uneven lipstick wiped off and reapplied with a better color of their liking. Reapplications continued 'til they were satisfied with their reflection in the tiny mirrors. Smiles stretched from cheek to rosy cheek as they proudly displayed their made-up faces.

Joy. Just pure joy. Reaped from sale samples.

Our fun wasn't limited to makeup. We played with Barbie dolls. Strawberry Shortcake. Cabbage Patch dolls made from scraps by a talented Grammy. My mom had made her and her two cousins, Bobbi and Roni, each one for Christmas—one of Sunny's prized possessions. Even learning to make the scrunched-up face just like her doll. Making funny faces with weird throaty voices, she kept me entertained.

We goofed off in the kitchen of our mobile home after dinner one night. As I started putting the Cool Whip away after serving it on her red Jell-O, I dared her to lick a huge dollop of Cool Whip off a plate. Not yet privy to my plot, she grinned in anticipation of a victorious lick. A dare done and accomplished. She thought.

I plopped the creamy whip on the plate. Then held the plate lower for her to lean down to lick. As she bent down to execute the dare, I smashed her face into the white blob. Up she popped with her face covered in cream. I bent over laughing hysterically.

"No fair!" she screamed as whipped white drops dribbled down her chin to her shirt. I don't think she knew whether to laugh or cry.

I scooped Cool Whip out of the container and flung the glob at her. She did likewise. Tentatively at first. Wondering if she'd be in trouble for throwing food. My eyes twinkled impishly as I grabbed for more. We both dug into the container coming up with a fistful of white. *Plop!* She hit my cheek! *Plop!* A big daub landed on her long strawberry-blonde tresses, slowly inching downward, leaving a sticky white streak in its path. On and on went the food fight. 'Til the container was empty. I glanced around. Whipped cream everywhere. Covering the floor. Dotting the cupboards. Most of it on Sunny and me. We collapsed to the floor giggling. So much fun. Frolicking fun with my Sunny. The only cost. A container of Cool Whip. A small price to pay for the forever memories. Especially with what our future would hold.

If I could only go back to the "nico" days. The days of her innocence. Her joy. Kept intact. Kept safe.

But she wasn't. I didn't keep her safe. So. Much. Sorrow. To come.

Oh Deer—1985

The city lights of Bozeman, Montana, reflected in the rear-view mirror of my yellow Volkswagen Rabbit as I headed down Interstate 90. I glanced up to bid a light-hearted farewell to my college town. I still loved Bozo, as it was commonly called, and was thrilled to visit it, however briefly. I had the honor of representing the director of the Department of Agriculture at a dinner function, being his administrative assistant. I smiled broadly, remembering the warm fuzzy feeling of favor when picked as the stand-in for the head honcho.

Wearing a title tag displaying my name above Montana Department of Agriculture, I proudly mingled with other event attendees 'til I glanced up at the clock indicating the late hour of 8:30 p.m. A 90-minute drive was still ahead. Although the roads were clear with no recent snowfall, the temperature had dipped below the freezing mark. Best to head down the highway. I bade farewell to the farmers and walked out on cloud nine. My red-carpet walk made possible by special selection.

Pumped up by a self-satisfaction endorphin high, I tapped my fingers on the steering wheel in time to the blaring radio music. I was rocking out to the 1983 chart-topper "Every Breath You Take" by The Police as I headed home. No moonlight shone on the interstate asphalt. But it was a beautiful, clear, precipitation-free winter night. I tapped my brakes, slowing the car as I neared the turn-off for Helena. After exiting, I turned right on Highway 287 to drive my final 65 miles home.

I saw small, beady eyes reflected in my lights. I slammed on the brakes hoping to lessen the impact. *Bash!* A crash into my right front fender.

Oh my God! I hit it. A beautiful, swift dashing deer. It came out of nowhere as they often do. *Please don't let it be hurt. Or dead*, I silently pleaded, worrying more about the deer than the fender bender damage.

I hate hurting animals. I considered every living deer a Bambi descendent. There's no way I could've been a hunter, even though I love eating venison. A little ironic. Hoping for a bruised Bambi rather than a dying doe, I turned my attention to the damage.

My Rabbit didn't fare well against the darting deer. I pulled to the right side of the road. Put it in park. And got out to take a peek. No dead deer lay in the road. Breathing a sigh of relief, I peered as far as I could into the darkness of the night. No sign of the deer. My attention then turned to the wreckage. My right headlight swung limp and loose from its housing. Electrical wires holding it like a swing. The now-dark lamp lay looking at the ground. Its once-bright light now extinguished. Pieces of the grill were split, broken, missing. My heart sank. I was sunk.

What am I to do? No cars. No trucks. No semis. No traffic traveling whatsoever. Fifteen miles from the interstate turnoff near Three Forks and 20 miles from Townsend, the next nearest town. No phone within walking distance in the dead of night. Temperatures plummeting. I climbed back in the driver's seat. I took a deep breath and turned the key. My engine started. I exhaled with a sigh of relief.

I wondered if I could make it back to Helena. It was running a bit rough, but it was running. I nervously laughed and thought, *This bashed bunny, minus a headlight and grill, has a few hops left, fingers crossed*. I hoped anyway. Dinged up by a dang deer, I decided to drive. Emergency flashers on, traveling at a top speed of 35 miles an hour, I crept along the shoulder of the road. Praying. All the way home.

By the time I arrived, my back and neck were feeling the effects of the impact. Although it was late, I called my mom and Jeff. As my insurance agent, Jeff insisted I get checked out in the morning. It seemed unnecessary with no gash gushing blood.

Obediently, I headed to the emergency room the next day. After thorough examination, I left with a whiplash diagnosis. Pain pills and muscle relaxers on the mending menu. With a recommendation for physical therapy. The beginning of treatment after treatment. Headache after headache. Because of hitting a road-dashing deer driving home on agriculture department business. All leading to a workers' compensation settlement approved by the Montana Supreme Court. My saving grace.

Or so I thought.

September 1996—Hill County Jail, Havre, Montana

"Can you sing 'Amazing Grace' real loud?" said the note handed to me by Larry, the night shift guard.

"Who's this from?" I asked Larry.

"It's from a guy downstairs," referring to the men's jail cells in the basement of the building. "The men can hear you sing and really enjoy it." Referring to the evening time when Sharon and I would sing praise songs. First of all, to give glory to God. But also, to keep us occupied while sitting in a cell with little to do. Television can keep you occupied only so long. So, we'd started singing.

Margie, one of our fellow cell mates, would sit on her chair, eyes closed, swaying back and forth in time to the music. Feeling the Spirit. Feeling Jesus. Praising Him with us. It's interesting the depth of faith you find behind bars. Broken people needing a Savior. Desperate for miracles. Clinging to a promise they're loved in spite of their crummy conduct. Their seemingly unforgivable wrongs that they never get right. Over and over.

"Are you going to write him back?" Larry asked.

"Oh! I didn't know I could." I responded in surprise. This was my first introduction into the power of connection through note writing. In jail.

Larry half smiled and said, "I'll pick it up later."

I sat down to write. Not sure about this jail-cell-to-jail-cell note writing, but clearly a crucial connection to a young man needing a bit of cheer.

That's what I did. Encouraged this man to stay out of trouble. Read his Bible to realize that Jesus cares about him no matter what he's done to be locked up. And we sang "Amazing Grace" really loud that night.

The reply came the next day. I learned his name was Robert. He opened up a bit about his pain. His past. His failures.

They keep saying I have a past. Why do they keep bothering me about it? I try not to look back on my life but look forward. And try to only learn from mistakes of the past, though that don't seem to be working either. At least when I write to you, my headaches go away, my anger dissolves, and I get sleep. Jesus, I turn my life completely over to you. I ask that you walk with me, guide me, and lead me away from temptation.

My heart ached. A soul lost, searching. A past constantly pulling him backward. Stuck in his muck. Yet, his heart desiring to do right. Influenced by a God who reaches down to care. Through an unlikely source. Me. From an upper room jail cell.

Ten-time loser. Convicted felon. Mentally ill. Paranoid. Labels that have been placed on me since age 14. I've been in and out of jails, drug and alcohol treatment, prison. I guess a life of crime is what I chose. It was a way to escape reality . . .

A wounded young man. Inwardly accepting responsibility, yet continually labeled by a system. Outwardly, he acts the tough guy. Can't tarnish his tough image. But in his notes to me, the depth of his soul was exposed. I encouraged him, *The only label God has put on you is "Beloved Son." His label is the only one that matters.*

I have a few friends like you who care, so with that I will make it, he responded. *One day at a time. I still read the Word and believe it, and still have to repent and ask for forgiveness on a daily basis, but it says in the Bible that He forgives 70x7.*

A few penned notes passed to encourage a soul loved by God. Scorned by many. How do you measure the worth of a human being? Man focuses on looks and actions. God looks at the hurting heart.

You sometimes remind me of my mom. You pray too much and I can't sleep. So, okay Mom. I mean old lady, a.k.a. Raylynn. What's so damn funny up there? I can't be depressed when I hear you laughing. Sure makes me happy, Robert wrote.

God used my annoyingly loud laugh to bring a smile to Robert's face. I sat and grinned, visualizing his jailhouse joy.

Right now, I'm really pissed off. And sick and tired of everything, including this thing we call life. I thought I could blow up a door and set us all free, but Jamie took my bomb project yesterday. So, I hope Jesus hurries up, he wrote, another day.

It wasn't always a joy-filled day. Anger raged. Loneliness and soul sadness created raging anger. Deep-heart digging created dangerous depression.

Do you remember what it's like to dream, Raylynn? Do you remember what it's like to have goals? Both long-term and short-term goals? Do you know what it feels like to have someone who is supposed to be an idol, an icon, a role model, look you in the eye and tell you that "you are the stupidest person I have ever known"? Have you ever been told, "You are worthless, you won't ever do anything more than stamp license plates at Montana State Prison?" Do you know what it's like to desire the comfort a prison offers? Where your word is as good as a handshake? Where you are accepted for who you are whether you're a killer, drug dealer, thief, or common criminal?

Nevertheless, prison is what we make of it. As is life itself. I myself I lived in a manmade hole, constructed by my own bare hands, through blood, sweat, tears. My own prison, where I suffer no matter where I am. This is the toughest of all prisons I have ever tried to live in. There is no escape, no parole, no death sentence. In this prison, I don't know what to expect. I have to be my own friend and my own enemy, and the only one in this prison who helps me is myself. They say God helps those who help themselves. God, help me. Jesus, help me. I pray to you, that you may guide me, walk with me, and help me live a more prospering life. Help me remain free from drugs and alcohol, and most of all, help me love myself so that I may continue loving you.

My heart wept. I held this latest pencil-written note, surrounded with carefully drawn beautiful red roses. And a cross. No physical prison walls could be as confining as those he'd built in his heart. The aloneness, the depths of despair, the cry to a God he hoped was hearing. For help to ease his hurt. Wipe clean the darkness in his soul. Yet the heart of the broken for the burdens of brothers or sisters can bring light to a darkened cell. It did mine.

After hearing I had additional charges in another state, I was devastated and poured out my heart to my jailhouse pen pal. His hurriedly penciled reply:

Don't worry about your new charges, Raylynn. He doesn't want us to worry. You've helped me remember a few things:

1. *One day at a time.*
2. *Tomorrow is tomorrow. Get every bit of good out of today as you can. And remember, for every bad thing that happens today, I'll bet you can find ten good things to overcome that one bad thing.*
3. *Keep your faith. After all, in the end that's what counts.*
4. *Don't give up hope.*

Remember you are not alone. If they don't drop your charges pretty soon, I might just have to confess I did everything, including your charges. After all, I don't mind being in jail.

A gesture of kindness from an unlikely source. Soothing words putting salve on my troubled soul. Willing to take mine as his. Loyalty of an unlikely note-writing friend. Followed by concern and a depth of perception I should have heeded.

You are the only woman besides my mother I have ever trusted. I think there's nothing I couldn't tell you. Raylynn, my gut feelings are that somebody used you in a way that wasn't right. Somehow, someone took advantage of your vulnerabilities. As a friend, I want to say be honest with me. And most of all be honest with yourself. I have gotten to know you better than my own family. All because you have taken the time to listen, care, and open your heart to me—not prejudging me—and accepting me for who I am. I owe you so much for that alone.

Soon after, I left for Ward County Jail in Minot, North Dakota. Robert was transferred to Montana State Prison. Although correspondence was banned between correctional facilities, somehow, someway, letters still were sent and received. For a time. Our pen-pal friendship ended soon after. But my care and concern for this convict comrade remained. Now and forever.

Red Hot Mama—1985

"A Red Hot Mama Contest? You've got to be kidding me!" I scoffed at the suggestion. Carol and I had become best buddies. We both had begun working for the Department of Agriculture about the same time. She was the director's secretary. I was his administrative assistant. We were partners on projects. And both single moms. A commonality had drawn us together.

"Remember Ron mentioned it when we were down at the Park Plaza on Saturday night?" she said, as if Ron's name would convince me.

I burst out laughing. "Me?! Yep, I'm *definitely* a Red Hot Mama," I said scoffingly, shaking my head with a resounding "no." But my sarcastic husk covered my secret I-wish-I-was-good-enough yearning. My passion to sing lay passive. Pushed to the depths of my soul.

Months ago, Carol, an avid music admirer, had twisted my arm to head to the Park Plaza Hotel where world champion honkytonk and jazz piano player Ron Trotta often entertained. We'd become well acquainted with this great musician during our frequent fun-time outings. On slow nights, the loyal-listeners-turned-aspiring-songsters gathered around the piano as he plunked out catchy ragtime tunes on the keys. Entertaining times for tired, single moms needing a bit of reprieve from everyday duties of 8–5 state government jobs and raising our fatherless kids.

Over the last few months, Ron's excitement for the upcoming 1985 Helena Jazz Festival spilled over into our mommy-to-musician interludes. He and Don West, a fellow musician, were the organizers. Ragtime, Dixieland, and contemporary jazz bands from all over the country would descend upon the capital city of Helena for three solid days of music. The June jazz jam sounded exhilarating. His uncurbed anticipation was contagious.

The March fundraiser for the jazz festival was none other than the Red Hot Mama Contest. A mic-slinging, fringe-swinging songster to be selected. The best belt-it-out buxom beauty. Reluctantly—after arm-twisting—I agreed. To enter the race for the most suitable sizzling, spirited soloist. Auditions narrowed the contenders to seven. Hurdle one. Jumped. I was in!

Only six days away. Sultry song selection for a wannabe Hot Mama. With limited learning time, I needed a song I knew well. I grew up listening to Bobby Darin, the 1960s rock 'n' roll sensation who made it big with hit songs "Splish Splash" and "Dream Lover." His "Baby Face" hit was one of my favorites. I could sing it in my sleep. With snapping fingers keeping the beat, I tried out my recall. Relief! It's branded in my brain.

Next, a swanky dress desired. Who else to call but super seamstress, Mom. Yards of forest-green satin pulled from her fabric stash was hastily sewn into a Hot Mama large ruffled collar crossing over the front. Leaving a bit of cleavage uncovered. Tight fitting. Bottom ruffle above the knee. Silky. Slinky. A wee bit sexy. And my mom had made it especially for me. Her hope-to-be Red Hot Mama offspring.

Rehearsals began. Countdown to Saturday.

Manion's Supper Club was overflowing wall to wall. Every seat filled. Standing room only. A hundred and fifty were disappointingly turned away at the door. I stood near the back awaiting the 9 p.m. start of the show. A newly built stage stood ready for ragtime action. The contest crowd was drinking. And chatting. And laughing. And joking. And smoking. And drinking. And anticipating the action. The Hot Mama musicians ready to entertain.

Jitters jumpstarted the dread in my head. I took a deep breath, attempting to sedate the panic of my upcoming performance. The pit in my stomach produced barfing butterflies.

I'm. Not. Hot. I'm fat and ugly. The negative affirmation drilled into me by Jeff fueled my failure fear. *Who am I fooling?*

My eyes darted to the door. Engage exit strategy. I gauged the distance. Then measured the disappointment. To Carol. To the contest crew. To me. Self-doubt left me feeling less than a mess. I.

Can't. Do. This. I closed my eyes, attempting to flatten the fear. Beef up the bravery. Heat the feet. That had gone cold. They'd call me Runaway Raylynn. Not Red Hot Mama.

Through the brain fog of apprehension, I heard my name. And "Baby Face." Setting the stage for my song. Announcing my performance. Still in a daze, my legs started moving. Like dragging cinder blocks. Step by slow step. Toward the stage. I made it up the small flight of stairs. Without puking.

Now that would be quite the projectile performance, I sarcastically smiled to myself, rolling my eyes. I heard the crowd clapping. *I can't back out now.*

The band began the first bars of the song. *Open your mouth and just SING!* I commanded myself. Deep breath in and . . .

"*Baby Face...*" I launched the lyrics. And just kept on going.

With my eyes closed, I envisioned being home with my hairbrush microphone in hand. Dancing in the kitchen. Singing with silly Sunny. I belted out "Baby Face" with boldness. As I finished, I opened my eyes to see the audience erupt into hoots and hollers and heard huge applause. I grinned. Feeling good. Actually, feeling great! *I did it!*

No matter I didn't win the contest. I won that night. I beat my crippling fear. My not-being-good-enough. A glimmer of beauty and self-love glowed. With boldness. And bravery.

Prayin' It—1985

"Hi Raylynn. It's Don West," said a familiar voice on the other end of the phone after my initial hello greeting. I was a bit perplexed by his call.

"Hi Don! What have you been up to?" I hadn't talked to him since the night of the Red Hot Mama Contest two-and-a-half months ago. Don had been one of the organizers, along with piano player, Ron Trotta.

We chitchatted a bit about the contest. We laughed about the cheering crowd's hoots and hollers, the costumes and the customers, the goofy and the great. Finally getting to the reason for his call.

"Would you be willing to sing the Lord's Prayer at the Jazz Mass on Sunday? It's at the Cathedral." Before I had a chance to utter a response, he continued, rapidly firing convincing justifications for me to say yes. "I just found out Jay Fleming who usually sings at the Mass is sick and can't make it and it's only five days away. I heard you sing the Lord's Prayer at a friend's wedding so I thought you might be willing to help us out."

Well, flattery will get you everywhere. A compliment-infusing Cheshire Cat smile stretched from ear to ear. I closed my eyes and pictured myself standing on the altar of the beautiful historic cathedral, belting out the 1935 Malotte version, a majestic masterpiece of the Lord's Prayer set to music. This version captures the intimacy of a simple prayer, rising to soaring praise, returning to a quiet ending Amen. Each time I sang it, a deep connection to the heavens opened up in my heart. The thrill of possibility enveloped me. Without delving into the details, the window of opportunity flew wide open like my mouth when I enthusiastically said, "Yes!"

I heard the sigh of relief in his response, "You have no idea how glad I am to hear this. You're doing me a big favor to jump in at the last minute. I'll be in touch with the details."

After disconnecting our call, I didn't even hang up the receiver before I dialed my mom. "You'll never guess what, Mom! I get to sing at Mass at the Cathedral!"

Her enthusiasm fired confidence-boosting bullets at the bravery-building bull's-eye. Direct. Heart. Hit. A hope-infused high. A drugless buzz.

The next few days were filled with 8–5 Agriculture Department work, but in the evenings I sang my heart out, practicing for my cathedral debut. The excitement kept building to sing in the building, the magnificent cathedral building. A whole lot of anticipation mixed in with a bit of nervousness. I kept telling myself it's just singing for Mass in a bigger building. Phew. No issue. 'Til the phone rang.

"How do you spell your name?" asked Don, on a Thursday night phone call.

Perplexed, I spelled both first and last. "Why do you need to know how to spell my name?" I asked a bit baffled.

"For the radio," he answered matter-of-factly.

"Radio?? I thought this was for Mass!" I repeated as queasiness invaded my intestinal tract, beginning in my throat. I could feel the intrusion advance like a parasitic piranha. Blood sucking. Courage siphoning. Creeping. Crawling. Cunning. Covert-operating cockroach. Scurrying down the gut. Stealing my gutsiness to sing.

"It is. The Jazz Mass. You know, the one we do each year for the Jazz Festival. We usually reach maximum capacity of 2,000 people, so we broadcast it on the radio for others to hear," he said, a bit surprised at my lack of understanding. He continued, hoping an explanation would suppress my surprise and suffice for my continued participation. "We have a nine-piece band to accompany you. Different members from different bands join together to play for the Mass. You'll sing with them."

Like this was supposed to calm my feathers. Unruffle my fears. *Yep, Don, you've totally eased my apprehension*, I thought sarcastically. Instead, a few jitterbugs blasted my bravery. *I'm doomed. Crap!*

Crap! Crap!!

"And by the way," Don continued in his matter-of-fact expectation, "Will you be the cantor, too?"

Well, the courage-less me kept shrinking shorter and shorter. I'd been a cantor in smaller Catholic church parishes, leading the congregation in their prayer responses. Starting the sing-along worship songs. But here? In front of 2,000 people? And the non-watching radio listeners? *This is turning into a double-seated, outdoor shitter sitter*, I thought snickering anxiously to myself. Through the scrunched up, unseen-by-Don face, out of my mouth popped, "Sure!"

"Great!" he said, like he expected no other answer. "I'll let them know." *Click.*

The call abruptly ended. I sat staring at the cordless phone silently cradled in my hand, an Indianapolis 500 fear-induced pulse rate rapidly racing. Faster and faster. *"Oh dear, Lord! What have I done?"* Backing out now. Not an option.

Friday festival festivities began with a public procession. A parade of brass instrument players. Master musicians with puckered lips blowing toe-tapping trumpet toots, trombone slides playing in perfect pitch, and saxophonists belting out their top-ten tunes. One by one the ensembles proudly strutted their stuff all the way from the 1920 Moorish-Revival-style civic center, with its towering minaret, to the historic gold strike-it-rich Last Chance Gulch. Where Victorian-era buildings were home to saloons, bars, and a walking mall, the musicians dispersed to their designated places. To play for the people. Thousands of attendees roamed from location to location enjoying the weekend jazz jamboree.

After a restless, nerve-jumping night, I bolted out of bed Sunday morning at 6:00. Grabbing my fuzzy pink bathrobe from the wall hook, I slipped it on, tying the belt tightly around my waist. As I tiptoed down the narrow trailer's wood-paneled hallway, I glanced into Sunny's room to see her curled up on her left side, one arm draped over the Cabbage Patch doll my mom had made her for Christmas. She constantly practiced the same goofy, wide-eyed O-shaped mouth expression of her doll, invoking chuckles from any captive audience. I smiled. My goofy little Sunny girl.

It was a chilly 52-degree morning in Helena, so I quickly brewed a pot of coffee to warm me from the inside out. Opening the front door, I fetched the *Helena Independent Record* newspaper that had been tossed at the bottom of the front steps. Sitting at the small kitchen table, I unfolded it and began reading the front page. The headlines read, "Fireworks could spark tinder-dry grass."

July Fourth isn't too far away, I thought. I leisurely continued my coffee sipping and newspaper-page turning. And skimming. 'Til the "Around Helena" section on page 6A. "Gulch is hoppin' with Dixieland."

Queasiness quickly began percolating in my caffeine-infused stomach. *Ugh. It's THAT day.* SUNDAY! Jazz Mass day. I tried to dismiss the thought of it while enjoying my morning breakfast beverage. But it boiled up and bit me. Dragging my feet wouldn't delay the time as the clock hands continued marching closer and closer to noon.

I glanced up at the round wall clock hanging above our kitchen window. My mom and sister Brenda would be arriving at my house in an hour. They appointed themselves my nerve-calming cheering section and Sunny sitter. Their support was the sedative to my shakiness. I hoped. Time to wake up Sunny.

By afternoon, it would increase to over 90 degrees, so I encouraged Sunny to pick out clothes accordingly. She was the Punky-Brewster-style dresser. Nothing matched. Not even her socks. But her independence and pride in donning her desired dress was more important than the sock-matching, color-coordinating clothes. This battle I'd lost a long time ago. I shook my head and grinned as she gleefully tore through her dresser drawers in search of the perfect ensemble.

Just like Sunny, I tore through my closet, second-guessing my last chosen outfit. Piles of clothes sat staring at me from my bed. *Pick me! Pick me!* Running out of time, I finally settled on the one I'd initially chosen. A white V-necked blouse tucked into a simple mid-length black and white houndstooth plaid skirt. I slipped on a tailored, black, lightweight jacket to complete the outfit. No more changes.

Even in the morning chill, I could feel the clamminess crawl from skin cell to skin cell, invading every nerve in my body. Hopefully the Cathedral wouldn't be an oven with the rising afternoon temperature or my pits would be puddles.

"Knock! Knock!" I heard my mom holler her usual "I'm here" greeting as she opened the door and walked in, followed by my sister.

"I'm *so* nervous, Mom!" I blurted as I felt her arms wrap around me for a calming hug.

"Oh, for goodness sakes, Raylynn," she said with a bit of motherly annoyance. "You are going to do great. You've sung the Lord's Prayer many times. All you need to do is open your mouth. You'll be fine."

Her confidence in me helped bolster my bravery a bit. A hug from my sister. Another boost. My cheering section now numbered three. Mom, Brenda, and Sunny.

After a bit of chitchat and last-minute instructions for Sunny, I headed out the door, sheet music in hand. My security blanket. Rehearsal with the band to begin shortly.

I entered the side door of the Cathedral closest to the altar. I glanced around frantically searching for the one person I would know. The smooth-talking organizer who got me into this mess. I spotted Don visiting with the priest and a musician. I approached and stood at a respectful distance not wanting to interrupt. He turned and grabbed my arm, pulling me forward to make introductions. Smiling, handshaking, nerves shivering, knees knocking. I followed the musician to the altar where the band was assembling. Over the commotion, he called out names and pointed to each band member. As they heard their name called, each turned to wave. I nodded politely, knowing full well no names would stick. Each were flying through my brain at lightning speed, not stopping long enough to be deposited in my memory bank.

Oh no! What if the same thing happens with the song? Panic began bubbling up. Deep breaths needed. Slowly. In and out. In and out.

My panic bubbles were interrupted by Don's voice. "Raylynn, I forgot to ask you earlier. Will you also sing 'Amazing Grace' at the beginning of Mass?"

I could have made Don a dart board and nailed his bull's-eye.

"What?" My eyes wide, I had no clue how to respond. A hiccup in my carefully memorized Mass music timetable.

"You do know 'Amazing Grace,' right?" he innocently asked.

"Of course."

He took my response as an affirmative to his request. He turned to the musician, "She's onboard."

Inwardly, I hollered in protest, *Wait! I didn't really say yes*—Too late. This thought train was out of control on my fear track.

The musician's voice boomed to be heard. "Okay, everyone. Let's run through the songs with Raylynn."

Like a mannequin, I was propped up in the proper performance place. As the song intro began, I took a deep breath and belted it out. I made it through without puking. A feat in and of itself. The positive head nods of the band soothed my chaotic thoughts, creating a small pittance of composure. In our short break, I stumbled to the bathroom, making sure my bladder had not a drop left.

"Fifteen minutes," I heard the in-charge musician announce. "Places everyone."

Sitting in my designated altar spot, I scanned the incoming crowd to see if my cheering section had arrived. I spotted a little red-haired, pigtailed Sunny standing on the pew, waving with all her might hoping to get my attention. I grinned at her antics. My arm raised slightly, giving her a small wave. Smiling broadly at my recognition of her, she went from waving to clapping her hands in anticipation, finally sitting down.

I sat mesmerized at the number of people streaming through the doors. The Catholic cathedral became a sardine packing plant of people. Churchgoers filled the pews butt cheek to butt cheek. With no more standing room available in the back, the outer perimeter walls were lined shoulder to shoulder. With intestinal knots tied by stomach spasms, my body began to shudder and shiver.

I think I can. I think I can. I chanted the mantra of the Little Engine. *I think I can. I think I can. Oh my God! What if I can't?* Then...

Music cued. Mass had begun.

A slight nod from the lead musician was my signal. Rubbery legs lifted my torso. I stood. Walked to the microphone. Took a deep breath as I heard the intro notes of the opening hymn.

"*Amazing Grace, how sweet the sound* . . ."

One by one, hundreds and hundreds of voices joined mine as each verse filled the building. So far. So good. So thankful. As Mass continued, I automatically fell into the Cantor role, leading responses at the proper time.

I watched as the musicians raised their instruments. It was time. I stepped to the microphone. Focusing on my trio of cheerers, I shut out hundreds and hundreds of eyes staring expectantly at me. Fear tears threatened to flood my face. I looked down at the floor. And prayerfully begged, *Please Lord. Don't let me make a fool of myself.* Slowly, I raised my head. Closed my eyes. Opened my mouth. And sang.

My first few notes were a bit shaky. Then I reached "*Thy Kingdom come. Thy will be done. On earth as it is in heaven* . . .." These words signify the intimacy and majestic connection between heaven and earth. Between an omnipotent God and mere sin-filled humans on earth. I was drawn in by the power of this prayer. The overwhelming awareness that we stood in the presence of a forgiving God. He literally brought heaven to earth, making it holy ground. At this moment, I felt His holiness envelop me. All awareness of my surroundings dissipated. It was just me and God. Consumed by His love, I sang to my Savior.

In my limited understanding of the Godhead, I still felt a desire to do His will. I prayed for His forgiveness. Each word coming forth was an expression of faithfulness to the King. I raised my voice in praise. In worship. In adoration. It was my communion with God. No more. No less. The high notes I'd once feared were a crescendo of power. Of prayer. Of commitment to Him.

"Amen." As I reached this ending word or "so-be-it," as-truth declaration, the realization of my earthly locality jolted me into the present. The Jazz Mass. I heard not a word. Not a rustle of clothes. Only an eerie silence. My self-confidence plummeted. I had no clue their thoughts. Their response. Did I take a nosedive down the rabbit hole of rejection as the talentless off-key songbird?

Anxiously awaiting the final, "The Mass is ended. Go in peace to love and serve the Lord," I heard the congregation ending response, "Thanks be to God."

I stood as the closing hymn was played, watching the priest, deacons, and altar boys proceed down the aisle. Noise erupted as the people chatted and began making their way out the wide double door. I knew it would take my cheering section a while to escape the crowd. I slipped out the side door closest to where my car was parked. My knees were still shaking.

Halfway to my parking spot, in a bit of a daze, a car pulled up beside me. I stopped and turned; a bit startled. A middle-aged couple sat smiling. The window was being rolled down as fast as the wife's arm could crank. I sensed their excitement.

"Hey young lady! We're so glad we ran into you! We wanted to let you know that when we found out that Jay Fleming wasn't going to be here, we hesitated to come. We figured no one could be as great as her. Well, young lady, you were! You exceeded our expectations. The Lord's Prayer was absolutely magnificent!"

My mouth fell open. I stood in shock. "You have no idea how much that means to me—"

Interrupting me, the wife asked, "How do you sing like that? Have you had a lot of training?"

I half chuckled, and replied, "No. I've had no singing lessons. It must be because I was prayin' it rather than singin' it."

After a bit more chitchat, they drove away happy and smiling, hands waving out the window.

I just stood there. Taking in the kindness of connection. Of positive feedback from total strangers. *As great as a professional performer?* Still in a bit of unbelief, I thought maybe I did okay then. I continued my trek to the car. My confidence escalating with each step. My stride a bit springier. My smile a bit broader. I allowed a minuscule amount of self-satisfaction to seep deep into my soul.

A Slide Encounter—1986

A new business venture began. Busy busting my butt to get it off the ground. Two new part-time jobs to help pay the bills. Busy. Busy. Busy.

I had left the Department of Agriculture after my Volkswagen Rabbit took on a wandering, road-blocking deer, wreaking havoc on my neck. Eight hours at a desk were no longer possible. A part-time temp job at the Small Business Administration provided needed income while I founded my new business venture. Professional Event Planning, or PEP for short, was born.

Working from my small home office. Soliciting clients. Planning memorable weddings. Convention trade shows. Special occasion parties. Keeping my budget low, my home phone had become an 8-to-5 business phone. Strict rules were set down for its daytime use for Sunny. No answering the phone 'til after 5 p.m. was the rule. Dutifully she hadn't.

She loved doing her "work" sitting beside me at my desk. She loved answering the phone. After 5. *Brrring. Brrring.* Sunny would spring to her knees on the chair and grab the phone. She knew exactly what to say.

Putting the receiver to her ear, she'd say, "Special cun-vent planners. This is Raylynn's daughter speaking."

The first time I heard her greeting, I couldn't help but burst out laughing. Indignant Sunny just looked at me. "I said it just like you, Mom. Why are you laughing?"

I quickly swallowed my laughter and apologized. Then told her how wonderful it was to have an assistant like her. We were partners. In PEP. In life.

****

Ever since buying a trailer and moving to McHugh's Trailer Park, we hadn't attended Mass at the Catholic Church as often. Yet this unseen God kept pestering me. Drawing me. Curiosity piquing more and more. Who is this Jesus? My Catechism taught me that my only connection came through the priest. Yet it seemed that everywhere I turned, someone was talking about a personal relationship with Him. Sharing their life with Him. Pushing me toward Him. My neighbors. Sunny's new babysitter. All brought a different perspective than I'd ever known.

At the babysitter's invitation, we attended her church. As I walked in the door, I felt a bit disloyal. After all, good Catholics attended Mass—and this definitely wasn't it. No holy water. No kneelers. No people sitting, quietly praying before the priest entered. Instead, people stood singing and clapping their hands. Smiling. Swaying. Raising their hands with their eyes closed. Worshiping. I'd never seen such a sight. Odd but slightly intriguing. I felt something draw me. Twanging my heart strings.

As we sat down and listened to the pastor speak, tears welled up in my eyes.

What the heck?

Embarrassed, I hung my head and coughed, acting as if I had a bit of a cold. I had no clue what was happening. And why. Sunny sat quietly beside me. Enthralled by the sermon. How interesting at only the age of five. Unbeknownst to me, it was the Holy Spirit. Drawing. Pulling. Probing. Each of us in our own way.

****

I began delving into the deity drawing me. I wondered, who was this Jesus? Who was this God you can talk to. Pray to. Cry to. Who loves you in spite of you? Your shortcomings. Your failures. Your crap. And despite my confusion as to how to connect, I had a deep-seated longing to have a relationship with Him. I began earnestly searching for Him. Seeking Him. And He, in His patience and love. Sought me. And Sunny.

Sunny came bursting through the door after school as she normally did. Always exuberant. Always full of life. And stories. Today was no exception. "Mom! You'll never guess what happened!"

Of course I never did. Not because I might not guess it. I could never get a word in edgewise.

"MOM," she said with even more emphasis. Obviously my "What" didn't come fast enough. "We need to pray for Amanda. Her brother is doing awful things to her. You know, really *bad* stuff!"

My heart wept for her little friend. "Does she know Jesus, honey?" I asked concerned, knowing there wasn't much I could do.

Sunny puffed out her little chest and crossed her arms. "She does now."

Oh no, I thought. "What happened?" I asked.

In only Sunny style, she burst forth with, "I was standing on top of the slide and the power of God hit me. I turned to Amanda and said, 'Do you want to know Jesus?' And she said yes. So, I led her through the sinner's prayer. Now she knows Jesus!"

My mouth dropped open. I stood looking like a baby birdie waiting for a bite. *Who is this kid of mine?* I thought. *How in the world did she even know what the sinner's prayer was? Let alone what it was for? I hardly knew.*

After announcing her spiritual slide encounter, she flung her empty lunch box on the kitchen counter and asked, "Can I go play with Melissa?" Her bestie.

I silently nodded my head. Still in shock. Out the door she went. Prayer forgotten. Pigtails flying. Ready to play.

Unburied Wound Eruption—1987

I was alone in a hotel room in Billings, Montana, where I was coordinating a trade show. My business, PEP, was on-site. Making sure all went well. Without a hitch. The day's events were over. A successful day, yet long and tiring. I was finally getting some well-earned rest in the hotel room before the final day of the show tomorrow. Then this.

Down time. Finally. I sat in the uncomfortable chair at the small desk nestled in the corner, drinking the pop and eating the cookies I'd quickly snatched at the coffee break but hadn't had a chance to enjoy. I looked around. Typical hotel room but it felt like a palace today. Feeling on top of the world, I sat reflecting. Smiling. I was thrilled to see the last couple of months of hard work paying off. My new business venture using my organizational skills was beginning to gain clients one by one. I loved planning events. After all, I was quick on my feet. A fast thinker. Problem solver.

I learned well how to make junk look pretty and smell like roses. After all, Jeff's type of love for me taught me well. *Thanks for the lessons, Your Highness. Now I can anticipate any failure, any error, any missing link, anything less than perfect.* These are the attributes of a great event planner. And today's event in Billings proved, once again, that I could make it not stink. No matter what.

My clients were pleased with the success of the day, despite the unanticipated failure of a keynote speaker showing up. I felt pride in what I'd accomplished. Averting the trainwreck, with participants none the wiser. I called my mom to share my excitement, as I always did. Her approval of me was a deep-seated need. And I sought it whenever possible. After my non-stop chattering subsided, my mom and Jeff's split became the topic of conversation, as it had been for quite some time.

Mom had recently attended Family Week at the Rocky Mountain Treatment Center in Great Falls, Montana, to learn more about alcoholism. We talked about all the signs, the symptoms. There was no doubt that Jeff was an alcoholic.

Then she calmly said, "I don't think his only problem is alcohol." Bomb drop. Direct hit. Explosion.

A volcanic eruption of once-buried hurts seared their way to my consciousness, leaving a trail of burned ash. Dark. Black. Past pain. Locked down. Too painful to remember. Too hard to discuss. Too embarrassing to relay to anyone.

Till now.

I took a deep breath and said calmly, "Mom. You're right."

Untapped memories of sexually charged encounters were spoken for the first time. Unwanted touches. The bathtub. Him the peacock. Dug out of the deep recesses of my brain. The violation. The hurt. The shame. Bringing them to life. Again.

It was hard for her to hear. Still, in some ways, not wanting to believe it. I found out later she had been referring to his use of drugs as an additional problem—not sexual abuse toward his adopted daughters.

In shock, I hung up the phone. *What now?*

The door that had kept each painful memory imprisoned flung open with one statement. *Not just alcohol.*

Mom had inserted the key and I'd turned it. The rusty door of fate flung wide open. Spewing forth that which I'd buried. On purpose. Too distressing to recall. Too hard to discuss. With anyone. Exposing memories. Exposing pain. Exposing the betrayal of a young innocent girl. Me.

Sitting alone in the hotel room in Billings, Montana. No one to listen to my heart breaking. No one to cry with. Just no one. Alone in my memories of pain. *God. Are you…maybe here?*

"Please hold my hand," I pleaded as the pain of recent remembrance flooded over me. "Jesus, if you really exist, please hold my hand."

I fell to my knees between the two full-size beds, flinging my torso on top. Face down. Palms up. My nostrils inhaling the smell of freshly used bleach. Tears wet the well-worn bedspread as I sobbed uncontrollably. Pain ripping my guts out. My hands lie open, inviting heaven to come down to a lowly little hotel room. Waiting for this unseen God to reply. To show up. To show Himself real. To real people. In real pain.

Burning. Deep burning in the center of my palms. Both hands. I leapt to my feet and stared. *Are they on fire?* The burning intensified. No pain. Burning without pain. Just heat. Boring a hole in my hands.

Lord, is that you?!

The comforting words were clear. "I understand your pain. They nailed Me to the cross. Betrayed by those who vowed their love."

I stood staring. My hands burning. Believing they'd burst into flame any minute now. Searing hot, but no pain. All thoughts of past pain flew out of my brain. Instead, the showing up of an unseen God in such a tangible way became my focus.

Holy crap! No, HOLY SHIT! Sorry, Lord. Not quite the "holy" thought. I stood staring open-mouthed at my red, still-burning hands. *What now?*

I clumsily sat down on the edge of the bed, fulling expecting if I didn't sit, I'd fall. My brain was having trouble comprehending what had just happened. Hot. Flaming. Healing.

The searing pain I'd been experiencing from the volcanic eruption was no longer a thought. Holy-Spirit salve on unburied wounds. Eruption had slowed . . . stopped. Frozen in place. The hot-lava leak of long-ago pain plugged. Blocked shut. God. This heat-searing, hand-holding God. Really exists. Here. Now. No doubt. Ever again.

No Sh*t Sunshine — 1987

I'd been intrigued about this man, Jesus, since my hand-holding episode and church attendance with Sunny's sitter. "A personal relationship with Him," the pastor proclaimed.

Really? How much more personal could it get than attending Mass each Sunday, saying confession, and taking communion? This is how I'd been raised. But this non-Catholic church pastor had emphasized a deeper personal connection was possible. All I had to do was ask.

I didn't realize I'd asked until that day…

"JUST BE OBEDIENT," boomed the voice.

The words thundered through my mind, my heart, my soul, my body. Every cell of my entire being shook with fear. Not fear like you're dying, mind you. Not fear like someone's scared the total bejesus out of you! Fear like, you know, GOD just spoke.

I knew beyond a shadow of a doubt that the Voice I heard was Holy. It sounded like hurricane-force winds crashing into my trailer. Like thunder and lightning colliding in one spot. Direct hit on me.

I had been lying in bed half asleep, dreading another day of my working-single-mom life. These three words literally threw me off the bed. I hit the floor, trembling, on my knees, face smashed into the carpet. My hands lay ahead of me, palms up in submission. Never in my life had I experienced such pure fear. It's kind of weird to think that fear could be pure, but this was. I knew I was safe. I felt an indescribable peace. Yet every hair on my body stood up.

What I knew: I was on Holy Ground. The God of gods. The Lord of lords. The King of kings had just spoken to me.

Little ol' me. In Helena, Montana, living in a trailer park. Working to support my 6-year-old daughter. No one special at all.

So, what now?

As the fear subsided, my bewilderment grew. What had just happened? The words kept roaring through my mind. *JUST BE OBEDIENT!* Up to this point, my relationship with God had been through the priests I had encountered in my journey as a Catholic. I had been taught that God spoke through them. Never in my wildest dreams did I think that God would speak directly to an unholy person like me.

But He did. He had. And there was not even a fraction of a doubt in my mind that it was Him. The almighty God I revered. From this day forward, my life was driven by a need to know this Jesus. This God who had told me to obey. Obey what? I continued to search.

****

I began spending time with a gentleman I'd met at a local bar where my friend Carol and I hung out for some girl-time fun. Nothing serious. Just nice to be noticed by the opposite sex. I'd invited him over to dinner. As we were finishing up, we noticed a Jeep parked on the street facing the kitchen window. Angry cuss words and door slamming caught our attention.

The displeased driver marched to the front of the vehicle and flung open the hood. Frustration written all over his face. His misfiring motor became a downright debacle. My friend headed out to assist.

After a brief discussion with the Jeep owner, he headed to a friend's house to get jumper cables. He said he'd be back in a flash. The annoyed auto owner jumped back in the Jeep seat and sat dejected. Waiting. For a battery boost for his breakdown. As I cleared the table, my heart went out to the poor pissed-off guy.

The doorbell rang. Sunny opened it. Seeing Melissa, she hollered over her shoulder as she headed out. "Mom! Me and Melissa are going outside," she announced.

In the meantime, I turned back to the sink to wash the dishes. As I finished, I turned and looked out the window. No Jeep. And no friend of mine in sight. That's odd. *Did it just start?* Mulling this over in my mind, the door flew open. Sunny burst in. Grinning from ear to ear. Oh no. That look.

What now?

I calmly asked, "What are you up to?" Before she could answer, I asked the question that was nagging me. "Did you see what happened to the guy in the Jeep?"

Another grin. Ear to ear. "Yep. He left."

Believing the only way it would have started is with the use of jumper cables, I asked. "Did he jump it?"

"Nope!" The shit-eating grin, as my mom would call it, crossed her face again.

Now a bit baffled, I asked, "So what happened?" Knowing Sunny, I was braced for her off-the-wall, out-of-left field Sunny-style answer.

"Weeell . . .," she drew out her answer dramatically. "I walked over to the Jeep and put my hands on the front and said, 'In the name of Jesus, start.'" After using all her air on this long statement, she took a deep breath and continued, "I went to the window and told the guy to try and see if it will start. He looked at me really weird but he did. And it started!" She said triumphantly. "Boy, Mom, when it did, he stared at me *really* weird."

No shit, Sunshine, I thought. She was oblivious to the magnitude of the miracle. The jaw-dropping faith of a youngster. The innocent belief in the miracle maker. Pouring out prayer power. And the vastness of the vehicle victory. An amazing God looking down on this wee one. A child. Chosen. Cherished. And boosted the battery. Turned the turbine. Jumped the Jeep. Holy-Spirit style.

****

On another occasion, Sunny had yelled, "Mom! There's an angel in my room! He's on my bed." In response to her declaration, I stuffed my sideways snicker and said as seriously as I could muster under the circumstances, "Sunny, there can't be." My skepticism was more than likely obvious, though.

"Mom, *please*! Come look! You'll see."

I followed reluctantly. Sunny stood near the door to her room.

"See!" she said excitedly as she pointed to her bed, waiting for my awed admiration answer. I saw nothing. My delay in approaching the room caused her hand to beckon me closer. "PLEASE, Mom! Look!"

I got within two feet of the door and stopped cold. Barred. Forward motion impeded. My feet felt fastened to the floor. Presence of an unseen power prevented my progress. Oh. My. God.

Sunny pointed again, giggling, "He's way too big for my bed. His feet are hanging off. He's huge, Mom! Now he's smiling at me. He's really nice, I think. Can't you see him, Mom? He's right there!"

She grinned back at the invisible entity inhabiting her bed. On top her covers. Lazily lounging around. Lying down. An angelic apparition of the Almighty. A mysterious manifestation. Holy. Moly. Miracle. Maker. Wonder. Creator. But I was blind and couldn't see.

Disappointedly, Sunny looked up at me, "He's gone."

An amazing appearance of a holy agent. Deity dispatched. A glimpse of a heavenly being to boost the belief of a little bitty believer named Sunny.

Somehow. Someway. Spiritual gifts given to my sweet Sunshine girl. I had no clue their immensity. Their intention. And why? What did the future hold for this delightful daughter? Only. God. Knew.

Toxins and Tears—1987

"You're going where?!" I asked in shock.

"Salt Lake City. Tomorrow. I have an appointment on Monday," my mom replied.

Adding the departure time and a minimal explanation for my anticipated next question, "Why? What for?" My interrogation continued not satisfied with her skate-the-issue reason. Her beat around the bush B.S. raised my worry monitor over the top.

She explained that she hadn't felt well for a few months so made an appointment with her future brother-in-law, Doctor Gayle, at the local Whitehall Medical Clinic. After numerous tests, his lack of wacky blood-test-results expertise led him to ship her off to Salt Lake City for blood specialist oversight and further testing.

"Mom, I'll take off work and go with you!" I said as my mind raced through a list of potential sitters for Sunny.

Emphatically she said, "No! You stay here and take care of Sunny. I want to go alone."

I was heartbroken. Never had my mom refused to let me accompany her somewhere important. *What in the world is going on?*

"But Mom, you can't drive there all by yourself! I can go with you. You shouldn't go alone."

Her perturbed answer was raised a few decibels, "Raylynn! I said *no!*" This intense tone indicated her stubborn mule heels were dug in and no way could I talk her out of her go-alone appointment plan.

"When are you leaving?" I asked, resigned to a gather-information-only tone.

"At 9 o'clock in the morning. My appointment is Monday."

With her rejection of my tag-along offer, I begged for a bit of continual connection, "Will you at least let me know when you get there? And how your appointment goes?"

She assured me that she would and then said, "By the way, I don't want Uncle Ron or Brenda knowing about this."

In shock, I agreed. And the phone went dead.

I sat staring at the phone in my hand, forgetting to hang it up. The fear trickled down to my toes. Foreboding entered my entire being. *What in the world is going on?* I thought. *Why would she shut me out like this? And not tell Uncle Ron or Brenda?* Freaking fear flooded my bones.

The next afternoon promptly at 3:45 p.m., my phone rang. It was a Sunday. Minimal conversation took place. Only an arrival notification. I asked questions to probe and pry a bit, but she answered none. "I'm tired from the long drive, honey. I'll talk to you later." *Click.*

After a fitful night, I dragged myself out of bed and woke Sunny up to get ready for school. Even at her young age, she was perceptive. "What's wrong, Mom?"

I knew I wasn't myself, but I was sworn to secrecy.

"Nothing honey. I didn't sleep too good, so I'm still a bit tired."

Satisfied with my answer, she dressed, ate her Cheerios, and dashed out the door. I watched as she raced across the street to her friend Melissa's trailer. Before she could knock on the door, her friend scrambled down the steps. I breathed a deep sigh and stared a bit enviously at their carefree chitchat and giggles as they walked side by side to school.

I went through the day in a daze. I limited my calls so my phone line would be free. I glanced at the clock. School was almost out. Time to pick up Sunny. Melissa had been picked up early by her mom for an appointment, so that would have left Sunny walking alone. After a bullying incident a few weeks previously, I didn't allow a walk home alone.

Only ten minutes tops gone from the house, but I rushed to check my voicemail. No message. No call from my mom. I sat down to wait. Each second of a minute ticked off as slow as an hour. Each hour felt like an eternity. About 4:45 p.m. the phone rang.

"Hi honey," Mom said.

I could tell something was wrong, very wrong. My panic button was punched. Slapped. Slammed.

"What's wrong, Mom? What did they say?" Dread slithered down my windpipe like a boa constrictor limiting my ability to breathe.

"I have some kind of problem with my blood. It's not good. They said I may have about three months if things don't change."

Three months for what?! My mind screamed for clarification. "Oh my God, Mom! What are you saying?" Tremors of an internal eruption started in the pit of my stomach. Radiating from its central point, the quivering became contagious, awakening each and every nerve cell in my body. Head-to-toe trembling emitting fear morsels that were swallowed up. Vomit was churning. Bile was building.

Sobbing uncontrollably. I couldn't breathe.

"Honey, it'll be okay. Please don't cry." In the midst of her horrifying news, she was trying to console me.

I gulped hard, trying to plug the ducts from which they fell. "What's making you sick, Mom? Are they sure? Can't you get another opinion?" I firebombed questions at her, trying to find a positive twist to the fate in her future.

"They said there's toxins in my blood. It's what's making me sick," she explained.

"Toxins? How on earth would you get toxins in your blood?" I questioned their expertise. Trying hard to find fault in their fatal diagnosis.

"It's from all the years of stress. It's causing some kind of toxins to build up in my blood. They said that stuffing emotions for so long can cause problems with my heart. I guess it's affected my blood quite a bit."

My mind raced backward through all the Jeff-torched trials of breakup, divorce, discovery of his infidelity and drug use. Not once do I recall her crying. She'd bottled up her emotions for years. All I ever saw was a few raging fits of anger. At the intense hurt.

"Why can't they fix it? Flush it out?" I offered, questioning their lack of fixable solutions.

"They gave me some new kind of medication. They haven't used it a lot for this yet so they aren't sure if it will do any good. But they thought it was worth a shot."

I could hear the fear tremble trounce on her hopeful words, dashing them to pieces.

"I'd say so!" I shot back. "Of course it's worth trying! Mom, *please* don't give up."

My plea was met with a silent struggle. One I could feel, not hear. A river of tears fell as I dealt with my own silent struggle. "I don't want Brenda and Uncle Ron to know" were her next spoken words.

"Mom, why? Don't you think they have a right to know? This is serious!"

My question was met with more silence. I waited. Pleading inside.

"I just don't want them to know, okay?" she said quietly. No rational reason for secrecy. No logical justification for concealment. Her dogged determination driving this decision was unshakable. "Honey, I'm so tired. I need to get some sleep so I can drive home tomorrow." The discussion was done.

"I love you, Mom. Please let me know when you get home, okay?"

"Okay. I love you, too," she said softly, as emotional and physical fatigue rudely intruded on our mother–daughter heart connection. The phone went dead.

I sat stone faced. My inner turmoil swirling and twirling in a thousand directions. My thoughts were fragmented with no ability to connect. Unlinked chains created confusion unable to conceive the consequences of our conversation.

The front door swung open. Startled, my heartbeat skipped a few.

"Mom! Can I eat at Melissa's? Her mom said it was okay!" Sunny announced, still hanging onto the doorknob, expecting to depart again.

I looked at her and nodded affirmatively.

"Thanks! See ya later!" Inseparable besties they were ever since we moved into McHugh Trailer Court.

Tonight, I was grateful for the alone time. The think time. The cry time. Without Sunny.

A childlike fear of abandonment smacked me upside my devastated heart. The secret seclusion of the toxic blood demise left me in panic. It was a solitary concealment confinement. I was riding solo with her secret, imprisoned alone in my fear.

Bewilderment became my daily state of mind. The next few weeks passed in a blur. Daily phone calls with Mom reaped no additional information or resolve. Disclosure discussion was off limits. The only response was, "I don't want to worry them."

Worry them? I thought. *What about me?* The fuse leading to my internal trepidation was lit. The emotional explosion was coming.

I had been seeing a counselor at Boyd Andrew Chemical Dependency Outpatient Services after the realization that Jeff was an alcoholic. The kind, young man was assisting me in identifying my laundry list of adult-child-of-an-alcoholic behavioral traits. During our last session, he had been keenly aware of my ramped-up emotional state. Initially, I refused to let him in on the don't-tell secret. But prying open slammed soul doors was his specialty. His probing questions wrecked my resolve. I was sure I'd be chastised for my lack of secret keeping. As he kindly responded, without scolding, I realized he wasn't a "Jeff."

As we talked through Mom's demand that I keep her secret, he asked, "Do you think it's right to request this of you? Do you think that it's fair?"

Our discussion led me to realize that I could choose. I believed that to remain silent was unfair to all of us. Uncle Ron and Brenda deserved to know. Mom deserved to have a caring family encircling her in love. Bearing the burden together.

My next phone call to her put me in the driver's seat of deciding the emotional pain I was willing to carry. Or not.

"Mom, I'm asking you to tell Uncle Ron and Brenda. If you don't, I will."

I stood firm as she spat out her fear-fueled fury. In the end, she knew I was right.

Six weeks of medicine and stress-relieving activities led to a miracle. Her local doctor took follow-up blood tests. Prognosis for the dire diagnosis changed. The outcome was an opportunity at renewed life. And for me. The strength to make a stand for my own sanity. Sadly, this lesson left me later in life. When it almost cost me my life.

February 14, 1997—North Dakota State Penitentiary, Bismarck, North Dakota

"STRIP! Everything off," demanded the prison guard. She opened the swinging bathroom stall-like door to the tiny, little bare-walled cubicle. Her head nodded toward it, indicating her expectation for me to enter. Her eyes darted from head to toe with a bit of a sideways grin. I had begun processing into prison life a brief five minutes prior. From the transport van to the prison doors, I broke out in a sweat. From fear. From anxiety. Or maybe from all the clothes I was wearing.

As of today, I wasn't just a jailbird. I was an inmate. Convicted North Dakota State felon. A prisoner. A number.

And it was time to bare everything. To the guards who stood outside the cubicle, this might be an everyday thing. Not to me. I slowly began to undress. For you to fully understand the next few minutes, let me take you back to yesterday. In the Minot jail.

My cell bunk mates had been giving me advice. They weren't first timers like me. They knew the ropes.

"Been there," they'd said with pride, sadly enough. "Wear as many clothes as you can. You get to keep what you have on when you get there!"

Really? I guess I better layer up. I planned. I practiced. I had it all worked out. Beat the system. Follow the rules with stretched boundaries. And stretch them as far as you can. That's what I had to do with my clothes, too, with an extra 20 pounds to stuff in after all the cheap, carb-ladened jail food I'd been eating.

I'm no dummy. I was raised in Montana, in the cold country. I know how to layer clothes to stay warm. I'd do the same. *I got this!*

I was determined to keep all that I had. Possession is nine-tenths of the law . . . unless you are the law.

It started with the handcuffs. The leg restraints. The slow shuffle to the transport van. *Ugh. I have to lift my leg all the way up THERE? How can I do that with chain-tethered ankles?* My short, and now fatter, Polack legs weren't serving me well in that moment. And neither were the number of clothing items restraining my body.

I stared out the van window, enjoying the scenery on the hour-and-a-half drive to the next stop on my incarceration journey. From Havre to Minot, now to Bismarck. To the North Dakota State Penitentiary. A prison, not just a jail. *Lord will this ever end?* my heart cried.

Arrival time. Slide down the van steps. Shuffle to the prison door. Herded in with the other new inductees, we stood in line waiting for the next command. *Tough. Act tough*, I thought. *Yeah, right. I'm a badass chick . . . NOT!* Nope. Just a chicken. Did it show? Maybe. Probably. Most definitely a newbie.

Two female guards headed my way and ushered me down the hall to a conference-type room. With the turn of a tiny key, leg restraints and handcuffs fell to the ground with a clank.

Phew! What a relief.

Into the tiny room I waddled, as she commanded, "STRIP! Everything off and hand it out one at a time."

So the undressing, the unrobing, and the unlayering began. A coat. A sweatshirt. Three T-shirts. A bra. Another bra.

By this time, I can hear the hint of snickering. The process continued. Jeans. Sweatpants. Panties. Panties. More panties. By now the guards' giggles were no longer suppressed.

Oh, no! Socks! I forgot to take off my socks! A black one. A white one. A tall one. A short one. And repeat.

As I stood buck naked in the cubicle crossing my arms over my breasts for less exposure, the guards were rolling in full-blown, hold-your-gut laughter. "Is that all?" they asked, trying to act stern.

"Yes," I whispered embarrassingly. The neck-high door swung open and every cavity, I mean *every* orifice on my body, was examined. The very definition of degradation.

Shower time. Disinfecting time. I tried to let the lukewarm water wash out the fear. No go. Still there. Terrified thinking about the others I'd soon meet. Behind the bars. In a state penitentiary.

"Hurry it up," the guard hollered. "We don't have all day!"

I hurriedly dried and donned the not-so-stylish orange jumpsuit. "What about my clothes?" I asked. "I brought all my own clothes. Can't I wear them?"

"Not while you're in orientation," replied the guard. "When you're done, you'll get two pairs of panties, two bras, two shirts, two pair of pants, two pairs of socks," she went down the list.

"What? I don't get to keep all my clothes? They *told* me I could," I pleaded. No way. *All that work for NOTHING?*

Although deflated, I saw the absurdity of the situation. No wonder they were laughing. *Way to show your badassery, Raylynn*, I thought to myself. Well at least I made them laugh. And laughing is good. Especially here. In this dark, depressing hole.

Fingerprints. Check. Mug shots. Check. Prison life had begun.

Follow the Rebel Brick Road—1987

"He's my cousin, too!" Curly said with a grin. "What a coincidence."

I sat open-mouthed, staring at Curly Thornton sitting in McDonald's in Helena, Montana, on a Friday night, mid-November 1987. It was my usual Friday night, end-of-the-week date with Sunny. I made sure I had $5 each Friday so I could treat Sunny. I splurged. As a single mom, $5 was a lot. And sometimes I felt guilty wrestling with responsibility. I should pay it on a bill. No matter how little. When you owe money, you pay it before anything else. That was responsibility.

But a single parent mom friend had said, "What about time with Sunny? $5 isn't going to pay much on a bill, but it will go a long way in time with your daughter. What's more important? You're all she has. She needs fun times with you. You can't ever get back the time you didn't spend with her. You can always make more money. So take the time."

I took her words to heart and so here I sat at McDonald's, Friday night. In a booth. Reading a romance novel. Glancing up often to watch Sunny play. Up the steps. Down the slide. Her strawberry-blonde pigtails bobbing. Giggling with another little girl. I smiled. Thrilled she'd made a friend and was enjoying the night out.

I went back to my love story, then heard the door open. I looked up and watched the dressed-up crew walk in single file. Business suits. I stared. I couldn't help it. The one walking in front was the spitting image of my cousin Bob, down to his mannerisms. Uncanny. Crazy. He and a striking dark-haired young woman walked in my direction and sat down across from me. The other two men went to the counter to order.

He saw me staring at him and smiled. Invitingly. I smiled back. "Hi," I said stiffly, a bit embarrassed. I couldn't help but continue. "You look just like my cousin, Bob Thornton," I blurted out.

His eyes widened and he said, "Bob? He's my cousin, too!"

My eyes widened, I said, "He is? Really?!"

"How are you his cousin?" he asked.

I explained the connection. My grandma's nephew. My mom's first cousin. My second.

"Unbelievable," he said. He chuckled and said, "I'm Curly Thornton. Butte born and bred," he boasted. His Butte pride was evident. He went on to explain his connection to Bob's dad. He turned to the dark-haired beauty sitting quietly beside him. "This is my wife."

I smiled and said, "Hi. Nice to meet you."

She smiled back, seeming amused at our conversation. The guys returned and set the tray of food and drinks in front of Curly. He picked up the cup of coffee, pushed the tray aside, and introduced us.

"Randy. Dylan. Meet my newfound cousin," immediately claiming me as his own.

A warm feeling of acceptance flowed through me. Head to toe. Sipping the hot liquid, he began quizzing me. About what I did for a living. I explained that I'd recently started an event planning business. I was pretty proud of my business venture and it showed. I handed him my card, trying to act important. Spiffy suits might translate to significant success. Affluence. Financial finesse. Prosperous occupation. Possibly in need of a bit of event planning. Right up my alley. And deep in my pocketbook.

After sharing briefly about me, I asked him, "What are you in Helena for? You live in Butte, right?"

He grinned and sat up a bit straighter like *Look at me and take note.* "I live in Billings. I was attending an event for the gubernatorial candidates. I'm running for governor."

Wowzer. Knock me over with a feather. My mouth dropped open unconsciously. "Wow," was all I could say.

My thoughts swirled a bit, intimidated now. In the presence of important people. A step above my pay grade. Intimidated by perceived importance. Impacted by influence. Sideswiped by significance. He's bigger than, better than. Me.

The couple-hour conversation became a Curly-boasting session. I was awed and starstruck by this man of God. Recovering alcoholic with a foot in politics to become a voice for the underdogs. The underlings. The less thans. The has beens. The have nots. His calling. His ministry. As the head guru of a nonprofit called On the Wings of a Dove. I was in awe. A Roman Catholic turned evangelist. An anointed action-taker. A heaven mover and celestial shaker. A—

My awe party was interrupted by his question, "In your event planning, have you ever managed a political campaign?"

My thoughts whirled. *Nope. But maybe I could.* I had worked for the government. Spent time serving cocktails at the governor's mansion. Worked with the governor's press person on communications as the agricultural director's administrative assistant. *I had a bit of clout, didn't I?* Probably not, but I could convince him I did. *Couldn't I?* I did my best to give a plug for PEP. He leaned in. Listening. Intently. Silently. Looking back now, even a bit eerily.

With the long travels ahead, he gathered his groupies and headed out the door. He grinned at me as he said goodbye. "I'll be in touch."

I watched the dressed-up crew trail after Curly as they headed out the door. One by one. I sat in wonderment. In a bit of what-in-the-heck-was-this-all-about feeling. *Excitement? Amazement?*

As I tore Sunny away from her McDonald's playhouse fun, I felt a bit giddy with anticipation.

What if he did ask me to be his campaign manager? I could learn. It's just managing details with a political twist, right? How hard could it be? What a professional promotion. A notch on my business belt. Advancing. Progressing. Prospering PEP. A huge smile crossed my face as I herded the less-than-thrilled-to-be-leaving daughter of mine out the double door.

Saturday morning phone call. "Mom! You'll never guess what?" When excitement happened in my life, the first one I called was my mom.

I began relating the details of the Friday night encounter. "It would blow your mind how much he looks like Bob. Totally unbelievable!

Do you know anything about him?"

My mom told me the little she knew about the family affiliations. Not much, really. But the connection to family made all the difference in the world. Family was a sacred bond. An untie-able attachment. And he was family of a sort, just a bit removed. This could be an awesome adventure. With recently discovered family.

Or so I thought.

****

Monday morning. A couple weeks later. The shrill ring of the phone caught me off guard as I looked through a catalog of trade show table drapes for an upcoming event. "Hello. Professional Event Planners. This is Raylynn. May I help you?"

My heart skipped a beat when I recognized the deep voice that said hello even before he announced, "This is Curly."

I mustered up my best business voice portraying a confidence I faked often. Counterfeit confidence. A phony professional. Masquerading as a manager. Campaign that is. I'd be a class act. A champion. At charades.

We chitchatted about his trip home and weekend activities. I laughingly said, "I checked you out," recalling my conversation with my mom.

He chuckled. "I checked you out, too." He said he'd prayed and his Father said I was his choice.

Whoa. He's quite tight with the guy upstairs, I thought. Reverential. Open-mouthed. Awestruck. Admiration.

"Will you take the job? Will you be my campaign manager?" he asked.

My heart was thumping so loud I was sure he could hear it. *Calm down!* I told myself. *Tryouts are over. I landed the part!* My professional persona paid off.

"Yes! I'd love to," I replied with a calmness in my voice that the rest of my body didn't feel. I was jumping out of my skin with excitement. *A campaign!* A gubernatorial campaign. And I, an insecure, single mom, a wannabe entrepreneur trying to make a life for her little sunshine, Sunny girl, was now a bonafide honest-to-goodness campaign manager. For Curly. One of God's elect. Sure to be elected. As governor.

At that moment, my life changed forever. A simple yes defined my destiny. Fixed my fate. My fear-filled future. *Hadn't I been praying for a closer walk with God?* Maybe he was the tool to get me there. God's answer. My religious route. Follow the rebel-brick road. To Oz. Curly the wizard. *Who does that make me?* Maybe the cowardly cat. Or the scatterbrained scarecrow? Who didn't think. For herself. 'Til it was too late.

A lookalike drew me in. Captured me. Caught me. Seized my soul. And I almost sold it to the wrong side. The dark side. The evil side. For a season of life. Almost destroyed. Almost dead. Almost demolished. Bulldozed by a bully.

That night, under the Golden Arches. I was captivated. By Curly. A charismatic con. A mesmerizing minister of his own death-driven doctrine. I swallowed the bait. Caught. Like a sucker. And I sank. Deep.

A Wolf in Sheep's Clothing—1988

"Alcoholics are God's chosen people," Curly repeated, slowly emphasizing the last three words. "God's. Chosen. People." I sat mesmerized as he continued describing the vision he'd had years ago. "Vast amounts of money will come to you in the mail. Take what you need and give the rest to the poor and the needy." He went on to explain further. "In September 1980, God told me I'd have problems with drugs for three more years. Then He'd set me free. Three years to the day, I was done. No more alcohol. No more drugs."

This charismatic man stood in front of a captive audience of fifteen, sharing his stupendous story. I was invited to attend a campaign meeting. I thought, anyway. Sunny and I headed to Billings in December 1987 to meet the gang. To strategize. To lay out a plan to win.

We sat shoulder to shoulder in the living room of a woman he grew up with in Butte, Montana. Tall oak dining room chairs smashed together side by side to provide maximum seating in front of the built-in decorative bookshelves. Dark-blue damask chenille covered the three-cushion round-backed sofa holding four attentive listeners a bit uncomfortably. Comfort was no issue, however. The words spewing from his mouth were electrifying. Exhilarating. Intoxicating. I snuck a glance at the face of our Butte-native hostess. Smiling. Nodding. Agreeing. Her involvement with the new and reformed Curly gave credibility to his vow of sobriety and religious restoration, having known him in his younger wild and wanton-filled days.

He boasted of gunshot wounds, barroom brawls, cocaine snorting, wife beating, adultery and divorces, gambling and bankruptcies, DUI's and arrests. Just the tip of the iceberg we heard of his checkered past. Yet he convincingly demonstrated his sobriety and spiritual conversion. I was dazzled by him. Besides, he was a newfound cousin. Family is faithful. Committed. Loyal. I quickly dropped my gaze to my lap as my grin crossed my face. I was related to this charming candidate for governor told to run for office by Jesus himself, he had explained. How much better recommendation can you get? Than God.

Recently I had attended Family Week at the Rocky Mountain Treatment Center in Great Falls, Montana. After my mom left her constantly drinking husband Jeff, she'd been given special permission to attend even though he refused treatment. Undeniably, the behaviors he exhibited were those of an alcoholic. So, at her urging, I followed suit and went. The stark reality was that not only was my adoptive dad, Jeff, an alcoholic. So was my dad, Raymond.

I knew that I had the potential to fall into this same category after drinking my way through my last year in college. It wasn't just your normal college partying I drank to drown my disappointments. To stave off my stinkin' thinkin' and shortage of self-worth. Each time life's troubles tracked me down, I drowned them in drink. Addiction was my nemesis. Even crappy food found its way to my fork as my faithful friend. Filling my desperation for attention. Drinks and sugar-induced endorphins fixed my need for love.

So, I fit the bill. Curly had just validated my value in spite of my addictive flaws. I was special. Chosen by God for a high and mighty purpose. How flat-out flipping fabulous!

I hung on every word. He presented himself as a prophet. Preaching to the people. Campaigning for governor on the platform of promise. To heal the alcoholics and set them free for Jesus.

This wasn't political. It was preaching. After an hour, he crooked his finger and motioned me forward. I was a bit embarrassed and a lot mesmerized. This was a cross between an Alcoholics Anonymous meeting and a Pentecostal church service. My experience with both were limited. All I knew, I'd never heard anyone talk about Jesus like this. Or openly admit the lousiness of their past.

Impressive. Really impressive, I thought.

After I nervously stood up, I walked slowly toward him. I stopped about two feet from him. Face to face. I outwardly flinched as he took a small step forward and put his hand on my head. Weird. Just so weird. I could feel my heart racing. Fear or anticipation, I couldn't figure out which. In my peripheral vision I could see other attendees smiling and nodding. *Okay, so it's just me. I'm the weirdo who's wigged out.*

I heard Curly say, "Repeat after me."

I did, not truly knowing what they meant or why I was repeating his words. Later I learned it was my acceptance of Jesus as my Lord and Savior.

"Amen," I said. Then I felt super funny. Like every muscle in my body became rubber. Just like Gumby's clay body was a bit wobbly, so was mine. I fell backwards, not even caring or knowing where I'd hit. Gentle hands caught me on the way to the floor and carefully laid me down. After a few moments of floating on cloud nine, my brain engaged, common sense returned, and embarrassment flushed my cheeks. *What just happened?*

Although horrified and humiliated, I finally got the guts to open my eyes. Curly had started to preach again and all eyes were on him. No one was paying any attention whatsoever to me. I slowly sat up. Curly stopped mid-sentence and reached out his hand to help me up. A grin was plastered across his face. "Pretty amazing, isn't it?" he said with eyes twinkling.

Never had I ever experienced this in the Catholic Church. This wasn't just sitting in the pews listening to a priest. This preacher man had called me up. Singled me out. I felt specially selected. Handpicked. Included. A lost sheep found and taken into the fold by a deeply caring, charismatic shepherd. I just didn't know he would turn into a wolf. Proudly wearing the clothing of each innocent, unknowing sheep he captured. Sadly though, it takes a slaughter, a destruction of life to remove the hide. To collect them one by one regardless of the ruination caused. The exposed tender souls left naked to bleed. Then to die. Slowly slaughtered by a self-seeking, seductive maniac.

****

The year 1988 began with a title and validation. An inexperienced campaign manager for a hifalutin gubernatorial candidate. The allure. I really had no clue about political campaigns, but I knew about management.

Could it be that hard to learn? I chuckled a bit. I was the "don't say no" expert in more ways than one. One positive aspect of my upbringing was learning that work is just work. If you have a brain, use it. Do what you need to do to accomplish the job. Don't have the tools? Figure out a different way. Don't have the knowledge? Look it up or ask someone who does. Don't say I can't, say how can I accomplish this?

A great work ethic was drilled into me. Even at a very young age, we were assigned chores on the ranch. Gather the eggs. Milk the cows. Weed the garden. Pick the strawberries. Pluck the chicken feathers. We didn't get an allowance. We got a roof over our heads and food on the table. The entire family worked. And worked hard. So, managing a campaign couldn't be that hard.

I spent hours in the Lewis & Clark County Library researching the trade and the tactics. Poring over previous winning campaign pamphlets, how-to books on fabricating a frenzy of favor, marketing the magnificence. With Curly as the candidate. My job…to present a professional persona to the public. And pump up the publicity in the press. I wrote news releases and creative campaign literature. Television, newspaper, and radio reporters called requesting Curly quotes.

I've hit the big time, I thought. I'd have clients busting down my door for my organizing expertise. On cloud nine, I sat dreaming of my potential to be picked. The fantastic fate of my future. *And Curly needs me, doesn't he?*

After all, he and his guru-groupies drove my white Voyager van across the state of Montana sharing the "Good News" of the deity-designated candidate's campaign. My workers' compensation lump-sum settlement, thanks to the deer, came in handy for a God-given goal. To fund the food and the fuel funneled through On the Wings of a Dove Ministry. A manipulative way to stay campaign-contribution compliant. Presentable nonprofit protocol. Such perfect pilfering.

Feelings of importance I wore like a badge of honor. I was point person for the prophet. My self-worth magnitude increased tenfold on the Richter scale of shocked selection. Of being pursued for a powerful political purpose. Me. Now I mattered.

And so did my money.

Cozying up to the camera at a local Helena video studio sat Curly. Dressed sharp in his dark, gray suit, sporting a fashionable red polyester tie. Relaxed and ready for his videotaped campaign pitch to preach a message of restoration. Of recovery.

"Whether I win or whether I lose makes no difference. I still win because I'm doing what I'm supposed to be doing right now. But ultimately, the campaign and the ministry are the same in terms of what I'm called to do. The campaign is God. When I say Jesus and me are a majority, I'm not kidding. The ultimate result of my campaign is that this state is going to have restoration," he had adamantly proclaimed.

I was mesmerized. He spoke so eloquently. Articulate and charismatic, he sat comfortably on the studio stool with legs crossed, and hands relaxed on his lap.

He's a natural and so convincing, I thought. *I'll vote for him*, I chuckled to myself.

The half-hour pitch was taped and ready for marketing. One thousand VHS copies to be handed out across the state in lieu of expensive television and newspaper ads. Cash from my coffers paid the cost. The conventional way of marketing wasn't for Curly.

This was my mountaintop mission. The view from the top looked fabulous. I felt needed. Then seven months from management commission to conclusion. Curly's last-place finish in the June 1988 primary election ended my gig as the campaign chief organizer. *Now what?*

I continued to be used. And pursued. Unaware of the pitfall. My pocketbook was the prize to be won. Not me.

Suck-Duction—1988

The House of "Suck-Duction." It sucked, all right. It nearly sucked the life out of me. And it began, oh, so seductively.

It's a story of the cunning spider and the gullible fly. Flattery is the bait which seals the fate of the fly. I was oblivious to the dangerous spinning of the web wrapping inch by inch around me. Slowly enveloping me in its trap. Dragging me into its den of duplicity. I was the fly. The feast for Curly. A master of manipulation stealthily attracting his target.

Alluring actions of care and concern drew me in. Catching me off guard. The persuasive pledges promising a place in the Kingdom of God were depriving me of inner strength to stand against the unsuspected venom being injected into my mind. My heart. Paralyzing me. He pounced purposefully. The captor slowly sucking the life out of my soul. Creating helplessness against the poisonous infusion of captivating control. Wounding limb after limb, creating ever-increasing weakness 'til total reliance on him existed. Captured. By the cunning spider.

The hardship of the last few years had taken its toll. My support system had been undercut by my mom's and Jeff's split. I had become the supporter rather than the supported. I was mom's sounding board for the years of drunk-and-disorderly-caused mental anguish she'd endured from Jeff. I was Jeff's sounding board for my mom's so-called bizarre behaviors after he violated their vows. His ability to coerce me into believing his bullshit was uncanny. After all, hadn't he come to my rescue when my dad died?

I was like a dog lapping up every lick of attention. My attachment to the domineering daddy hard to break. Difficult to decipher the truth. Who be the teller of it? Mom or Jeff? Back and forth my brain flew. Mom was a mess from the betrayal. But Jeff pulled our strings. Still. By his skills of debate. I had heard someone laughingly say he could talk the Pope out of being Catholic. It wasn't laughable when it came to the matter of the heart. For my mom. And the masterful manipulation of mind. For me.

In this state of uncertainty. Enter the savior, Curly.

Each wrap of the web progressed with Curly's save-the-single mom moves.

"I heard your swamp cooler isn't working. I'm sending Randy over to fix it. He's good at handyman tasks. While he's in Helena, he'll do whatever you need. He's there to make it easier for you," he had offered.

I half laughed at the mental picture of me attempting to unscrew the rusted bolts on the not-so-cool broken swamp cooler, sitting atop my 1972 Marlette 14' x 65' mobile home. My mama didn't raise no wimp.

At least I tried, I had chuckled to myself. Then the chuckle became a sigh of resignation. My shoulders were sagging with the weight of my aloneness. Mentally and physically exhausted. A dash of helplessness eroded my self-sufficiency, leaving a trail of neediness in its wake.

Like blood to a shark, Curly followed the scent of vulnerability. Creating a subtle dependence. A reliance on his ever-evolving relief tactics. His take-charge helper maneuvers. Invaded. Covertly. Silently. Secretly. Totally oblivious to the outcome. Gullibly, I had begun humming my responsibility-reliever melody. All the while the web was woven. Tighter and tighter.

"Will you do something for me?" Curly had asked casually.

My heart skipped a beat. A chance to serve the savior of my single-mom sanity. "Sure!" I replied, thrilled to hear his request. I'd most certainly do my best. A people pleaser for a mere drop of positive attention.

"Do you remember me talking about Lisa?"

I nodded attentively, listening to his request.

"She needs some womanly instruction." He stopped and hesitated. A pause as he searched for the right words. "Like how to be more feminine. You know, how to apply makeup, how to dress, how to wear her hair. You do that exceptionally well. Would you be willing to teach her?"

Somehow, he sensed that flattery would be the fuel to fire up my affirmation, my willingness to take on the task. And it was.

"Yes!" How simple this would be! I was a Mary Kay Cosmetics Master Makeover Class graduate. How fantastic to practice my artistic abilities. I grinned, eagerly wanting to please.

"Plus she'll need to keep busy. I'm sure she'll be willing to babysit for Sunny. Since she's part of the ministry, you won't need to pay her," he explained.

My heart leapt at the prospect. With my dwindling nest egg, the thought of not having to fork out the babysitting bucks seemed like a win-win for me.

How much better can this get?!

Curly the self-appointed savior came to the rescue. He had already offered me the position of Executive Director of the ministry. Another title. Validation. Acceptance. Support in the midst of my aloneness. He persuaded me to experience the House of Restoration to fully understand the vision of the ministry. It had been a done deal in his mind when he offered, even though I had much to consider.

Come into my house said the spider to the fly. Luring. Leering. Lunging. For its paralyzed prey. Never should I have given into flattery and false words. They meant nothing. Only seduction. That led to downright destruction.

When you think of being seduced, the first thing that usually comes to mind is sex. Much more powerful is feeling important, worthwhile, and valued. This is what seduced me. It was intoxicating to be wooed by a smooth-talking seemingly God-seeking man who played on the fact that we were distantly related.

Family was the foundation, the cornerstone of life. My Polish grandparents drilled that into my mom and her brothers, who drilled it into my generation. My sister, my cousins, and me. Family loyalty was treasured. A priceless gem in the rocky road of life. So, who much better to exploit me than someone claiming me as family?

I wanted a validation stamp of "ACCEPTED" and "WORTHWHILE" imprinted on my heart. My upbringing taught me that hard work demonstrated value and worth. Being worthwhile was necessary to matter in life. And I deeply longed to matter. Yet, I always believed I had to prove my worth to really matter.

The title of campaign manager then later executive director was bestowed on me by Curly. This signified acceptance. What more validation did I need than this? A gubernatorial candidate. A senatorial candidate. A presidential candidate. A preaching evangelist. A recovered alcoholic who believed his "Chosen" message would be heard by the masses through his aspiring political office ambitions. All these titles signified success in my eyes. Curly's success. He was somebody and this somebody was validating my entrance into the kingdom of God. He'd given me a golden key I thought would unlock the heavenly arches. Instead, it unlocked a living hell.

Careful What You Wish For—1988

Chosen as his ambassador, Curly sent me on an On the Wings of a Dove ministry mission. An inmate, Curly's long-ago friend, at the Montana State Prison had requested help from his now prophecy-proclaiming friend. A parole plan with employment placement and living accommodations was needed to secure his release.

I was familiar with the protocols for prisoner visitation. As a young, impressionable, and sheltered high school girl, I'd accompanied my grandma to visit a cousin during his incarceration at the Montana State Prison in Deer Lodge, Montana. Initially, my cousin was locked up in the old historic prison, constructed in 1871. Thick sandstone walls surrounded the buildings, their height reaching 24 feet and their depth four feet below ground surface. I can still recall the deafening sound the first time the metal bar door had slammed shut behind us. Briefly locked in a small enclosure awaiting our escort intensified my fear as my claustrophobia sent me internally spiraling out of control. I'd close my eyes, take a deep, calming breath, and wait for the clanking sound to signal the door opening in front of us. By 1979, he had been moved to the newly constructed 66-acre compound. Much more livable, and from an outsider's perspective, much less frightening to visit.

Curly knew my desire to help the downtrodden and underdogs, the oppressed, the hurting. Like my ex-husband, Jerry. Curly knew my heart to help. He knew my devotion to my cousin and the joy of seeing his eventual release. Who better to send on a saving mission to those in need of saving. A visiting pass procured, I embarked on a new mighty ministry-mission assignment. Curly's friend and I became well acquainted after numerous encounters in the closely guarded visitors' room.

But my last visit with Curly's inmate friend ended in a dispute. His demeanor was dastardly. As my voice raised a decibel or two, I called him on his crap. As I saw it.

He glanced quickly around, leaned forward, and hissed through gritted teeth, "You have NO clue what it's like to be in here, so don't you go judging me and my attitude!"

Shocked, I pulled back at his intense response.

"Visiting hours are over."

I glanced over as I heard the door-stationed guard announce the end of family and friend time. Abruptly, he exited with no backward glance. He was gone.

I stood up and joined the get-out-of-jail line. Exiting and leaving their loved ones behind. My thoughts had no direction. Misunderstanding hurt. Heavy hearted, my internal dialogue said, I've failed again. Consumed with exiting etiquette, I put the conversation aside briefly as I headed to the parking lot.

Perplexed and puzzled, I prayed, "Lord, he's right. I truly don't understand what it's like to be locked up night after night, day after day in a cell. Surrounded by walls and barbed wire fences. Will you please help me to understand?"

Dumb. Just a really dumb prayer. Be careful what you pray for, you just might get it. And you might not like the answer.

April 1997—North Dakota State Penitentiary, Bismarck, North Dakota

"You have a visitor," the guard had said, smiling as she opened my cell door. "Head to the showers." It was a double-edged sword to have visits.

All of us lucky inmates being ushered to the visiting room stopped off in the bathroom. Not for a shower but a total degrading strip search. "Strip!" she hollered to all of us as we stood in the shower stalls. We did as we were told. We knew the drill. We followed the rules so we could be privileged enough to see outsiders. All at the price of our dignity. For family. Friends. Loved ones who dared to enter the walls of NDSP.

After hurriedly dressing, we walked single file down the hall to the visiting room. A guard in the front. A guard bringing up the rear. And yes, they had seen *all* of our rears. Literally. Many times. The strip search strips. Not just your clothes but your dignity. It strips away all sense of modesty.

We entered the visiting room. Male inmates from the other side of the prison were already there, brought in through a separate door. At a separate time. We each scanned the room looking for our visitor. Once located, we looked down and headed to our designated table.

A fellow member of Curly's ministry had come to visit. She had been arrested with me but had been released. She understood, in some ways, what I was enduring. We visited. She shared all the current Curly news. The happenings seemed so far away. I was grateful for the cement walls and bars that kept me safe from his reach. How weird to feel safer in prison.

I heard a bit of a commotion and looked to my right. A young man sat visiting with his mom and sister. Another inmate stood staring down at the man. Intimidating. Sneering. Threatening. Bullying. Anger rose in my throat. I had a difficult time breathing. I wanted to jump out of my chair and beat the shit out of him. How *dare* he degrade this young man. Especially in front of his family.

ASSHOLE, I thought. *You're a complete ASSHOLE!*

I was horrified for this young man. But in prison, silence is your friend. It's your safety net. Your security. So I sat fuming in silence. The rage of indignation permeated every cell of my body.

The guard yelled, "Visiting hours are over!"

We knew this meant women proceed to the front. Men proceed to the back. After saying my goodbyes, I made my way through the tables. Asshole was making his way in the opposite direction. At the point where we both wouldn't fit between the tables, I assumed he'd step to the side and let me pass. Most men with manners would. Not the Asshole.

He started past me and shoved me with his shoulder. The inference "Get out of my way. I'm important! I'm better than you. You lower-than-scum obstacle in my way." As he shoved, the rage I felt for his treatment of the young man erupted.

I got in his face. Nose to nose and said with vengeance, "FUCK YOU!" The words spewed out of my mouth with no filter. My usually cuss-free mouth had definitely engaged. I had been pushed beyond all decency.

At that moment, I didn't care about consequences. *Go ahead*, I thought. *Hit me!* I know how to take a punch. I've been trained well. I expected rage in return.

I expected beady eyes of hatred at my so-called disrespect. Instead, I saw fear. I saw his eyes change from arrogance to total fear. He stumbled backward over the chair, his eyes locked on mine.

Holy crap! What just happened? I continued forward to join my fellow female inmates.

Two Native American sisters, my self-appointed bodyguards, stood staring at me in shock. One said, "Oh my God, Raylynn! Do you know who that is?"

Anger still raged in me. I said, "Yes! He's an *asshole!*"

She said with a slight tremble of fear in her voice, "I don't think you understand. He runs the prison. You better watch your back. He's going to get a message to his girlfriend about what you did. You're fucked!"

I froze. My face turned pale as the anger drained away, leaving behind a trail of fear. *Should I beg the guards to lock me down 24/7? Oh dear God! What have I done?*

After our follow-up strip search, we were locked in our cells. I laid on my cot staring at the ceiling. Playing over in my head the happenings. The reactions. I was confused. If he was so tough, why did he stumble backward? Why had I sensed fear in him? Why didn't he react like Mr. Tough Guy? And why in the world would I say *that*?

The thought came to me, *It's the only language he would understand. It wasn't you he feared. It was Me in you. He saw Me. Not you. Evil fears Me.*

That might be true, Jesus, but what's going to happen NOW? I'm going to die, I wailed inside. This silent conversation with Jesus didn't give me total reassurance that a violent ending wasn't coming at the hands of an enraged girlfriend defending her man. *Shit!*

Nothing.

Nothing happened. Dinner in the cafeteria. Time in the yard. Sitting alone with my back to the wall. Watching. Fearing. Waiting. Nothing. Nothing happened. Never.

Four Hundred Buckaroos—1988

With Curly monopolizing my time with the ministry, my PEP business was going bankrupt. No time. No money to devote to my event planning enterprise. My baby built from the ground up. Implosion was inevitable. My future reeked of failure. My biggest fear.

An event gone awry. Amiss. The participants wanted a refund of their fee. No funds left to return. I was hopeless. Helpless. Dejected. Defeated. Sitting alone in my leased one-room office in the basement of the Knox Flower building on the corner of Villard and Last Chance Gulch in Helena, Montana. Tears splattered as they reached the tabletop.

I sobbed, *Please Lord, help me! I don't know what to do!*

Silence. Nothing changed.

Until...

I heard my office door open. I jumped to my feet, wiping my face as quickly as I could. Surprised, I saw Donna, my physical therapist, walking tentatively through the door. She'd been treating me since the collision between my Volkswagen Rabbit and a rural-road-crossing deer blinded by my headlights.

As she tended to my whiplashed neck month after month, we became good friends with the common denominator being our love for Jesus. She knew of my Curly campaign connection, but I never shared the status of my collision-cash stash. Or lately, the lack of it.

An unsure look crossed her face. I became concerned. *What in the world is her worry?*

She'd never entered my door before. As she stood ill at ease in front of the table, I noticed her hand tightly clutching a piece of paper. Her arms held stiffly to her side. I wasn't sure what to say.

I finally mumbled, "Is everything okay, Donna?"

Her hand flew out and flung a small rectangular piece of paper on the table. Seemingly out of breath, she blurted, "I don't know why, but Jesus told me to bring you this."

Perplexed, I looked down at the paper sitting sideways on the table. I picked it up. I recognized the paper. The size. The date. The signature. The cursive writing spelling $400. It was a check. A $400 check.

Shock shook me. The thin paper between my fingers literally felt like burning flames of fire. I dropped it in shock. The exact currency needed for cancellation paybacks. Four hundred buckaroos. A perfect God had heard an imperfect person's prayer. And had set in motion His answer before it was even prayed.

Tears fell again. This time in thankfulness of a God who hears. For a special servant who obeys. And gives. And loves unconditionally. Speechless, I looked up attempting a response. My office door opened. She walked out. As quietly and quickly as she'd come.

It was a brief moment of saving grace. As I faced failure after failure. No funds. No future. The finish. My dream had become a nightmare. It wasn't even a matter of swim or sink. It had already sunk. Desperation set in. Maybe I should consider Curly's offer.

I'd Like to Solve the Puzzle — 1989

It was a frigid February evening, the soft purple pillow of sunset visible out the living room window. Thirty minutes before, Sunny had happily left the dinner dishes to me as she headed out to play with her neighborhood friends.

"Bye, Mom!" she said with her quirky little smile, knowing she was getting out of her chores . . . again, the little sneak. I just chuckled to myself, shook my head, and turned on the TV. Time for my daily dose of the *Wheel of Fortune*.

I picked up the dish towel and began drying. The game show antics became background noise as I began to think about a decision ahead of me. Curly had asked me to move to Billings to become the executive director of his ministry. I was astounded that he would choose me for this position. I knew I had great organizing skills and abilities. I had management experience. But Executive Director? Of a ministry? A bit overwhelming. It stroked my ego, however.

I wanted to feel accomplished, worthwhile, and feel I mattered. Feel like my life really mattered for something. After all, hadn't he chosen me fifteen months before as his campaign manager? I felt needed and valued . . . again. I would have a new title that made me feel important. It seemed natural to consider the possibilities ahead. I could really make a difference in my life. I could *be* somebody! For me. For Sunny.

But was it God's will? For me? For Sunny? Since the day of my holy "Just be obedient" encounter, I pressed into my relationship with God. So, with dish towel in hand, I prayed, *Jesus, should I go? Should I uproot Sunny? She'd have to leave her best friends and the only school she's ever known. Should I leave my family who live close by in Whitehall? After all my mom has endured with her health and the divorce from Jeff? What would this do to her? Would you really want me to do this, Lord? This decision doesn't affect just me. It affects those I dearly love.*

I was torn. So many emotions running through my head. *How in the world will I know His will?* It was so hard to tell at times. How do you figure out what an unseen entity wants you to do? *I need to know, Lord*, my heart cried.

I thought of the 1976 StarKist commercial with Charlie the Tuna. He wanted to be a Hollywood star. His answer came via a note attached to a fishhook descending from above. "Sorry, Charlie!" the note said. I laughed at how absurd this would be. But how defining it would be. *Hey Lord! Drop me a note, would ya??* How ridiculous this thought was.

All of a sudden my ears pricked up to the TV. I heard the contestant say, "I'd like to solve the puzzle. BILLINGS, MONTANA."

Are you serious? Billings, Montana? The puzzle answer on *Wheel of Fortune*?

Most people don't even have a clue where Montana is, let alone Billings. I stood with a dish towel in one hand and a fork in the other staring at the TV. A ray of sunshine flooding through the window shone directly on the solved puzzle. *No way. Just flat out NO WAY!*

My heart was pounding. It couldn't be. *Are you serious?* I stared at the TV with my mouth open the disht owel and fork falling to the floor. I had pleaded with God for an answer. His answer. *Could it really be? A sign? My sign? The one I'd jokingly asked for?* I sat in shock.

How on God's green earth could this be a coincidence? The magnitude of what just happened overwhelmed me. The tears rolled down my face. Would God really have done this for me? Would He really have been this direct? Was I really important enough for Him to make this happen? Speak to me through this?

Un-fricken-believable.

The House of Restoration—1989

We walked single file up the stairs. Paula pushed open the corner bedroom door. "This will be your room," she explained.

Sunny excitedly shoved past me and plopped down on the twin bed closest to the second-floor window looking out over the backyard. She loved new adventures. I stood in the doorway, surveying the small room. Two twin beds neatly made, a wooden nightstand sitting evenly between the headboards. A lamp decorating its center. A worn but functional four-drawer dresser sat near the small closet door in the corner of the room.

From a three-bedroom trailer to one little bedroom. I sucked in my breath. Anxiety-filled nerve impulses attached to my diaphragm, crippling its ability to function. I forced myself to intake a massive amount of oxygen, hoping to neutralize my nerves. A flashback of my *Wheel of Fortune* Billings, Montana, message came front and center in my brain. Breathing a bit easier, I was certain God had something here for me. After all, I'd prayed and an answer had been broadcast across the television screen. So I arrived. At The House of Restoration.

The House of Restoration—coined by Curly's On the Wings of a Dove Ministry—was designed, in theory, as a spiritual in-house treatment center. After his seven treatment center stints and counseling training, Curly had it all figured out. He knew the techniques to fix the floundering, to deliver the deranged, to lessen the stinkin' thinkin' thoughts of the lost. And it seems, he thought I fit all three. With a fringe benefit of family. We were related. Sort of. A common cousin connecting us by marriage, not blood.

A hand-selected household. A ménage of deliverance-needing individuals specially selected for saving. We were chosen. By Curly.

To be fixed. Curly style. Group therapy hot-seat style for our behavior modification. Dark deception digging, puffed-up pride pulling, excuse-making extraction. In other words, shoveling the shit out of your soul.

Scriptures were his method of doing that. Preaching hour after hour. We sat taking it all in. At least trying to. My Bible learning wasn't up to par, it seemed. I'd heard Curly preach many times throughout the campaign. Plus, over the last year, the meetings I'd attended had ministry on the menu with a sprinkling of campaign. But my personal Bible study had been limited. Lacking in spiritual knowledge, I was determined to dazzle. After all, I'd been brought here as the executive director of the ministry. A title that spelled worth. So I better impress with more than just management skills.

School had started. Sunny, with her sunshine disposition, started making new friends. With her hours at school and my hours spent on the in-house treatment aspect of my residence here, time with my sweet Sunny was limited. Curly wanted me to get control of my past demons, as he called them. To do so, he suggested Sunny stay with another couple and their kids for a short time.

"Dealing with your defects should be your focus for now, which will help Sunny in the long run," he'd explained convincingly. I agreed. Reluctantly.

Hot-seat methodology. The twisted rationale he used for administering this sometimes-painful strategy was procurement of our eternal rewards. The Army of God must march forth in unity, pure and proud. Without character imperfections marring our heavenly appearance.

I'd observed this hot-seat practice put in play. "Tearing down the flesh," he called it. The attitudes and actions not worthy of a Godly servant were addressed. I hated to see others torn down. I was, by nature, a defender of the underdogs. I could blast and berate a bully if needed. But it was difficult to express words that would intentionally harm another's heart, even it if was "for their own good." It went against my nature. Speaking up when witnessing injustice was one thing. Sitting in a room with a leader focused on weakness weeding, defect digging, and pride pulling was another. The justification was made swallowable encased in a sweet-tasting, salvation message.

"Raylynn, put your chair in the middle," Curly instructed calmly with a nod of his head directed at the circle center.

Our group therapy sessions were held circular style in the overly expansive living room of the large ministry-rented house. I slowly stood and carried my folding chair to the middle. I carefully set it down, making sure it faced Curly. My fearful anticipation slowed my movements. I slid into the chair and awaited further instruction. Anxious suspense of what was on the agenda caused a cold sweat to break out on my skin. I crossed my arms, placing each hand on the opposite forearm trying to rub the slight sweaty moisture in. Or off. Trying to unfluster my freaked-out feathers. Stop the shakes and shudders. And out-of-control heart palpitations. I gulped down the apprehension rising in my throat.

This is really not a great time to upchuck my breakfast. What now?

Curly continued to read and teach. Calm, coolheaded, and composed. Unlike me. I felt a bit awkward sitting alone. I was the new kid on the block. The latest house invader. Now I was going to be the bully's focus. Who's the bully? What's the focus?

My jitters jerked the pinball plunger, launching panic-thought pellets into every cognizant brain cell anticipating the likely negative emotional encounter.

It began. Curly switched subjects from scriptures to hot-seat sitter. Me. "I've heard complaints about how you've been treating people in the office."

I gulped. My mind raced through daily interactions, business activities.

"This is your chance to let her know how you feel," he said as he looked around at the circle sitters.

"She's more focused on business than she is on prayer," Dylan said.

I'm just trying to get the work done! All you want to do is boss us all around and tell us to pray instead of work when Curly's gone, my internal defense screamed silently.

"She acts like the computer is still hers and no one else can use it," Rachel said.

Well, it WAS mine and I know how to use it.

"I can't do anything right. She's always correcting everything I do. She acts like Miss Professional," Paula chimed in.

If you're not doing it right, isn't it my job to make sure you do? "Miss Professional?" *Maybe you should try it . . .*

"She's like a drill sergeant," Bruce piled on.

You're always goofing off. I'm just asking you to do your dang job.

"She acts like she's the boss," Randy said.

Well, Curly brought me here to be the executive director. So I'm just trying to direct and nobody listens!

With each statement, my worth plummeted into the pits. Person after person hammered a not-good-enough nail in my heart. Curly's eyes scanned the room. His eyes stopped and stared at Jill.

"You haven't said anything yet, Jill. What do you have to say about Raylynn?"

In shocked dejection, I locked eyes with her. *Not you, too, Jill!* I silently screamed. My heart was crushed. I had a soft spot for her and had spent many hours comforting her as she poured out her pain.

I heard her soft, sweet voice say, "I don't have any complaints about Raylynn. She's been really kind to me. She's taken the time to talk when I needed somebody to listen. I really like her."

The gratitude and love that I felt for her in this moment was off the chart. As sweet and satisfying as a thirst-quenching water sip, offered in the midst of a bone-dry desert crossing. Her words were salve to my ripped-to-shreds soul.

Curly sat back crossing his arms. "I asked you all to let her know how you felt. Jill is the only one who focused on something positive."

I could feel a bit of uncomfortableness descend on the word-slinging participants. Always a flip flop to the purpose of the session.

"You all had complaints. How many of you took it directly to Raylynn as the Word instructs, 'If you have ought against your brother or sister, go to them one on one. Did you go to her? Did you do what Matthew 18 says? Did you go privately to her and point out the offense?'"

Those in my line of sight slightly shook their heads side to side.

He continued his group chastisement, "Then why did you bring the complaints to me? Why did you air them in front of everyone here? She's doing the job that I brought her here for."

My deflated and tramped-on ego started puffing up. From the prophet's praise, or so I presumed. I bit the bait.

"How do you feel now?" Curly asked conversationally, as if I'd just had a relaxing massage.

I wanted to shout, "Vindicated," but I figured that wouldn't win me any friends, just make enemies. Wrong attitude.

I mustered up my humility and said, "I wish they would have come to me. I don't want them to think badly of me. I just want to do my job." I felt this was a proper response to please all. The people and the prophet.

The end of it, right? Wrong!

Curly's slightly smiling eyes became dark. Intense. Digging holes in my soul. "They were right. Everything they said was valid."

Well, there went my vindication. My victory.

"Tomorrow Rachel will be in charge. You will take direction from her." The first of many demotions and promotions. Round and round we go, who you'll be the next day, only Curly knows.

****

You see, the thing about worth—especially when you don't have much of it—is it comes at a price. The price was my sanity. My soul. And my sweet daughter Sunny. My hands to defend us and the brains to bolt were tethered by fear.

This price was paid one coin at a time. Little by little, he assaulted my identity. My inner self was stripped away. Unknowingly, a gradual erosion of my personality, my values, and my intellect weakened my ability to recognize reality.

A subliminal strategy was used to mold our brains like putty. Ideas were planted below the level of consciousness. Did Curly truly plan it that way? I don't think so. I think his narcissistic, psychopathic tendencies and desire for power and prestige created an internal storm driven to control. We were his subjects to control, to manipulate, to do his every bidding. And he sucked us in by caring for the lost. The outcast. The needy. And this was us.

We each had our own empty hole of neediness. And Curly filled the need. He projected a belief in belonging. A sense of security. The promise of a prosperous future. Giving us all purpose for ourselves and our families. Clustered together. One big family. Sharing kitchen and quarters.

To lure me in, he'd called and interjected himself in every aspect of my life. With no husband and a dad who dropped out of my life, I welcomed his fatherly advice. He'd sent a crew of men to help me fix my roof. He'd sent support during difficult business dealings. He'd shown up to spiritually steer me in the right direction. Or so I thought.

Truth became enveloped in a puffed-up cloud of intense spiritual teaching. He knew the Bible. I didn't. I was intimidated, yet in awe of what I saw as amazing discernment of the scriptures. Hour after hour he'd study. Hour after hour he'd preach to us. Night after night 'til exhaustion set in. That's where the brain is the most susceptible to suggestion and manipulation. No one else could give us this insight, for he was holy.

He professed to be anyway.

July 22, 1997—Transport to Yellowstone County Detention Facility, Billings, Montana

"Whatcha in for?" I heard the young man seated behind me ask. It's the equivalent of asking, "How are you?" The small talk. The convict chat. Not your usual howdy-doodie dialogue. We all had one thing in common. Common criminals *in* for a crime. Some innocent, some guilty. Some lifers, some short timers. Same talk. Same chat. Same question. "Whatcha in for?"

We'd left the Cass County Jail in Fargo, North Dakota, a couple hours before. Taking the scenic route back to Montana. Not like the numerous Greyhound buses routed through the states, there were limited prison transports heading west to Billings. Instead, Fargo to Rapid City, to Miles City, to Billings. It was going to be a long, tedious trip. Overnight stops in countless jails. No Comfort Inn. No Motel 6. Just jail cells. And hard bunks. Thin blankets. And strangers.

Watertown, South Dakota. Two hours south of Fargo. We took the exit and headed to the Codington County Detention Center. More prisoners. More passengers. The bus began to fill.

I watched as he boarded the bus with the sideways step-up and shackle shuffle. He made his way to a seat behind me. He looked like the rest of us: orange jumpsuit, tan plastic shower slip-ons, handcuffs, and leg irons.

Stone faced. Emotionless. Typical inmate, I thought. I stole a sideways look as he shuffled by. Bulging muscles stretched the jumpsuit sleeves to their max. There was an air about him that was intimidating. But of course, who wasn't? To me anyway. The coward. The I-run-from-violence chicken.

As the gears shifted and the bus started climbing the hill, I turned slightly to answer. "Bad checks." His question inferred an obligatory one back to him. "How 'bout you? What're you in for?"

His quiet answer exploded in my yellow-belly brain. "Murder for hire," he said self-assured. Cold. Heartless.

I was thankful for my ability to face forward. Operation stone face commence. *Execute an I'm-not-the-least-bit-shocked face. Ugh, execute—good choice of a word.*

Carry out a death sentence. Paid executioner style. He said it so casually, like he'd just said nanny for hire. *Really? A job? To kill?* I'd watched TV cop shows many times, but to come face-to-face with someone who actually took human lives. Pulled the trigger. Stabbed the knife. With absolutely no regard. No regret. For a paycheck. Chills ran down my back. Horror hit my heart. This life terminator sat right behind me. Fear ripped my insides to shreds.

Our conversation continued as he casually described detail after detail of the company he'd formed. The clients he accumulated. Like a businessman discussing the financial empire he'd built through blood, sweat, and tears. The difference: this man had caused blood to run cold at his appearance. Caused blood to run as he killed. Caused tears to flow because of grief. Those marked for death. Kills for customers. Cash for casualties. Murder for hire.

God, how did I get here? Traversing with murderers. Conversing with killers.

As our conversation waned, I focused on my tightly clenched hands. Handcuffs rubbing harshly. Nervously, I began twisting and pulling. My hand came out.

My mouth fell open. *Holy cow!* It slipped right off. My head jerked up looking at the guard. *Did he see?* I giggled gleefully to myself. I watched as the second came off as easily as the first. I was grinning from ear to ear.

A tiny glimmer of freedom leapt in my heart. No, freedom was not at hand. At all. But both hands were free. In the midst of imprisonment. In a place of confinement. My hands were free. I felt free for a brief moment. I looked up. The face of a nervous young prisoner seated just ahead came into view as he sat with his back against the bus window. His peripheral vision caught my movements, spotting my cuffless wrists.

Eyes widening in alarm, he hissed under his breath, "You better get those on or *all* of us will be in deep shit! Escape is no joke!"

Escape? Are you kidding me? I looked down at my leg cuffs. Looked up at the armed guards. *Escape not happening today! Nope. No way,* I quietly laughed at the absurdity. *Busting out of the bus? Really? I'm trying not to bust a gut. You betcha, I'm a badass broad. A Bonnie with her Clyde. A bus-wreck breakaway*, I thought sarcastically.

Laughter bubbled up. Laughter patches up pain. Pushes away fear. Fear of backseat murderers. Fear of new jail mates ahead. Fear of my future. Without Sunny. With Curly. Without Curly. Fear of failing. Fear of hell. Just plain. Flat-out fear. A few minutes of laughter pushed it away for a few moments. Resignedly, I slipped the handcuffs back on. Closed my eyes. And wept inside. Quietly.

****

Rapid City. Just ahead.

Pennington County Jail. I stepped sideways off the bus, careful to stay upright. The guards stood by as we filed off the bus one by one. Deputies were our welcoming crew escorting us into the jail. *One night please. What time is checkout?* My coping mechanism was always humor. Processing in for a night. And what a night it was.

Our shackles were removed as we entered the building, no longer needed with jail security in place. I was directed, along with my meekly mannered fellow passenger, to sit on benches resembling church pews lining two walls of an office. I looked around. A desk. Two doors. And metal rings cemented above the bench backs. *What in the world?* Soon I found out their use. The officer unlocked my left wrist handcuff and clamped it to the three-inch metal ring. Me on one bench. My nervous friend, who'd spotted my cuffless wrists on the bus, on the other.

We sensed the tension in the place. A commotion was heard in the distance. A lack of visibility to see what was happening created more anxiety. More wondering. Curiosity. We looked at each other, a bit worried. No one seemed to be close by. We both sat looking like puppets with one arm dangling from the handcuff attached to the wall.

Claustrophobic thoughts kicked in. Confined to a wall. *Breathe.* Coping skills set in motion. Escape techniques activated. Not so much the brain. As I slid the handcuff off, my buddy almost had a coronary.

"*No!*" he said through gritted teeth. "You're *really* going to get in trouble now!"

Laughing, knowing I really am not an escape risk, I peeked out the door. I looked back at the handcuff swinging side to side against the wall absent a wrist. No longer attached. I smiled deviously. I really felt free. Free! Literally free! An impish look crossed my face as I stood grinning from ear to ear.

I stuck my head out and saw no one. I heard footsteps. Close. I launched myself at the bench, grabbed the handcuff and slipped my hand in place just as the guard came through the door. I wasn't sure what my fellow jailbird would say.

Was he a snitch? Better not be. Absolutely a no-no in jail. He just swallowed hard, took a deep breath, and looked innocently at the guard, mimicking the look on my face. A fast learner. Maybe there's hope for him after all.

Time for lockdown. Shenanigans were over. Fear slapped me in the face. I wondered how many women there would be. How would they treat me? An outsider entering their territory. Stopping by for just a night.

The guard inserted the key. The door to the common area swung open. In we walked. Handcuffs off. Fear on full throttle. I scanned the room, not meeting anyone's eye. I noticed a table unoccupied and headed toward it. Away from the throngs of women roaming around. Sitting in tightknit groups. Talking. Staring. The newcomer. Me. Creating curiosity. I sure hoped that's where it would end. If trembling was audible, the noise would have been deafening. But it isn't. And wasn't. I looked down at my hands resting in prayer-like position on the table, so I prayed. For courage. For calmness. For toughness. For safety.

Please God. Deliver me. Save me. Protect me.

****

I felt her presence before I heard her voice. I looked up at a Native American woman, probably in her 60s. She grinned shyly at me with her almost toothless smile.

"Want some coffee?" She showed me the small amount of instant coffee crystals nestled in the middle of the cone-like container fashioned out of paper. "I don't have much, but I'll share it with you. If you want." The kind eyes of the elderly woman searched mine. Offering kindness. Offering what little she had to a stranger. Feeling my fear. Understanding it. Desiring to calm it. With kindness.

I walked to the dirty steel sink with her. She carefully poured crystals into two of the cups stacked underneath. One for me. One for her. Reaching up, she turned on the water and filled the cups, handing me one.

"You'll have to stir it with your finger. They don't give us spoons." I did as she said. The water was tepid. Lukewarm at best.

I put it to my lips and drank. Now, the taste was truly horrible. But it felt warm and comforting. Each drop was filled with the heart of a woman incarcerated for who-knows-what, caring, sharing, giving, loving.

In this moment, I felt the presence of God. She was Jesus with skin on in the jail. He used her gift of coffee to show me His love. He says He will never leave us nor forsake us. Not now. Not ever. Not even in jail. And He used a woman who gave with her heart. And was willing to give the little she had. I swallowed the last few drops. I choked up as I thanked her, knowing I would be okay. Tonight. In this place. This jail. I headed to my cell. The door shut. Locked. Lights out. Time to sleep. Safe in the arms of Jesus.

Those Darn Socks—1992

"Do you know Wally likes you? He finds you attractive." Curly stated matter of factly as we sat across from each other at his kitchen table.

I'd been summoned to the king's castle to chat. My face turned beet red as I watched him put a coffee cup to his lips. The slow, slurping sip gave me a moment to lasso the emotions running untamed and bucking through my brain.

A lump of fear caught in my throat. *Did I do something unintentional to entice him? Is he picking up the wrong vibes? Am I in trouble?*

Yet, I couldn't help but be a bit flattered. Someone was attracted to *ME?* What a farfetched idea in light of the personality put-downs I constantly received from Curly. My worth could be measured by the pennies put in a piggy bank. Not dollars deposited in a bank account. So, Wally must be the highest bidder for the bumbling broad. What in the world did this mean?

"Are you attracted to him?" Curly asked.

Stumbling and stammering, I murmured, "I don't know." My mind went to the oversized football lineman–looking man with a crooked smile. I hadn't really thought of him in any amorous entanglement way. Romance was not on my agenda. But obviously it must be a God thing for me if Curly brought it up.

I began watching Wally watch me. A bit weird. Not your usual hookup in the bar. Nor your fall-in-love-at-first-glance romance. Relationships were not my strong suit. My past was sprinkled with failure confetti. Colorful connections lacking commitment. Limited loyalty. A faithfulness farce. A masquerade of mismanaged emotional attachments. My romance track record listed last place finishes. It was more hanky panky than lovey dovey. Would Wally win the Pulitzer prize of pursuit? Maybe, according to the prophetic proclaimer.

Could I be attracted to him? Not trusting my own feelings, I thought maybe it was my own insecurities and past failures blocking me. Nerves negated my interest indicator. A scale from "not really" to "maybe." Finally, uncertainty was dispelled. Curly had a vision. The Raylynn and Wally matrimonial match-up. Nuptials for the self-appointed deity devotees. Just a hifalutin hallucination hookup.

And hook up we did. On June 21, 1992. Curly even popped the cork on the pocketbook and provided a pittance for the wedding. Experts in stretching dollars, we cut cash corners where we could. A wedding cake and reception goodies bought with a fellow follower's food stamps. Bridesmaid dresses sewn by seamstress-inclined ministry members. A short white dress and a stylish hat were fantastic finds on the clearance rack at Herberger's.

My mom and Jeff attended reluctantly but came separately. Their divorce had left them at odds, understandably so. They were united on one front, however. Their underlying disapproval of my seemingly foolhardy, hasty hookup. And their dislike of my Curly devotion and my increasingly limited family interaction tainted their outlook on any new nuptials. Plus, I hadn't batted a thousand in the dating game. Ever. No homerun hit for choosing my preceding marriage mate either. It was a strikeout and now I was up to bat. Again.

Their mistrust of the mysterious matchup simmered under the surface. My own misgivings were buried by the misconception that "God" organized this union. My warped allegiance to the source of the so-called godly vision clouded my connection to the bonafide heir to the heavenly throne. Intuition of truth lay buried at the bottom of the not-smart enough, not-good enough, not-spiritual enough, self-perception crap pile. Resulting in a super shitty situation. Sanctity of vows soured by a dutiful "I do" but a deep down "I don't." Unspoken dread of the marriage bed.

****

Dutiful Wally wife. But dutiful wingwoman to the wacked-out one. Relationship responsibilities collided with Curly's day-to-day demands. Who dictated my daily duties? Always. The one who fostered fear. Fanatical fear.

A couple's confidential conversations were privy to the prophet. Overheard words were delivered high-speed express on the hotline to the Royal Highness. No privacy prevailed with the snoopy tattle-tales. No telling who would tell your secrets. About everything. Even socks.

As we prepared for a Curly-called afternoon gathering, Wally donned his undarned socks. Grumbling about the holes in the heels he'd asked me to fix started the fight. Defending my neglect of his so-called wifely duties, I argued that darning socks came second to my daily duties doled out by the dictator. The usual underlying fear of the upcoming meeting was a catalyst to a continuing contentious conversation. Nothing resolved, we headed to the meeting.

Snooping snitches let the undarned socks situation out of the bag privately to Curly. No squabbles concealed. All secrets shared. Allegiance to the almighty was paramount.

"So Wally," Curly calmly began. "Show me your socks."

Wally looked flabbergasted at the request.

His hesitation resulted in a further command. "Take off your shoes. Now."

Wally's face flushed red as he bent down to untie his tennis shoes. One by one, he pulled them off and set them on the floor to the right of his still-socked feet.

"Now take off your socks." Slowly they were removed and remained in his hand. "Show them to me."

Wally stood up and tentatively approached holding the white sport socks.

"It looks like you have some holes in them," Curly said casually as he lifted his piercing eyes from the socks to Wally's face. This smooth tone of voice was a bit unsettling.

Wally slightly shook his head in agreement.

"So why are you wearing holey socks?" Curly inquired.

Wally began stammering and stuttering, "I asked Raylynn to darn them but she hasn't had time," he answered, in defense of his lack of a darning wife. He was the star contestant in the blame game we all played so well. I sat in shock wondering what was next as I stared at the floor.

"Go get all of your socks," demanded Curly.

Wally sat down, a bit confused. His brow furrowed as he put socks and shoes on. I could sense his fear. His worry of what's next. He left to fetch the rest.

Not skipping a beat, Curly began teaching out of a new "End Times" book he'd been studying. "But you, Daniel, roll up and seal the words of the scroll until the time of the end," he read from Daniel Chapter 12.

Of course, Curly was talking about his role as "Michael, the Great Prince." It was a tough concept for me to wrap my head around. From Curly the Prophet to Michael the Prince. Name-changing mania. Presumption or pretense? A whirlwind of wonder words whipped by my brain but didn't land.

I figured it was because I was not spiritual enough. Maybe if I wasn't such a screwup and so stupid, as I was oftentimes reminded, I'd be able to comprehend more. A flashback of a face, fierce and seemingly hate-filled, staring down at me. Shook me. Intense words had berated the inadequacy apparently evident in me. I froze.

Worried he was going to detect my mumble jumble mental mess. Insufficiency exposed. Ineptness uncovered. My thoughts would betray me. I took a deep breath. *Straighten up soldier and engage. Just pretend you weren't daydreaming.* I looked up and shook my head in agreement so he'd believe I was on the same page, so to speak. Literally and spiritually. We better have our Bibles turned to the proper passage. Or else.

A doorknob turned. I heard weatherstripping drag over the rug as it opened. Then it slammed shut. Fear flew to my throat, almost choking me. Wally's back. *Now what?* I pretended to look at the Bible in my lap so that I could glance sideways at Wally. I saw a plastic grocery bag gripped in his hand. I was sure everyone could hear the thump of my heart, my stressed-out heartbeat. I'm going lose it. Really lose it. *Quit it, Raylynn*, I scolded myself. You better focus. Or else.

Curly didn't even acknowledge Wally's meek entrance. He kept preaching and teaching his too-scared-to-not-be-attentive God's army soldiers. How long would this go on? I couldn't breathe. The anticipated fear was sitting on my chest, blocking my ability to inhale. Exhale. Inhale. Exhale. The effort it took to do this automatic life function was exhausting.

Interrupting his teaching flow, Curly looked directly at Wally and raised his hand, beckoning him forward. "Give me the bag," he demanded.

Wally stood and obediently walked to stand in front of Curly, holding out the socks. He motioned for Wally to sit back down. Curly took each pair of socks out slowly. One by one. Unfolded them. One by one. Examined them. One by one.

He finally raised his head, "I see you've got quite a few with holes."

Wally nodded in agreement, a bit of relief on his face, feeling the conversation was headed in a positive direction. For him, anyway.

I almost puked. *I suppose I'm going to be in trouble for not darning his dang socks. Isn't it always my fault?* I thought sarcastically. Apprehensively. Tables were always turned. Who knew who would be under them. Tonight, I feared it was me.

"So, you think Raylynn should darn these for you?" Curly asked inquisitively.

Wally silently nodded.

"And why should she do that?"

"Well . . . they've got holes in them?" Wally answered unsure of himself. "And she knows how to darn. I don't."

Strike one for me. No threading of the needle. No mending of the holes. *By golly, it's just a stitchless marriage.* My inner dialogue sidelined the mounting panic.

"You're saying she's not fulfilling her wifely duties? Is that it, Wally?" The calmness of his words sent shivers up my spine.

I felt the conflict in Wally. Should he say yes or no? What was the right answer? It was always the dilemma. It was the anticipation of potential punishment that shaped each answer we uttered. It was never just what's truth. It's about what kept you out of trouble. What met the expectations of the lunatic leader. The issue, though, we couldn't perceive the insanity, the lunacy of it all through our survival-mode tactics. Fear was the action and answer influencer.

"Yes," I heard Wally whisper.

"Speak up, Wally. Are you sure about that?" Always questioning our conviction.

"Yes!" Wally said a bit stronger. He'd made a stand with his first simple yes. He'd jumped aboard the blame game train.

Curly stood. My whole body tingled with fearful anticipation. He walked slowly toward me, his beady gaze drilling dread holes in my head. I dare not even blink.

At his approach, I sat rigidly still, clenched my teeth, preparing for the expected blow. Towering over me, his now-downward stare never moved from my face.

"Why didn't you darn his socks?"

My turn to tell or tattle. But which was which? "I should have taken the time to do it," I said, accepting my lack of darning duty. Maybe accepting accountability will void the vengeance. I swallowed. Hard.

Curly turned and sauntered to his seat. "Get me a pair of scissors," he demanded. Someone jumped and a pair appeared in his hand. I held my breath. *What for?*

Curly bent sideways and picked up a sock from the pile. He held it up examining it from top to bottom, making a bit of a production of it.

"It definitely needs fixing with these large holes in it," he said, like it was a new revelation. I heard the blades of the scissors open as he raised his right hand. *Snip. Snip.*

"How about now? It's going to take a bit more than darning with these large holes, don't you think?" he sneered, staring at Wally. The severed sock fell to the floor, its mate now in his hand. *Snip. Snip.* Down to the floor it went. Another. *Snip. Snip.* Every sock. Snipped. Sliced. Dropped.

In these moments, no one dared to even breathe. Each sensed the intensity. All on high alert, feeling like deer blinded by brightness frozen in fear, awaiting an anticipated impact. The hit. Hard. Relentlessly. Without braking. No stopping the snake-like strike.

But it didn't come. At least. Not now.

The midafternoon game commenced. Football. Guys only. The darning-duty delegation was still being dealt with. Physically. Disguised as football hits. Wally the hittee. Curly the hitter. Hard. Harsh. Heartless. Hits. Over. And over.

Back to begin a meeting. Again. Back to berate Wally. Again. Although my heart went out to him, I sat wondering if I was next. For shirking the socks. My wifely duties. Instead, tonight I was given a reprieve. Pardoned from any punishment. Phew.

And Wally was rewarded with cash for the cut-up socks. Moolah for handling the meanness. Of the master.

The midafternoon game announced. Football. Any of the damn-duty delegation was still being dealt with. Boys who Dwyalled a football bits. Wally the halfer Clark the Liter Hank Harsh, Heath on line twos. And over.

B.E.E. to begin a meeting. Again back to Paul de Vielle. Again. Although no heart went out to him. Lead sentenced. His name For bucking the sports. My watch during tonight. He was given a reprehensive commendation, any punishment. Three.

And Vl who was rewarded with a tribute line on the steps. Knocked for handling the firearms. Of the master.

Go Straight—1993

"Go straight," I told Loretta, who was my chauffeur from the hospital to home. She had been sitting outside the entrance to the St. Vincent Hospital where I'd had a not-so-pleasant crotch cauterization for endometriosis. When I saw the old brown Chrysler Cordoba pull up to the curb, the nurse wheeled me, hospital-exit style, to the car. My walking was excruciatingly painful. I waddled like I had a corncob up my backside. My instructions had been to go home and lay down. Let the crotch recover. I lowered myself gingerly into the lowrider seats. Slammed the door shut. Loretta put it in gear and hit the gas.

After my directional statement, she glanced sideways at me and I shrugged. Not really knowing why I said it. She drove straight ahead on 12th Avenue where the entrance to the hospital was located rather than turning right on Broadway, the shortest route to take me home. She braked as we reached the intersection of North 27th Street.

"Turn left," I said surprisingly, giving instructions like I had a game plan, when in fact I hadn't one. I only had a small, still voice in my head whispering directions. *Maybe I'm just hearing things*, I began questioning myself. I didn't trust that the Holy Spirit would be hanging around someone like me who wasn't quite "spiritual enough." Go straight. Turn left. *Really spiritual stuff*, I thought a bit sarcastically.

As she made the turn on 27th and headed up the hill, it happened. A fast-moving car didn't even hesitate at the stop sign of the side intersection. The collision of the non-stopping car and a boy on a bicycle sickened me. Shocked me. Scared me. I saw his body thrown into the air, landing hard on the black asphalt. Crumpling. Like a rag doll.

I screamed at Loretta, "Pull over!!"

Before the car had even stopped, I flung open the door, leapt out, and ran. I knelt down, staring into an innocent young face etched with fear and pain. He raised his head. I saw his fright-filled eyes searching frantically, then come to rest on his bike. Obviously, his prized possession. I encouraged him to lay back. I sat on the ground beside him and stroked his forehead. He raised his head and buried it in my lap, weeping uncontrollably. I continued to softly stroke his head and began praying for comfort. To ease the pain. To bring calmness. To heal his body. To help him though this tragedy. As I prayed, I felt his body relax. His sobs subsided, replaced by a sad, pitiful whimpering. I felt a tap on my shoulder and looked up.

"Ma'am, we'll take it from here." The paramedic knelt down and carefully held the boy's head so that I could get up. The boy's eyes again widened in fear. He tried to reach for my hand as if to say, "Please stay." I reassured him. I wasn't leaving. I'd be right here.

I moved far enough away to allow the first responders to do their job. Carefully, they transferred his crumpled body to a stretcher. As they began loading him in the ambulance, a worried couple came bursting from their quickly stopped car, screaming his name. Relieved to see his parents on the scene, I turned to walk back to the car. A knife-stabbing pain hit hard. Lightheaded from its intensity, Loretta helped me to the car and headed home. The shortest route. No more directions from me.

The next morning, I called the hospital and was told the boy had been admitted for observation. I had to see for myself that he was okay. Loretta and I headed back to the same entrance she'd picked me up from the previous day. Although the floor nurse couldn't give me his room number, after explaining the reason for my concern, she understood the situation and slightly nodded in the direction of his room.

I tentatively knocked on the slightly ajar door. It was opened by the woman I'd seen yesterday at the ambulance. As I looked at the boy, he grinned from ear to ear.

"Mom! That's her. She's my guardian angel!"

I was taken back by his enthusiasm. In a moment, I was enveloped in a lung-crushing hug. Tears streamed down her face as she thanked me over and over again for what I'd done for her son.

A bit embarrassed, I said, "Anyone would have done the same."

Her head shaking side to side, emphatically she said, "No! You were there when I wasn't. You took care of my baby for me. And you prayed for him. I truly believe God answered your prayers. He barely has a scratch. It's a miracle! They kept him overnight for observation, but I knew he was going to be okay after he told me about you."

I was totally flabbergasted at what she shared. *Really? A miracle?* We chatted for a bit. Then I excused myself, feeling my own post-cauterization pain kick in.

I was humbled. Jesus actually had been giving me directions to witness the accident. And He used me to pray for a miracle for an innocent young boy. Full of faith. I smiled broadly, and if I could have, I would have skipped like a kid out the hospital door.

I did feel like a guardian angel. And it felt so good.

January and July, 1997—Ward County Jail, Minot, North Dakota, and North Dakota State Penitentiary, Bismarck, North Dakota

The dawning of the day came. In the wee hours of the morning, a commotion was at hand. Although each of us was locked in our cells, we could hear it. The intense directives of guards dictating orders. Words weren't clear. Seriousness was. Hustle and bustle could be heard. Cell doors opening. Shuffling of shoes. A gradual crescendo of male voices. Locked-down inmates yearning to learn the news. The men's side of the jail was in upheaval.

Thirty minutes before, I'd been jolted awake. I had sat up; the stillness of the night was all that filled my ears. Only the typical jail sounds of jangling keys of the night guard walking in the distance. But no sound out of the ordinary could be heard. Only the usual quietness of the night in the Ward County Jail located in Minot, North Dakota. I listened but had heard nothing. So I prayed, "Lord, what is it?" A heaviness of heartache enveloped me. An urgency to pray for someone. A sorrowful soul. Hurting deep. Buried in darkness.

The intensity of my prayers was surprising. I had no clue why. But God did.

Then the commotion hit. Hard. Fast. Furious. I heard the panicked voices. But could not understand the source of the distress. I kept praying. And praying. Our cells stayed locked past the opening hour. The disturbance was not over. Yet.

Click. Doors finally unlocked. All cell occupants slowly emerged. Women wary of the yet-unnamed trouble. Rumors flew rapidly replacing our unrest with sorrow and sadness. For the lost but saved soul God had redeemed that night.

As the details of the drama unfolded, my heart was overwhelmed with humility. God had asked me to pray. He'd awoken me for His purpose. A soul He was after to save. His child, not destined to die this way, had been overcome with pain.

Discouraged, depressed, all alone. A young man had fashioned a noose from the ghostly white sheet ripped from its place on his steel bunk. Slowly and deliberately he worked, numbed by intolerable pain. As he sank into his self-induced oblivion, a merciful God saw his pain. His sorrow. His unbearable burdens.

As I had sat praying for an unknown hurting heart, the Holy Spirit whispered in the ear of his cellmate, prompting him to awake. To arise. In horror, he saw little life remaining in the limp body hanging from the bunk. Hoisting the hefty weight of his cellmate's lifeless body had eased the tension of the death-inflicting noose. He cried out to God for mercy for a miracle. For life to be restored.

And it was. Breath returned again.

As consciousness returned, heart-rending sobs engulfed the pitiful young man as his cellmate, a newfound God-believing friend, held him. Comforted him. Prayed for him. Telling him, "Jesus loves you, my friend, don't give up. He'll take all your pain."

I remembered this night when the North Dakota State Penitentiary guard unlocked my cell door. I'd been transferred to this facility on Valentine's Day a few months previously.

"Raylynn, will you help?" the female guard asked.

"Help?" I was a bit shocked at a help request. We were more like remote control cars started and stopped, directed and driven; not asked to help.

"Cathy is really struggling and wants to talk to you. I know your heart. I see how you treat others here. She's threatening suicide and no one can reach her. Will you talk with her?"

"Of course!" I answered as I jumped to my feet, following her out my now-opened cell door.

We walked up the steep stairs to the upper tier and headed to her cell. I saw the faces of fellow inmates smashed against their six-inch-wide cell door windows. Watching. Wondering.

"Now, I'm going to ask you not to mention this to the other guards.

You know it's against the rules for me to allow you into her cell. But I don't know what else to do."

Totally taken back by the privilege of breaking the rules with permission, I agreed.

I stopped outside her opened cell door and looked at the guard for final approval. At her nod, I walked in. Cathy was sitting on her cot, crying uncontrollably. Instantly my heart was filled with compassion, a desire to comfort. I sat down beside her and put my arms around her shaking shoulders. Another violation of the no-touch rules. She leaned into me, sobbing. The front of my T-shirt was sopping wet from her tears. I held her tight 'til the intense weeping turned to whimpers. Then we talked.

She poured out her pain. She puked out the poison of hopelessness. Of fear. Doubt. Depression. As she talked, I silently prayed that each and every drop of despair, each and every sliver of sorrow, would fall at the feet of Jesus. And I knew it did. I held her close to my chest like the precious child she was. God saw her. Loved her. Longed for her heart to be returned to Him. And it was. As I prayed, she prayed. Allowing Jesus to renew her faith. Dispel her fear. And fill her with extraordinary love. No matter the sorrow in which she sat. No matter what she'd done. Or not done. She was loved. Unconditionally.

As is each and every person. Inmate or guard. God makes no distinction when He deals out remedy cards for crises.

****

As the night cook for the guards, I had become well acquainted with those whose hearts weren't jaded by our confinement status. Those who chatted. Joked and laughed without judgment. One guard in particular was intrigued by my positive attitude.

"How can you be so happy in prison?"

I gave him a reasonable response. "Well, it's good to stay positive, right?"

Not satisfying his question, he asked again, "No, really. How are you so happy?"

The guilt of not giving God the glory invaded my brain. *He's a guard for goodness sakes, Lord!* I silently argued. But He poked me to profess the truth.

"Well honestly, it's the Lord who helps me be happy no matter where I'm at," I confessed. Then I thought, *Plus, I'm not in the self-proclaimed prophet's place to be put in my place.* Now, *that* combination could elicit a joyful attitude anytime. Anywhere.

As much as night kitchen time allowed, the guard and I would chat about God. My favorite prison pastime was reading book after book. I happily shared my favorites.

"Can you bring one of your favorites to me?" he asked.

"How can I do that?" I was a bit flabbergasted by his rule-breaking inmate-to-guard-giving request.

"You can check out books, can't you?"

I nodded affirmatively. He went on to explain, "Sitting all night in the tower gets boring so I read." He glanced around the dining room area. Spotting a small, skinny unused cabinet at the end of the counter, he gestured and said, "You can easily sneak a book in there. Then I'll pick it up on my dinner break and bring it back when I'm done. I need something better to read than the crap I've been bringing from home." He looked pretty pitiful in his plea. I almost burst out laughing. A guard asking me to fetch his faith-filling reads. A flip flop of the prison pecking order. I grinned. "Sure! I'll get you one tomorrow." Book after book, he'd read and return. We'd chat about the meaning, the gleaning and learning. A sneaking reading relationship. Guard and inmate. Soul to soul. God connected.

****

Side by side we sat in a tucked-away room on the upper tier of the cell block talking. My fellow inmate, Linda, and me. A bit of an outcast, she hung around me because I cared. Her constant attention neediness stirred up bullying and rejection from others. Her focus was ailments, assholes, and attitudes. She'd dealt with a lot of each in her life. I listened to it all. This day the focus was a lump on her neck. Hurting. Swollen. Sticking out. Knowing our unlocked time was drawing to a close, I reached up, placed my hand on the nape of her heck and said simply, "In the name of Jesus, be healed." Weird. My hand got super hot. I just figured it was skin-touching heat. Standing up, I headed back to my cell for count. Twice a day we were all accounted for to assure no one was out of place. Or escaped.

Before I hit the base of the stairs, I heard her holler at the top of her lungs, "Raylynn healed me!!!!" I froze. What in the crap?? She came bounding down the stairs, yelling excitedly, "It's GONE! My lump! It's just GONE!!! You healed me!" I reached up to feel her neck, and sure as heck the lump was gone. "Holy cow! He DID heal you!! It wasn't me, Linda. It was Jesus! He's the one who did it. Not me." I wanted no glory for God's miracle. I stood grinning at her exuberance. Another soul given a glimpse of God's goodness. His heart. Through me.

As my cell door locked behind me, I looked down at my hand. Still red. Still a bit hot. "Wow, Lord, how cool was that!" A hot shot of heavenly heat injected in my hand used to heal a lost soul. Her neck. And her faith.

Prison had its purpose. Punishment. Protection. Convict connections. And faith. In action.

Please Don't Ring—1994

I sat at the small desk in the basement bedroom of the home Wally, Sunny, and I shared with another Curly-following family. Staring at the phone; willing it to stay silent. "Lord, please don't let it ring," I sobbed silently. Tears showed weakness, Curly had said. No way did I want weakness to be heard in my voice should he call back. In the face of fear, my tears shoved into silence.

Have you ever felt the kind of fear that literally makes your butt pucker? You might find this humorous . . . unless you've experienced it. It would start in my stomach and spread like a deadly virus to every cell in my body. Hair standing on end. Heart pounding so loud I had no doubt it was audible. Trembling so deep I was sure my entire being was turning inside out.

I'm going to be sick. I can't! I'd have to run to the bathroom and I might miss his call. Oh God! No. Not happening. The beating would be worse, much harder, more painful. I was already in trouble. As usual. Did I ever do anything right?

At midnight, four hours earlier, Curly had called. "Why didn't you tell me we couldn't get any more cash from the credit card? You've left me out here with nothing! Now I can't go to the gym. I can't eat! All because of your inability to do your job. Your stupidity! I have no clue why I ever thought I could trust you! You're worthless. From now on, you'll babysit the kids. See how you like that! Don't you dare go to sleep! I'll call you back as soon as I figure this out with the guys."

I knew they had been sitting in his hotel room for hours after being summoned to serve. To sit. To stare. To endure whatever wrath spewed from his mouth. To endure whatever punches he decided each deserved for their "disobedience."

So I sat. I stared. Willing it to stay silent.

I thought back to yesterday before he had left town. All the guys were frantically packing the van that had once belonged to me. Everything had its place and, by God, it better not be even one fraction of an inch out of order. And nothing better be left behind. Shoes. Socks. Sweats. Suits. Books. Bibles. Bags. Should have been simple, right? Just make a list. Yeah, right. Major problem.

No matter how many lists were made, it changed. Even if the destination didn't. An invisible list existed, only known to Curly. It changed each time unbeknownst to the guys packing. Of course they got it wrong. That was the point. No one ever got it right. Not them. Not me. We were all useless to him. The self-declared God of us all. We were born to please him. To serve him. To do whatever he bid. We had been chosen. Specially selected, he had said. It was our job to obey him. Why? We'd go to hell if we didn't—and our families would join us.

I jerked upright. Fear hit hard. I'd nodded off.

PLEASE don't call right now. Somehow, he always knew. Fear continued to ravage my soul. *I must stay awake! Gum. I'll chew some gum.* I did for a couple of hours 'til my jaws couldn't take any more.

Now what? Read! I'll read for a while. That'll help. Read the scriptures he'd wanted us to study. That would keep me alert and get my heart right for when he called back, or so I thought. Panic! I couldn't find my notes with the scriptures. His fist flashed before my eyes. *Bam!* I knew the reality of this if I didn't find them and study. Fear. More fear. Butt-puckering fear.

That night, the phone didn't ring. I finally got in bed at 7 a.m. to sleep for an hour. Exhaustion replaced the fear. A typical night. On duty. For a monster.

Cemented by Fear—1995

Secured. Stuck. Superglued. The moment that sealed my fate to the fanatical. The progression was seductive. It pulled me in like a guppy. On a dangling line. Hooked. And choked me. With the bait. The debris of my destiny. Doomed.

Another early morning Curly commando call to arms. A moment's notice to depart. Summoned to his time-away-in-prayer retreat room, Rachel and I headed to Miles City, Montana, to do his bidding. Two-and-a-half hours later, we arrived at the Super 8 Motel located half a mile south of Interstate 94 in a rural part of town. He loved the sanctuary-type seclusion, away from the off-ramp hustle and bustle businesses.

We located the back entrance and headed inside. No front door entry for flunky followers. No one to see. No one to tell. No visibility of visitors was allowed. The dim hall lights illuminated the room numbers. We tiptoed quietly down the hall to avoid any attention.

My heart began pounding as we approached his room. Were we called for duties or discipline? It could be double trouble with a traveling twosome. We never knew. Would he blow a gasket about unperformed or less-than-perfect tasks assigned to his ministry management duo? Or would we be an attentive audience for his recent book-reading revelations?

Today it was neither.

Rachel stayed to be his motel maid. Or so I was told. I was the errand runner tasked with taking the car to get its tires rotated.

As he directed, I scribbled the tire shop address on a Super 8 notepad and headed out the door. Gripping the keys, I grinned as I located his vehicle. *My* former Voyager van he'd claimed when he and the traveling groupies would campaign-cruise for his almost-last-place race for governor. This made the car-driving errand less stressful since I knew how to operate it quite well.

I shivered with a twinge of excitement. This wasn't mission impossible. It was mission *importance*. I would prove my competence and win his validation. Praise. He needed me to do this. And I would receive a thumbs-up of approval. Ready to be puffed up by the prophet for a job skillfully executed.

That afternoon, tire job accomplished, I called Curly for instructions. My lips curled upward in a silly smile. I was ready for the raving review of the errand running sure to come my way. Various time-taking tasks were always assigned to tick off the minutes before returning to the ministry master. Speed was my superpower when it came to pleasing the prophet. Curly's impromptu plans were a test of my tenacity to carefully complete his chores. I was sure. Determined not to fail, I determinedly sailed through the assignments. After three phone calls, three delays, and at least three hours more, permission was finally granted to return.

Confidently, I strode from the street corner phone booth back to the newly cleaned van. I turned the key, started the engine. Believing yet still silently hoping and praying the job was done to his satisfaction, I drove back to the motel.

As the Super 8 sign came into view, my resolve to be rewarded teetered like a seesaw, worried about any possible blunders. I tapped softly on the brakes. *What in the world was I thinking? Praise for the completed projects?* Wishful irrational reality. More like fiction and fantasy. A self-propelled terror torpedo burst my bravery bubble. Mission approval. Might. Just. Be. Impossible.

Realness of my return stuck a fork in my flesh, pricking the fear pockets tucked in my brain. Where should I park? The spot I'd vacated a few hours earlier was now occupied by a beetle-bug green Volkswagen Rabbit. *Crap! Now what?*

I found a spot nearby and cautiously parked the car. Equal distance between the two white boundary borders. I made sure. I judged the distance from his previously perfect parking spot, measured against the further-away, second-choice location. Not much difference.

Please let this place be okay, I prayed silently. I exited the car, shutting the door with utmost care, and walked quickly to the memorized room-numbered door. I took a deep, calming breath. And knocked.

Newly rotated car tires weren't his focus. A stress-relieving run was. Continuing cleanup chores were assigned as he headed out the door in his black Nike spandex shorts, white T-shirt, and cap. Upon his exit, we hurriedly sprang into action. My heart pounded with worry of the less-than-expected cleanliness we might deliver by the time he finished his run. Less than could mean meanness emerging. Berating beginning. A nosedive plunge into punishment purgatory.

Should we dare straighten his books? His Bibles? It was always a game of chance. Gambling we would be good guessers straightening up the maniac's mess. *Eeeny Meeny Miny Moe. Where to place the books? Neither of us knows.*

I glanced around the double-bed room. One bed for sleeping. One bed for Bibles and books. Assessing every detail that he might see as still dirty. Dusty. Unclean. Not a wrinkle in the newly made beds. I brushed flat every petal of the olive-green and rose-colored flowered bedspread. Pillows propped up perfectly against the wall-mounted particle wood headboard. His brought-from-home Mr. Coffee pot was brewing on the table next to the cheap color television.

We heard a key turned in the lock. Rachel and I stood in the crevice between the bed and the outer bathroom wall where we'd just completed round two of book straightening and Bible placing. Wanting to get it just right. I held my breath and prayed he'd be pleased.

The door opened and shut behind him. As he entered the room, our bodies were literally flattened against the wall. Something eerie. Something spiritual. Something totally overwhelming entered, too. The hair stood up on my neck. My back. Even my arms. Fright sucked the breath from my lungs. A trough of terror was gouged all the way down my spine. Cemented by fear. To the wall. I. Could. Not. Move.

Eyes wide, I stared at him. His face had a peculiar, perplexed look.

"I can't believe what my Father just told me," Curly's voice spoke.

We knew it had to be something big. Or bad. Was it sinister or sacred? Menacing or majestic? All I knew was that something powerful had entered the room. It was intoxicating. Spiritually stimulating. But what spirit?

He sat down on the edge of the freshly made bed. No sound came from his mouth. No words emerged. Only fast, post-run breathing. Still stuck like scarecrows, we waited. Not daring to move. Too scared to even breathe. We stood. Backs against the wall. Like targets of a firing squad shooting firestorm-igniting bullets. Aim. We're not ready. But fire anyway. The prey. Praying in panic. So. Freaking. Scared.

"He told me who I am," Curly mumbled.

A mental picture of piety progression. A stairway to superior sanctity. Holy hierarchy achieved. Step after step. My thoughts flew through the name-changing transition. Each metamorphosis was validated by the verses he chose in the Bible. Hour after hour of indoctrination. Cerebral-matter manipulation. And purposeful persuasion. From Curly the Evangelist to Michael the Archangel. From Michael to King David. From David to . . . who again? Who was greater than the man after God's own heart?

"I'm Jesus," he proclaimed.

Holy shit. Oops—better not be thinking these cuss words. Not with Him. Here.

My mind raced. I had felt an overwhelming presence when he entered the room. Could he really be Him? Shock waves tore through my heart. We continued to stand. And stand.

In the silence. Unmoving. Cemented. By. Fear.

Finally movement. He grabbed his Bible and began flipping from page to page. Scripture to scripture. Forward and back. Back and forth.

We continued to stand. And stand. Cemented. By. Fear.

He began reading aloud. Scripture after scripture. Verse after verse. Validating his vision of his newly anointed holy vocation. Oblivious to our presence, no permission had been granted to sit. We dared not move. Barely dared to breathe. Noiseless and motionless. We stood. Silence was our net of safety. This spiritual presence was present. Pressing. In. Overpowering.

Trying to stay upright after the hours of wall leaning and listening.

Thoughts whirling. Twirling. Twisting. What did this mean? His past admonishment of being eternally damned for doubting him, ditching our destiny, had new meaning. Could panic make your stomach churn? Mine performed fear-induced bellyflops.

For the first time since he began tearing through book after book, Bible after Bible, he glanced up. His piercing look sent petrified slivers shivering down my spine.

"Raylynn! Pay attention! You've witnessed the most important revelation of your life and you're daydreaming? Do you realize you'll be called to bear witness to this very moment in time? In fact, get Dylan on the phone. You can start now. Tell him what just happened."

When Curly was absent, Dylan, the ex-marine, was in charge. Well versed and Bible schooled after having peer pressure drug problems early in life. Thus, Dylan's draw to Curly's "alcoholics are God's chosen people" vision. We were all ordinary outcasts, singled out for spiritual service. Earmarked for eternity. God's handpicked soldiers. An army specially selected for top-notch training we had been convinced. All because we wanted to believe in our heavenly worth after our own pain-filled pasts.

Relieved from my standing position against the wall, I moved to the nightstand where the black touchtone phone sat. I lifted the receiver, listened for a dial tone, then punched the numbered buttons in proper sequence of the memorized number, praying Dylan would answer quickly. I was relieved to hear his sleepy hello. By this time, darkness had fallen and midnight was approaching.

"Hi Dylan. It's Raylynn." I began tentatively testifying. Terrified. Sharing the super-*un*natural spiritual story I'd been asked to relay. I swallowed. Hard. "Something happened today and—"

"Oh, for goodness sakes! The most significant event of your life and you can't even describe any of the details? You're WORTHLESS! You can't even get *this* right!" Curly roughly snatched the receiver from my hand, pulling me off balance.

I grabbed the nightstand edge to keep myself from landing backward on his bed.

"Get away from me. Now!" The decibel of his anger increasing tenfold. And I was the cause.

Like an obedient soldier, I took up my sentry post. Back to the wall. Stand. And stand. Once again.

Cemented. By. Fear.

Exhilarated by his appointed, anointed, power position, Curly commanded the crew of guys to drive. Billings to Miles City. Time to blow his trumpet. Spread the word of his new anointed appellation. He sat puffed up and proud like a peacock awaiting his mating.

While we awaited the groupies' arrival, we were graciously granted a reprieve to sit on the floor. Waiting. Forcing ourselves to remain alert. Awake. Watching for any potential snare set by the self-appointed saintly snake. Continually preaching and teaching his treachery.

The devoted bunch of God's Army guys arrived anxious to hear the rest of the story. In the excitement to reveal his heavenly appointment, Curly's anger subsided. Rachel and I gave our account of what we'd witnessed. Each word elevating his ego. That was our job. Promotion of the prideful prophet. Designated dictator documentators.

The sun began to rise as the self-proclaimed "Son" sat with his unsaintly servants. Minute after minute. Hour after hour. We stood. We sat. We listened. And listened. And listened. Twenty-four hours on duty was taking its toll.

Early morning reprieve. Finally, we headed home. In the absence of the newly appointed son of the godhead, mental strain lessened. A bit. Muscle tension relaxed. A bit. Thought racing slowed. A bit.

But fear. Fear stayed. In its totality. Petrified people turned to petrified robots. Once organic cells of bruised hearts and broken brains. Turned to stone. By fear. Cemented to every living cell in the body. Every nerve fiber in the brain. No acid-dissolving antidote available to slow solidifying. The dread. Of the honcho head.

And now. The big-shot badass bully. Just. Got. Bigger. And badder.

August 1997—Yellowstone County Detention Facility, Billings, Montana

Stacy was half carried into my cell located on the main floor of the jail. It was where newbies stayed 'til they'd been properly oriented into jail life. I'd been there about a week. The cell was small with just one bunk. For one body. I looked around the small quarters . . . a bunk took up half of the room. The cold stainless-steel toilet and sink stood at the foot of the bunk near the cell door. *Where was she going to sleep?*

She slowly crumpled down the wall 'til her butt hit the floor. The jailer left her there and slammed the door shut, lock engaged. *Now what?* I thought as I quickly glanced her way. Who was she? What was she in for? What kind of person is she? Was she violent? Mean? Always my questions when encountering a new resident of each barred barracks I'd visited.

She didn't look too menacing in her current state. Head slumped forward, back against the wall. Eyes closed. The jailer returned with a small cot that sat about eight inches off the cement floor. She squeezed it in beside my bunk where I sat cross-legged. Unceremoniously, the jailer pulled Stacy up from the floor and plopped her almost limp body on the cot. As I watched, my concern grew for this blonde, wild-haired young woman sprawled out on the small temporary bed.

The jailer stood and turned to me. "I'm sorry but we don't have anywhere else to put her. She's been coming off drugs for a while, and she's still experiencing some detox. Not too bad of detox at this point, they assured us," she said a bit sarcastically. Then I heard her mumble under her breath, "We sure hope so anyway."

The jailer looked down a bit apprehensively at the cot holding Stacy as she turned and left the cell. Door shut. Lock in place. Silence.

I stared down at this poor young woman who looked like death warmed over. Not what I signed up for. Detox? *Ugh. Lord, I'm really not equipped for this.* I squeezed my eyes tightly together to keep the tears from escaping. No time for whiners. Or criers. Or cowards. I curled up in a fetal position, hugging the thin institutional blanket. Closed my eyes and fitfully slept. Until…

I heard her whimper. I sat up in my bunk and squinted in the almost-too-dark-to-see light of the cell at the body lying next to my bunk. Was she okay? She started moaning and slightly writhing on her small cot. My heart went out to her. No matter that this was the pain of withdrawal from self-administered drugs, she wasn't doing well. I slid down to the small crevice of space between the bunk and the cot on the floor. I put my hand on her forehead. A cold sweat. She continued to roll her head side to side, as if trying to shake off the pain. The drug effects. The withdrawal woes. When the night jailer made rounds about 2 a.m., he looked in through the sliver of a window in the door. Seeing me down on the floor with her, the door opened and I begged him to do something.

"Nothing we can do. No doctor's on at night," he explained. "She'll get through it. We'll check on her in the morning."

Jerk! I thought. *Heartless jerk jackass!* Under-my-breath name calling gave little relief. It was going to be an awfully long night.

I wiped her brow. I held her hand. I finally couldn't stand to sit by and just watch this human in so much pain, physically and emotionally, without having someone to care for her. I swept her up in my arms and rocked her like a baby. Eventually she relaxed. Eventually she slept. I watched over her 'til the cell darkness lifted. Morning jail lights came on. Another day dawned. Still behind bars. With my new prison pal.

Stacy sat up and put her head in her hands. "Fuck, I have a headache!" We talked about the process of withdrawal and the tough night she'd had. "Those fuckers don't even care!"

I didn't discuss the details of the long night. But I knew she knew. I could see it in her eyes. Feel it in her heart. She knew I cared. A perfect stranger in a jail who didn't make her feel less than. Didn't bring up her wrongs or judge her for her choices. Over the next few days, we became well acquainted.

She would watch me as I sat and read my Bible. "Why do you read that?" she'd asked with curiosity rather than contempt.

I simply explained Jesus to her. Who He was. What He'd done. Why I loved Him. Her slight nod acknowledged my straightforward description.

"Time to move!" the jailer said, opening the cell door. "Gather your belongings."

We both started picking up the few things we had. "No, not you," the jailer said to Stacy. "You stay. You're still in orientation."

A bit wide-eyed and uncertain, her usual tough exterior mask slipped a bit. I hugged her with my eyes. That not-allowed human touch. Stopped. Cold. Unfeeling. Not permissible to hug. To touch. To show simple compassion to another hurting, lonely soul. Not under the watchful eye of our guard. She stayed. I left.

The guard led me up the stairs to the left and opened the corner cell door and motioned me in. I looked inside worriedly at the two bunks. Wondering. Another roommate. *Now who? Please, Lord! Don't let it be another intimidator.* I'd been around enough of them to last a lifetime. I felt like the cowardly lion each time I met someone new. *Put 'em up, put 'em uuup! Which one of you first? I'll fight ya both together if you want. I'll fight ya with one paw tied behind my back.* The famous cowardly lion speech ran through my head each time. When my panic pressure lever turned on, it became my fear valve releaser.

I settled in my new abode. No roommate...yet.

Two days later, right after lockdown, I heard the key in my door. That was weird. The cell door had been locked for barely ten minutes. I looked up from where I sat on my bunk reading. I saw a mass of wild blonde hair peek around the door as it opened. Grinning from ear to ear, Stacy literally flew into the cell.

"Hi roomie!" She flung her stuff on the second bunk and sat down facing me. My mouth opened in surprise. "I told them I wanted to bunk with you, and they agreed! So fucking cool!" Stacy's manner of speaking always included the *f-word*. It was just who she was.

I laughed, jumped up, and hugged her. No one could see. We sat long into the night catching up on the jailhouse jabber. The goings-on. The good. The bad. The ugly. One person in particular was the object of our discussion. A tough broad awaiting transfer to the Women's Prison for murder. I warned Stacy. She's not someone you want to tangle with. This broad was tall with shoulder-length dark hair and medium build. And tough. Her demeanor said "I'm a badass bitch. Don't even try to mess with me." Her facial expression said, "Stay out of my way." And I was one who got in her way. Constantly.

Each day, she and her sidekick sat midway up the steps leading to the second tier. Waiting. Like a rattlesnake waits to strike. From her perch on the stairs, she'd calmly scan the room looking for her next prey. The target of her contempt. Slowly. Methodically. I would begin my ascent step by step. Bull's-eye on my back. Fear in my heart. Deep breathing. Kept climbing. As I reached their perch, not a muscle they moved.

"Excuse me," I'd say, as I stepped through the minefield of feet. Landmines of legs. Sprawling. Stopping. Scaring. Deliberate movement. Tripping. Catching me in the tangle of her web.

Down to my knees. "Be careful Bible Thumper. You might hurt yourself," she had sneered. Laughter. Mocking laughter. Erupted in my ears. Again. Every day.

Each night, Stacy watched me. Reading. Praying. Wondering. I asked her if she'd like to read with me. Sitting on our bunks opposite of each other, we started at the very beginning. Genesis Chapter 1.

She was intrigued. "Wow! The whole entire fucking world in six days? God is so fucking cool!" That *f-bomb* again.

I laughed at her exuberance. Her innocence. *This is definitely not your usual Bible lesson*, I thought. It certainly wasn't going as I'd expected. But I'd learned not to expect the usual from Stacy.

Our bibles now open to Genesis Chapter 3. "That fucking snake! I've known a few of them in my life," she sneered. "Why would she listen to him?" She was outraged at Eve's disobedience. "How stupid!"

I literally choked on the laughter bubbling up in my throat. I swallowed it quickly so she wouldn't see. She was deadly serious! "What??? Are you fucking kidding me?!" She shook her head in disbelief. "When I get to heaven, I'm going to kick her fucking ass!

The tirade continued. "It's because of her we have to put up with so much fucking pain when we have our babies? I'm going to kick her fuckin' ass!!" She looked up from her reading and finally calmed down. "Boy, this shit is really something!"

I fell on my bunk in gales of laughter at her indignation. Never had I heard anyone respond to reading the Bible like this. I can't help but think that Jesus was sitting in heaven splitting a gut, too. Stacy was His child. His creation. His daughter. Dearly loved. Even in spite of her "fucking" vocabulary.

Leave Now—1996

We sat in Curly's motel room after receiving a last-minute summons to appear. The obedient lot sitting attentively. Waiting. What did he want? To preach his personal proclamations? To correct the Curly-code-of-behavior breakers? To dictate his desired demands to deviant disciples? Before the long night was over, all three were on his serving platter.

He'd examined the prescription pill bottles sitting side by side on his nightstand. Opening each one, he counted the number of precious tablets remaining. Previous med run supplies were running dangerously low. As he impatiently threw them to the floor, the bottles scattered, rolled, then came to a stop. I glanced down and saw two bottle inscriptions facing me.

Julie Rocker. Take 1 every 6 hours for pain.

Gary Johnson. Take 1 or two every 4–6 hours as needed for pain.

Fictitious names. Fictitious patients. Fictitious ailments. For real drugs.

Three of us were chosen for the med run. The special supply stockers elected. We hadn't been on a run for a while, so Curly felt we were the least likely to be spotted as drug seekers. Skirting the authorities. The innocent ones. Chosen to supply drugs so he could atone for drug addicts. Or so he said. *Atone? Really?* It took me a while to understand what he meant.

During one late-night session, Curly had explained, "I'm the one who will suffer the penalty for all those with addictions. I will atone for their abominable sins. It will remove the effects of their sin from their hearts, thereby being able to reconcile with God again."

Pretty deep, I'd thought.

From his perspective, everything had to be atoned for. This was for the drug addicts. And we were the suppliers of the atonement substance. Drugs. Oxycodone. Hydrocodone. Loritab. Lorcet. Percodan. Ativan. Whatever we could con a doctor into prescribing after telling our tale of woe. Car-wreck-caused neck muscle strain, manual-lifting-caused lower back injury, football-tackle-caused knee injury, fibromyalgia all-over-pain, chronic headaches. We were pain-filled for the prophet. For the good of mankind, we lied and limped. Pleaded and prayed. For drugs. For him. Up to 100 a day he'd ingest. Erupting bursts of anger. Intense uncalled-for violence. We endured it all to atone for the sins of our families. For the salvation of the world. And our deliverance from a literal living hell.

Phonebooks in phone booths or hotel lobbies were our resource. Way before the Internet. We scoured The Yellow Pages for hospitals, far enough away to satisfy Curly's paranoia and close enough to get us back to his hotel before sunrise. We found the perfect one.

We headed down the road as fast as the road sign said was legal. No tickets needed on our way to our dastardly deed. As we rounded the corner, the bright red Emergency Room sign came into view, beckoning us forward. My stomach clenched and cramped. I hated it. I wasn't a great liar. *I can't do this!* Fear almost paralyzed me. What if we got caught?

Although, it wasn't getting caught that worried me so much. It was Curly's furious face that flashed before my eyes with the thought of a failed mission. Visualizing an empty treasure trove. No drugs defined disaster. Dredged up dread. Maybe even dead. If we didn't show up with the goods. The opioids. The atonement tools.

"What name are you using?" Sharon's question popped the panic balloon blowing up in my brain. My thoughts turned to the fictitious name I'd be called. Patty Snead, I'd decided. Now to remember it. First letters. P.S. Just remember "Pretty Scared." *Yep. I am.* Patty Snead. Pretty Scared. Living on 130 1st Ave E. Doesn't every town have a First Avenue? I sure hoped so. Phone number? Check. Social Security Number? Check. Courage? Not so much.

I'd drawn the short straw, so to speak. I headed in first. We planned to arrive at the automatic emergency doors with our forlorn stories five minutes apart. No recognition. No connection as far as the staff was concerned. I approached the check-in desk with my fake pain-filled expression. Thank goodness I only had to remember my name after filling out the form. In 1996, no need for identification. No need for proof of your existence. Just sign in and sit. Wait to be called.

I sat panicked, hoping I'd be believable enough to score a scrip. To fill the stash. To stave off the wrath. My heart pounded in fear.

"Patty Snead?" I vaguely heard the nurse call a name. "Patty Snead?" I heard it again.

Looking up I saw no one stand up. *That's me!* I leapt to my feet. "I'm here!" I waved my hand and walked toward her. "Sorry I didn't hear you," I apologized meekly.

I followed her into the inner rooms. Moment of truth. Well, untruth. How cool of a cucumber could I be? How convincing of pain? Of need for drug relief? Time for my debut. Time to sink or swim.

The nurse motioned to the examination table. I followed her direction and sat on the end. "What seems to be the problem tonight?" she asked in her professionally detached nurse voice.

"My head won't quit hurting. I feel as if it's going to explode. I had a car wreck six months ago and every once in a while I get excruciating headaches that just won't go away. I tried Tylenol but it's not cutting the pain at all. I just can't take it anymore," I said in an appropriately whiny voice.

I put on my best I'm-going-to-die-from-the-pain look. She scribbled notes as I talked then took my temperature and blood pressure.

"Your blood pressure is a bit high," she said, and made a note on my chart.

No shit, lady! If the doctor doesn't give me a prescription, I'll have more than high blood pressure! I silently screamed.

As she turned to go she smiled reassuringly, saying, "The doctor will be right in."

****

"Hello. I'm Dr. Schmidt. So, you're having headaches. When did they start?" the concerned distinguished-looking doctor asked.

I repeated my tale of the "car crash." Whiplash. Cervical strain. Headaches still happening. Pounding. Did I sound convincing enough? A stethoscope appeared in his hand.

"Heart sounds good," he half mumbled as his exam continued. He pressed the back of my neck. "Does this hurt?"

Of course it hurts, I thought. *Any place you touch will hurt. I just need drugs. Don't you get it?* Crazy thoughts played tag in my brain.

I nodded my head and winced. "Yep. It REALLY hurts," I replied sorrowfully.

He took out his pen light. Clicked it on. "Please look straight ahead," he said as he pulled my right eye open with two fingers. The light bore into my eye socket. I swear it lit up the hair on the back of my head. "Look right, left, up, down," he continued as I obediently peered in each direction as he requested. Releasing the right eye, he moved to the left. "Straight ahead. Up. Down. Right. Left."

Me. Obedient once again.

"Hmmm," I heard him say as he started the drill again. Same eye. "Again, please. Straight ahead. Up. Down. Right. Left." He released my eye, took a short step back. Then, with a furrowed brow, asked, "Have you recently hit your head?"

I shook my head no.

"Have you been hit in the head?" he continued probing.

The force of Curly's closed fist throwing my head sideways as it connected dead center with my left jaw flashed through my mind. "No," I innocently said.

His worried look began scaring me. He turned to the attending nurse. "Page Dr. Hinchley. STAT." She hurriedly left the room. "I think you may have a retinal detachment. You need to see the ophthalmologist right away. You're certain you haven't been hit?" The concern in his voice began tearing down my resolve.

Wow. Someone actually cares about me. *What if I told him the truth? What would happen?* Curly's frothing-at-the-mouth angry face front and center in my mind. He'd kill me. Fear gripped my heart.

Then a different self-preserving fear hit. What about my eye? The STAT announcement isn't used for a simple headache. *Now what? Tattle and stay? Or exit and escape?*

The nurse returned and said, "Dr. Hinchley isn't on call tonight, but I did reach him. He'll be here as soon as he can. Fifteen minutes is what he estimated."

Oh my God! This isn't what I came here for . . .

The doctor turned back to me saying, "Please sit quietly. We'll be back shortly."

I sat frozen in fear. No drugs results in a very pissed-off prophet. What to do?

Unbeknownst to me, Rachel had called Curly from the hospital waiting room, letting him know I was taking longer than normal. A doctor. A nurse. Back and forth. I hadn't been left alone for her to find out my status. Had my lies been believed? Ailments prescription aided? She couldn't report.

Alone. Afraid. No, terrified. I closed my eyes and wept silently.

"*LEAVE NOW!*" Rachel hissed through gritted teeth. "Curly said leave now! Let's go!"

My eyes flew open and there stood Rachel whispering intensely to me. I visibly jerked at the mention of his name. "We've got to get out of here," she said as she grabbed my arm.

With a slight hesitation at first, I slid down off the examining table. As soon as my feet hit the floor, I began power walking past the nurses' station and out the double door. Without a backward glance, the three of us who had been assigned the med run raced to the car, jumped in, and headed out of the parking lot. Looking in the rearview mirror, we prayed that no flashing police car lights were following.

"Curly could smell the enemy and said to get out now," Rachel explained, as she continued the return trip to the hotel where Curly held court with all his loyal subjects.

I was terrified to return. He surely knew what I had been thinking. What I'd almost done. What was in my mind to do. The divine God. In charge of the universe. In charge of his chosen. In charge of my thoughts, I was sure.

Fear began choking me. I could hardly breathe. No drugs spelled disaster. And the cause had been me. I felt the trickle of sweat roll down between my breasts. Under my arms. Down my lower back. I almost peed my pants in trepidation.

What if I just opened the car door and jumped? At least I wouldn't have to face him. But what about Sunny? My family? The ever-present fear of hell was the bait I bit in the trap. And trapped I was. By fear. By threats. By believing lies. No key labeled "Bullshit" to unlock the latch of the trap.

The car stopped. My legs were paralyzed by fear.

"We better go in. He's waiting for us," Rachel instructed. My legs wobbly as I opened the car door and tried to take a step. Internally, I laughed hysterically. Thoughts racing. Nerves wriggling. Stomach swirling.

Taking a deep breath, I resigned myself to the fact that I had to face the music. Face the fear. *Might as well get it over with*, I thought. The sooner I did, the sooner I could go to our room and maybe get some sleep. Boy, was that a far-reaching wish on a fallen star. Burned out. Busted. And that I was. Busted.

Only one score for the night. Sharon's back injury performance earned a Loritab scrip. Rachel had been too busy reporting my almost-caught situation. Her failure became my failure. Double-duty dread. How long would it take 'til punishment time? Curly was notorious for letting you squirm.

Sam was in trouble. Again. "I don't want to even look at you!" Curly screamed. "Get out of my sight! Go stand in the bathroom. Better yet, stand in the tub. Don't even move an inch. Or else. And you join him, Raylynn. I can't stand you right now! You allowed the enemy to use you. To steal from me. To get in the way of atonement! People will suffer because of you! How does that make you feel? You stink like the enemy. Get out of here. Now!"

I slunk into the bathroom following after Sam. I heard Curly holler, "Dylan! Go make sure they stand straight. Hands at their sides. Not touching the wall." Dylan came to the door as Sam and I stepped over the side and took our place side by side. Shoulder to shoulder. In the tub. A motel room tub. Small. Rounded sides.

Difficult to stand without slipping. No choice. Slipping. Moving. Swaying. Talking. All would come with severe punishment.

After our perfect punishment placement, Dylan returned to the meeting. I slightly turned my head to look at Sam out of the corner of my eye. He was doing the same. Cast-off comrades. No word passed between us. Just resignation. Acceptance. Of our discipline.

Time passed. How much? I wasn't sure. My legs were now most certainly like jelly. Wobbly. Weak. And getting weaker with each passing minute.

"Stand up straight!" I heard Dylan say sternly.

We both stood at attention, realizing fatigue had caused a bit of a slump in our stance. Stillness. Silence. In the outer room. It was sickening. I knew he was coming. Dylan stepped aside to allow Curly to enter the bathroom. Indescribable fear hit me.

Just as his fist hit me. My head flew sideways, almost knocking me over. I fell back against the wall. *Bam!* His fist flew again, connecting with Sam's jaw.

Oh God. Please help us. How can this be you, God? I cried to myself.

"Stand up straight or I'll do it again," Curly spat at us.

Sam and I recovered as well as we could with our ears ringing. Our heads splitting. Fear exploding. We stood. Again. Straight. Shoulder to shoulder. For six hours. Deserved discipline for the disobedient disciples of Curly. Another night. Of terror. Ended at dawn.

Wigged-Out Warrior—1996

"I need a credit card," said Curly's wife. We stood eye to eye in the basement of the house where I resided with Sunny and my then-husband, Wally. We were the basement dwellers. Another family lived upstairs. My designated responsibilities included the keeper of the money box filled with credit cards. Visa and Mastercard aplenty imprinted with the names of Curly's credit-worthy cohorts. We were the patsies for the pocketbook. The loyal crew conditioned to contribute all to the cause. Curly's cause. Get a card. Give the card. To Curly.

Supporting his household. Their every need. Their every want. More and more cash advances. More and more goods bought. More and more travel funded for the master head. In charge of charge cards. And cash. Payout only pending approval. By the prophet. A pittance here and there was given to us to meet our needs.

I'd been instructed *never* to give out a card without his prior approval. Permission from the power-hungry prophet was a prerequisite for disbursement. And no go-ahead had been given.

But this was Curly's wife. Conflicting emotions collided. Apprehension. Uncertainty. Turmoil. Trepidation. On a collision course to probable punishment. No chicken dinner winner here. Caught between a hard place and wrecking rock. Smashed to bits by the holy air blaster whenever he might return.

"I need to get some food," she explained, a bit agitated at my no-go attitude, hoping that reasoning would get me to loosen my grip on the grub-buying card.

This couldn't be happening. I swallowed hard. Gagging on the panic lump expanding in my fear-constricted throat. Choking me. The entire night had been a shit show. Only snippets of the happenings had been shared. Trying to protect not the innocent but the reputation of the self-appointed saint. All because of atonement.

That's what he called it. Atoning for the wasted druggies. The lost alcoholics. It was his job to redeem them all. After all, he was the holy anointed one. He took it on as a "sacrifice." His trumped-up justification demonstrated by his reluctant, "I really don't want to do this, but my Father in heaven is commanding me to do so." Yet he took to it like a duck to the water. After all, he'd been through seven treatment centers. But professed his sobriety over and over on the campaign trail. So, had he been truly sober or just an abstainer?

In his deluded mind, this drug downing had nothing to do with sobriety, or so he convinced us, quoting scripture after scripture into the wee hours of the morning. Day after day. Night after night. It was atonement. After all, he was the sacrificial lamb he had said. Over and over. Anything he chose to do was for atonement. This night was different.

Curly's house sat with the famous Rimrocks as the backdrop to the kitchen sliding glass door. This cliff of sandstone formation created a backyard obstacle course filled with huge boulders extending all the way to the upper edge, hundreds of feet high. An expanse masquerading as a spiritual battle ground to the wigged-out warrior. Curly.

After gulping down handful after handful of pain meds, obtained deceptively by his med runners he became unhinged from reality. Loose as a goose galloping across the rocks, raising unholy hell. Tormenting hallucinations caused out-of-control behavior. Swordfighting, unseen assailants in imagination-produced attacks. Yelling insane accusations at any moving critter or weed waving in the wind. Crouching behind huge rocks hiding from invisible, hostile combatants. The war was waged. Behind his house. Behind his neighbors' houses.

Second-in-command Dylan began a tour of reconnaissance, scoping out how best to corral Curly. Run interference with the aroused-from-tv-watching neighbors checking their watch dog barking alarm in their backyard. Stop the concerned cop calls. Intervene in the potential straitjacket-donned arrest wear.

So we gathered. In one accord. And stood. In shock. Fear of what might happen. Not knowing what to do. What would be right. What would be wrong. In Curly's eyes. Always measured against the yardstick of potential punishment.

This was exactly the dilemma with the credit card. Obey his command or give into his wife . . . no friggin' clue.

It was a basement chatterbox conversation. Fear. Concern. Unbelievable panic. At the absence of our fearless leader who wasn't so fearless now. Part relief. Part dread. Part what-in-the-heck-do-we-do? He hadn't prepared us for this.

Bruce spoke what most of us dared not to express. "I think he's having DTs." Delirium tremens, a potentially fatal form of alcohol withdrawal.

However, it wouldn't have been DTs since it wasn't alcohol he'd been ingesting. At least not recently. It had been the various types and massive amounts of drugs. Drug-induced psychosis, more like it. Liberating, irrational delusions. Lifelike hallucinations. Extreme paranoia created a head-on collision in an unseeable conflict none of us could fight.

In the wee hours of the morning, we heard from Dylan. He'd coaxed Curly to end the battle and head to bed. In relief, the rest of us dispersed and did the same. All with apprehension as to what the dawn of the next day would hold.

As we'd suspected and dreaded, a gathering was called by Curly. Come. Tonight. Belfry butterflies in the belly bit. Hard. All bravery busted. Nerves raw. We went.

Not a sound. We sat waiting in the living room of his home. The door to their bedroom was closed. We waited. And waited. Not daring to even breathe. What would be the outcome of the previous night terrors? For each of us.

He sauntered into the living room. His intense gaze scanned the room like detecting radar seeking who were the devotees and who would be devoured. None of us knew. He sat and stared around the room. In the stillness a dropped pin would have sounded like a bomb. Casual conversation began, but we feared it was a ruse for what's to come. No lead. No tip-off. No cryptic clue. About the catastrophic calamity he endured.

The shit-show explanation for his behavior he told was of a spiritual battle he had to wage. It was devils, demons, and powerful principalities of the darkness. He, the Holy One, had to handle it. Stave off the slimy serpents. Win the wicked war. Between heaven and hell. He made it all sound so . . . so spiritual.

He explained we were all put to the test. Faithful or faithless in the face of the fight. His Father knew and would tell him. Fear. A fear-slapping statement. *Oh dear Lord! Was I faithful?* My thoughts raced running rapidly over our gathering happenings.

"Raylynn." It wasn't a question. It was a pay-attention command. You are being addressed.

"Yes?" I answered shakily.

"My wife told me you wouldn't give her the credit card she asked for last night."

Full body clenching muscles indicated the intensity of my fear. "No. I didn't."

His inquisition continued, "Why didn't you give it to her?"

My thoughts did somersaults trying to land on an appropriate answer. Would the ramifications of truth result in dire discipline? I blurted out, "You told me to not give the credit cards to anyone, so I didn't."

A fierce gaze enveloped his face. He. Just. Stared. I. Just. Shook.

Then to my surprise, and relief, a smile spread across his face. "Good for you! I now know I can trust you to obey whatever I tell you to do."

My muscles relaxed. My heart slowed down. I could finally breathe.

He turned to Bruce. The berating began about his inability to understand spiritual things. "You thought I was going through DTs?"

Bruce slowly shook his head up and down bracing for the blast. And it came in the form of a fist to his face. Hard. Fast. With fury. "This has nothing to do with DTs. Don't ever forget it!" Curly admonished him.

Discussion continued about the previous evening events. Then he stood. Smiling, he walked to stand in front of me. Standing so close I had to strain my neck backward to meet him eye to eye. His sly smile kept me at ease.

CRACK!!

His raised fist connected. Cold-cocked. One. Hard. Punch. To my head. Sideways it snapped as far as my neck would turn. Instant pain. Sharp. Stinging. Swelling. Stunned. My eyes watered. I faced forward, pain ripping at my jawbone and my cheek. The shock of the blow burst my bubble from my earlier bravo. I had no idea what I'd done.

Unhurriedly, he walked back to his chair. And glared at me. Vicious. Intense. Hatred. Spewed forth from his eyes. "Don't you *ever* deny my wife access to whatever she asks you for! Do you understand me?"

I nodded. A petrified promise. Of yes.

The night meeting ended when day dawned. I silently slunk out the door. Shamefaced at my shakedown for stupidity. My inability to perceive proper behavior. The need for intense reprimand. I was hopeless. Still. Again.

September 5, 1997—County Courthouse, Billings, Montana

A call on the inmate phone, hanging on the gray cement cellblock wall of the Yellowstone County Detention Facility, had informed me of my immediate court appearance. My public defender, a woman I'd yet to meet, had begun her legal instruction. "They'll be transporting you to the courthouse for your initial appearance."

"Really? It's about time," I had said a bit sarcastically under my breath. The Yellowstone County justice system was a bit backed up. I'd placed call after call to her office after learning she'd been assigned my case, even before I appeared in court. This was supposed to protect my rights, as is usually explained the first time you head to court within 48 hours of arrest. But I'd been transported from North Dakota State Penitentiary via jails in Fargo and Grand Forks, North Dakota, and Moorhead, Minnesota. Then hitched a handcuffed ride on the prisoner transfer trail through Rapid City, South Dakota, and Miles City, Montana. Finally reaching my destination of Billings to stand my final charges . . . I hoped. In the place I'd begun my check-writing activity.

No answer. No return call. Until now. After sitting in the jail for over three weeks, it was finally time to learn my fate. *How many months will I get this time?* I thought.

She continued in her lawyerly voice, "I'll meet you at the courthouse and will walk you through what you'll need to do. This is only an initial appearance, so you won't need to enter a plea yet. I'll visit with you before that takes place."

Click. The call was disconnected. I stood staring at the black receiver in my hand. Totally shocked that this was happening with such little notice.

"Get a move on!" the guard said sternly. "We're leaving in three minutes. Line up at the door."

Those of us readying for a chauffeured ride in the prisoners-on-parade transport van stood in line awaiting our travel accessories. Nothing unique about this heading-out-of-jail jewelry. We each were gifted with a belly chain bound to handcuffs and shackles secured to ensure a shuffling stroll. Out the door we shuffled, one by one. Loaded in the van, one by one.

I sat in silence looking out the window searching for familiar landmarks. Remembered restaurants, neighborhoods, grocery stores, and motels flashed by. Motels. My heart skipped a beat, and I sucked in my breath when I realized we were near the dreaded Travelodge Motel. It was the location where Curly would go "get in prayer" away from us. Away from his family. He was the holy man needing divine devotion time. Many times, a call to that room meant nothing but a trip to hell. Nothing felt holy about it at all. If you were summoned to go, you prayed. I took a deep breath. Inhale peace. Exhale fear.

Interestingly enough, my fear of what I was soon to face at the courthouse paled in comparison to the mental images of the motel memories. When panic wormed its way into my body, my heart pounded. My lungs wouldn't take in necessary air. My leg started shaking. It shook so hard I was sure the floor of the van was vibrating. My wanting-to-take-flight leg bouncing maneuver didn't get me anywhere. But it was calming. My fast-twitching muscle fibers releasing fear-caused negative energy.

I looked away hoping to see something, anything to bring back pleasant thoughts. Nothing came into view, so I closed my eyes and thought of Sunny. The vision of her sweet, sunshiny smile was like an anxiety antidote.

I felt the van stop and heard directives being given by our excursion escort. One by one, we unloaded and entered the prisoner entrance at the back of the courthouse. Fear once again took hold. This time for my unforeseen future.

I stood at the defense table in my orange jumpsuit with my hands clasped in an upside-down prayer position. In my nervousness I thought of the nursery rhyme finger game. *Here's the church.* Hands clasped tightly. *There's the steeple.* I put up my index fingers. *You open the door and you see all the people*—now *that* one's impossible with my shiny silver bling binding my wrist movements.

My head was in my usual guilt-stricken bowed position—humiliation did that to a person. I glanced up without raising my head to peer at the black-robed somber judge. The scowl on his face didn't reassure me of any little bit of leniency.

He's probably going to throw the book at me, I thought. Fear began to slither down my back like a cunning boa constrictor wrapping itself around my midsection. Hanging on tighter and tighter, restricting my ability to breathe. Controlled panic set in. I'd been trained well over the years to stand quietly and internalize all reactions in stressful situations to minimize the potential explosive and abusive repercussions. This learned survival technique served me well in this moment. It seemed like eternity 'til I heard his voice.

"*How* long have you been incarcerated?" I heard him ask disgustedly.

Nausea traveled from my brain to my toes, not even stopping at my stomach. I didn't know you could feel nauseated in every cell of your body. In this moment, even my little piggy toe wanted to throw up. I get why. I'm just a pig in his sight. A stomach-churning, check-bouncing, revulsive Miss Piggy. If I opened my mouth, I was going to puke.

I glanced sideways at my new legal beagle, silently begging her to speak for me. Wasn't that her job? She nodded insistently toward the man who held my future in his hands. Her expression gave me no hope that she'd help. She was hell-bent on my mouth working, on me answering, with no consideration whatsoever of bailing me out of this predicament. Funny. Bailing me out. I half-hysterically laughed at myself.

My mouth opened automatically, and I said meekly, "Almost thirteen months, your Honor."

"Thirteen *months*? Are you kidding me? For bad checks?" he said horrified.

I held my breath, truly hoping to pass out. *I can't take this anymore, Lord!* I inwardly screamed. I opened my eyes brimming with tears, awaiting my fate of continued incarceration.

The next moments were like a slow-motion movie. I saw him snatch the gavel, raise it over his head, and slam it down on the wooden block. It sounded like an explosion. I jumped at the sound, ready to faint. My knees were knocking. My palms were sweating. My teeth were chattering. As I awaited the anticipated severe sentence. The words that came next totally rocked my world.

"You're outta here! Release her immediately!" the district court judge said sternly, pounding his gavel on the wooden sounding block positioned on the official courtroom bench.

Out of here? My mouth fell open. *I'm sure I heard wrong.* It must have been wishful thinking.

I turned to my attorney in total disbelief. "Out of here?" I repeated again.

She smiled kindly and said, "Yes, Raylynn. You're finally free."

Friday, September 5, 1997—Yellowstone County Detention Facility, Billings, Montana

"PRAISE JESUS!!!!" I screamed at the top of my lungs. We'd just returned to the cell block from our courthouse excursion. My exhilaration at the anticipation of tasting freedom for the first time in almost thirteen months had me literally jumping for joy. Thus, my proclamation of praise flew out of my mouth with no fear filter or mouth muzzle. I was flat-out walking out these doors with no jailhouse jewelry attached. Flat-out free!

The guard who unlocked the door for the out-and-about judge-appearance participants scowled at me and said, "No yelling like that." My Cheshire Cat grin spread from ear to ear. My first time being a bit mischievous and unpredictable felt fabulous. Is this how the cat felt in *Alice and Wonderland*? If so, no wonder the grin was plastered on his face. It was on mine. I'd lived with a submissive survivalist attitude for months, so a bit of out-of-the-box behavior was warranted.

"Go pack your stuff," the guard ordered. I flew up the stairs to my corner upper-tiered cell. Quickly changing out of the orange jumpsuit and pouring myself into my oversized sweatpants and T-shirt, given to me by caring Bible study ladies who kindly provided clothes to fit. The carb-laden foods had piled on the pounds. Picture an oversized thunder thigh being stuffed in a stiff denim jean leg—not a pretty picture of comfort.

One by one, my jailbird buddies came to bid farewell and wish me luck. My next-door cell neighbor was quietly crying.

"What am I going to do without you here to pray for me every night? I'll lose it!" Her slightly hysterical tone was created by anticipated apprehension.

Being extremely claustrophobic, my neighbor's panic would set in each evening prior to lockdown. I had made a pact with her to pray. "Put your hand on your wall at lights out. Mine will be just on the other side of the cement block right above your bunk, and I'll pray."

Each and every night, I had asked God to bring her serenity and provide peaceful sleep until she heard the pop of the electromagnetic locks opening in the morning. My heart was ripped to shreds. Freedom for me meant an escalation of fear for her. I reassured her, though, that it wasn't my words or prayer that protected her. It was Jesus and He promised to never leave or forsake us.

I snuck a quick hug despite the don't-touch policy.

"I promise, I will still pray at lights-out time. No matter where I go, I'm still praying. I still care. And so does Jesus," I reassured her.

She turned and walked down the upper-tier walkway, wiping tears with the back of her hand. I had no clue that leaving the detention facility would be so friggin' hard.

I returned to packing my limited belongings, placing them in bags provided by the guard. Out of the corner of my eye, I saw movement at my door. I stood up and saw the stair-tripping tyrant standing, arms crossed, with her back leaning against the open cell door. The slight smirk I knew well spread across her smug face.

My first thought, *Lord, what's this? Her last opportunity to get in a dig?* At least I wasn't climbing the stairs where she sat to perform her accidental-tripping technique on the specially selected suckers.

In her hostility, I'd become her bull's-eye target, her number one elected enemy, sitting at the top of her shit list. Why? I wasn't sure. I stood quietly, looking at her questioningly. She squinted and stared hard, as if trying to bore a hole through my eyes.

Well, shit. I could feel a tingle of fear trickle down my back.

NO! I stood a bit taller, drumming up courage and thought, *You're not going to intimidate me now, you murdering bitch! I'm outta here!*

Not a nice thing to think, but it did the job. Fear fell away. Pity took its place. My thoughts flashed to her future existence filled with lifelong prison bars day in and day out. Awaiting transfer to the Women's State Penitentiary, she was facing a life sentence for murder. My heart fell in shame for my name-calling courage builder at her expense.

Out of the corner of her mouth she sneered, "I heard you're gettin' outta here."

I nodded affirmatively.

I watched as her face began to slightly soften. She continued, "I guess I owe you an apology."

Had I really heard her correctly? Inwardly, a direct heart-shocker hit. Emotional explosion. Outwardly, I stood still, showing little emotion—a survival technique I'd learned while enduring Curly's abuse. It served me well in jail, too. It served me well in this crucial moment.

I quietly responded truthfully, "Yes. Yes you do."

Her position shifted and I sensed her uncomfortableness.

"Weeeell," she drew out while she seemed to search for words. "I guess I was a bit jealous." Her head hung down as she looked at the floor. She continued, "I used to have what you have, then I lost it."

The lost-sheep look in her eyes said it all. My compassion for her pain compelled me forward. Although prohibited, I reached out and enveloped this hurting young woman in my arms. A bit taller than me, she slumped forward slightly and rested her forehead on my shoulder.

I whispered intensely, "No! You've not lost Him. He's always been with you. All you have to do is ask forgiveness and turn back to Him. He's waiting for you. He loves you."

She raised her head and I stepped back. Tears were welling in her eyes as I looked in love and compassion at a woman I'd previously avoided. But Jesus never did. He loved her and wanted her back in his fold. She squared her shoulders and started walking slowly away. Her cockiness once again apparent. A necessary trait for this place.

She glanced at me over her shoulder and grinned. "See ya, Bible Thumper."

****

"Who's picking you up?" asked the cheerful guard as she stuck her head in my cell. My head snapped up from bagging my belongings at her question.

Pick me up?? I thought, staring at her in confusion, like she'd asked who's taking me to Mars.

"Your paperwork should process shortly. As soon as we get it from the judge, you're out of here," she explained, a grin on her face. Although responsible for law and order in the unit, she'd been extremely kind with no condescending attitude. No better-than-us-lowly-lawbreaking-jailbirds perspective.

A wide-eyed, jaw-dropping moment as I attempted to respond, but nothing came out. A sinking feeling of uneasiness slammed a double hitter directly in my gut. In my excitement of soon-to-experience freedom after months and months of my behind-bars abode, I had no clue where I was heading. Nor how would I get there.

The judge had reminded me that I had 48 hours to report to my parole officer in Bismarck, North Dakota. Although I was free, I had been given five years parole from the North Dakota State Penitentiary. A fleeting thought had crossed my mind, *I wish Mom could come get me*. The pain of separation tore at my heart. I missed her. I missed Sunny. I missed my sister.

But my lot had been launched. Cast by Curly the picker. It was a privilege to be pegged and handpicked by him, the chosen one predestined to save the sinners and select the saints. We'd be the saints if we did his bidding. He'd bullied and browbeat the bejesus out of us. Yep. Because he claimed to Be Jesus. No going against the professed big guy in the sky who brainwashed us into believing the beatings were best to test our trust. To fix our flesh. To decide our fate. Door one said heaven. Door two said hell. Our choice. However, from what I'd experienced over the last few years, there had to be an adjoining door flung open, letting heaven swoop in like white whipped cream to sit on the dark, dank drink of hell. Served on a fear-splattered platter of pain. Not much choice at all.

If we exited or escaped, our fate was in hell. A generational curse for our families there, too. A far-out fear maybe, but just what if it was real? Scripture after scripture was twisted to teach us truth—his truth.

"You will be hated by everyone because of me. But the one who stands firm to the end will be saved," Matthew 10:22. "If anyone comes to me and does not hate father and mother, wife and children, brothers and sisters—yes, even their own life—such a person cannot be my disciple," Luke 14:26. These threats and use of the Bible kept me in fear.

My heart sank. The 200 miles from my mom's home might as well be 2,000. I asked to use the phone. The guard led me down to the lower level and motioned to the phone. "Go ahead and make what arrangements you need."

I picked up the black receiver and hit zero for operator. "What number are you calling?" said the monotone voice of the switchboard monitor.

I recited the number and heard her dial. *Brrriinng. Brrriinng.*

"Hello?" said a male voice.

"Will you accept a collect call from Raylynn at a correctional facility?"

"Yes," my then-husband, Wally, said.

He's the only one I knew who was in a position to come. Someone who owned a car and could gas up without having to ask for money and permission to spend it. I knew he still cared enough to come get me. Over my year of a locked-up lifestyle, he's seen to it that I had money on my books for extras. Candy bars for comfort eating and behind-bars bartering. A rented 12-inch TV as a prison pastime.

Having escaped Curly's clutches while on the road with him in Minneapolis, Wally had eventually returned home to North Dakota to work. Resuming a halfway-normal life, he'd secured a job making good money and bought his own vehicle. And today, he agreed to fetch me from the slammer. Exit detention. Enter freedom. At least from a cement cell and bars.

My pickup car wouldn't arrive for almost eight hours. I had to fly the coop at five o'clock sharp when my get-out-of-jail card had to be played. The Wally Express departing Williston, North Dakota, at 3 p.m. couldn't be my transport. It was a five-hour trip, which meant an 8 p.m. arrival at the earliest. Panic set in. The idea of heading out the door alone to nowhere felt a bit overwhelming.

My soon-to-come freedom became laced with fear. From delight to despair in a millisecond.

Sitting on the edge of my cot with my bags of belongings at my feet, my eyes landed on my Bible near my left hand.

Oh Lord, I prayed. *What do I do?*

Out of habit, I picked it up and out fell a simple folded white notebook page. I picked it up from where it lay on the cold, gray concrete floor and unfolded it. A name and a number were scrawled on it.

The kind smile of the woman who'd given it to me flashed in my mind. "If you need anything at all, Raylynn, give me a call" she'd said as she slid the paper to me. I recalled her kind, compassionate eyes as she stood up from the table we'd used in the small conference room for Bible studies.

Each week Margaret arrived in our cell block with her Bible under her arm and a beautiful, sweet smile on her face. A gentle soul who gave of her time to bring hope to those she saw as lost lambs locked up in jail. She shared her life outside the walls to give us a glimpse of freedom. Laughingly, she told tales of her husband's pet chickens bringing joy to our cold world of confinement and cement walls.

I raced out my cell door and flew down the stairs. Maybe, just maybe, she'd come. After permission was granted to use the phone, I dialed the number and held my breath.

What if she wasn't home? What if she said no? What if she hadn't really meant it? The what-ifs bounced like a multi-ball pinball jackpot play in my brain. Targets tagged with *Yes. No. Not home. Can't come. I'm busy. No time.* And the bull's-eye target was embossed in big, bold letters, *You're not worth it.*

The phone rang four times. "Hello?"

I froze. She answered! "Margaret?" I asked, praying it was her.

"Yes?" she replied questioningly, obviously not recognizing my voice.

I took a deep breath and pushed forward. "Hi. This is Raylynn at the jail. I've been coming to your Bible study. Do you remember me?"

Doubt dripped droplets of potentially perceived rejection, slithering down my throat like a snake's deadly venom. I swallowed hard.

She chuckled and said, "Of course I remember you! What can I do for you?"

My heart leapt excitedly at the acknowledgment of knowing me. I squeezed my eyes in silent prayer trying to drum up courage to explain my stranded situation. *It's now or never*! I shouted silently to myself.

Tentatively I asked, "Is it possible for you to pick me up at 5 p.m. when they let me out? I just need a place to go for a few hours until my husband arrives from North Dakota." I barely finished telling her my tale of tardy transit when her exuberant answer was discharged rapidly through the phone line.

"Of course I'll come! You can come have dinner with me at my house and your husband can pick you up here."

Her hand of hospitality literally brought me to tears. A generous gesture from a woman I barely knew. But she knew God. God knew her. And He knew me. And He knew my need.

I asked permission to make another call. My collect call was accepted, and I relayed the address, directing Wally to where I'd be when he arrived in town. Now the countdown to freedom began. Ninety minutes felt like ninety hours. I stared at the clockface as the second hand slowly ticked its way around.

Tick . . . Tick . . . Tick . . . Tick. Can time move any slower?

My heartbeat was going twice as fast as the clock. *Thump! Thump! Thump! Thump!* I swore I was going to have a heart attack before the clock struck five. Pacing. Pacing. *Thump. Thump.* Pacing. Pacing. *Thump. Thump.* My brain was going to burst. I stopped cold. In my anticipation of freedom, I hadn't weighed the consequences.

Freedom equals a renewal of fear. Where was Curly? What would he say when he found out the deserter Wally was picking me up? Had they talked? Where were we going to stay tonight? Where was I going to stay in Bismarck? Fear. Flat-out flippin' fear had gained entrance to my freedom festival. A deeper, more intense fear enveloped me. It was different than the fear I'd experienced inside prison walls. I steered clear of antagonizing bullies and kept my head down. With Curly, I wasn't able to steer clear, or dire consequences would ensue. After all, I'd been chosen. And my only choice was heaven or hell, so he had said.

Knock it off! I chastised myself. *I'm getting outta here. That's all that matters.* I had to kick the crappy damper out of my post-prison party. No more Debbie-Downer disposition. I was going to be free and I was going to celebrate. At least for now.

****

Friday at five. Time for Happy Hour. It's Happy Hour, all right. Freedom at five on the fifth. September 5, that is. How crazy.

I took a deep breath, said goodbye to the smiling guard, and took my first step to freedom. No hand-hampering handcuffs. No shuffle-inducing shackles. No jazzy jail jumpsuit. Just me and my bags of belongings. One step forward out the Yellowstone County Detention Facility door, then I froze in fear. My feet felt glued to the ground. I almost jumped out of my skin when I heard the door slam behind me. Locking me out, not in.

What's next? What do I do?

Exhilaration and apprehension are like oil and water. They don't mix well. Should I shudder or shout? Puke or party? I really wasn't so sure. When you're inside, all you think about is getting out. But that first step—literally—the first step beats down your braveness. Blows up your balance. Normalcy no more. At least as a locked-up life defines it.

My initial beat-feet-out-the-door fear had clouded my focus. As my fogginess began to dissipate, I became aware of my surroundings. A car came into view. A friendly, familiar face smiling from the driver's seat.

Margaret! She'd actually come. For some reason I hadn't been sure. A "yes" is just a word 'til action backs it up. She came through. She came for me. My heart leapt in gratitude.

She reached across the passenger seat and opened the door. "Get in!" She said excitedly. "Throw your bags in the back."

I did as she instructed then climbed in the car. *Weird*, I thought. So strange to get into a vehicle one foot at a time. No strategic wiggle to get in with your ankles anchored together.

The car lurched forward as she hit the gas, seconds after I shut my door. Her feisty foot action fit her personality. Her adventurous, carefree nature reflected in her slightly reckless driving ability.

We flew down the street with her questions firing right and left, "When did you go to court? How did you get out so quickly? What sentence did you get? What are you going to do now?"

I could hardly get a word in edgewise, even though the questions were directed at me. I laughed at her exuberance. Her joyfulness was infectious. Before much more conversation ensued, we arrived at her house.

"Come in," she said invitingly as she climbed out of the car. "Don't mind the chickens. They're my husband's pets." Squawking chickens escorted me to the door. Such a weird feeling of déjà vu hit me. Chicken coops and cousins from childhood days on the ranch.

Three hours with Margaret was a much-needed gift. No expectations, no fear of doing wrong, no call for lockdown. She accepted me for who I was, ex-con status and all. This woman exemplified the directive, "Be Jesus with skin on." Loving. Non-judgmental. Accepting. She truly cared wholeheartedly.

The kindness from this woman was just what I needed today.

Tomorrow, will I be as lucky, Lord?

Facing Freedom—1997

Ding dong. It's Wally calling. Coming to get his ex-con bride. As the doorbell finished its chime, I looked at Margaret in panic. The realization that I would see a husband I'd not seen in almost two years hit full force. We really didn't know each other since his defection and my detention. My freedom euphoria took a nosedive off cloud nine, quickly falling to ground zero.

Terror tromped out flames of freedom that had ignited in my heart. Instead, fear took up residence, claiming my sold-out soul for Curly the Self-Proclaimed Saint and Savior. My year of freedom from his clutches had done nothing to dispel the spell he'd cast over my spirit. Fear of eternal damnation still spoke louder than my pursuit of peace and search for sanity. At this point, peace went out the window. What would the supreme-being wannabe say? Back then, it wasn't, "What would Jesus do?" It was, "What would Curly want me to do?"

As I stared at Wally's smiling face, dread danced darkly across the ballroom in my brain. *Breathe, Raylynn, breathe*, I told myself.

Hesitantly, Wally opened his arms for a hello hug. I obliged and gave him a have-to half hug. I quickly turned to introduce him to Margaret, allowing me a way out of the awkward embrace.

A bit of chitchat about her release-day rescue and his road trip soon came to an end. We stood up to leave. I prayed my gratitude for her kindness would be felt in my heart-to-heart departing hug. Choking back happy tears, I knew I would truly miss this beautiful, giving soul.

As we drove off, chickens were squawking and scampering out of our way. Now silence.

Wally must have sensed my nervousness. He said, "I made a

reservation at the Days Inn to get some rest before we head back to Bismarck tomorrow. I hope that's okay."

I silently nodded my head, affirming his decision. Yet uneasiness spread like wildfire fanning into flame, the fear firmly encased in each and every nerve ending. Unleashed now, fear spewed forth. I crossed my arms hoping to stop the internal trembles. The jumping-jack jitters determined to expose my apprehension.

How could freedom foster fear? I wanted it. But I feared it. I prayed for it. Yet I was afraid. In jail, I didn't make many decisions. Only very simply ones. What to read, who to talk to, what TV show to watch. But where I slept. When I went to bed. What I wore. When I took my meds. What food I ate. All was decided for me. Someone else was in charge of me. But I was safe. I was secure. Not like I felt with Curly. Each and every decision was questioned at one time or another. In essence everything we did then was filtered through a Curly's-way colander. His way or no way.

With the penal system putting up probation parameters, what would he say? Jilting justice sent me to jail. What would he want me to do now? Quaking shakes shook me to my core.

For now, I was free. As we approached the Days Inn, my stomach churned. The last motel I had visited was the place I had been arrested. It was the last place I saw Sunny. Memories of her face that day haunted me.

My sweet Sunny. Oh, how I miss you.

Wally parked the car and went to check in. I watched him walk to the entrance and disappear. I was alone. One hundred percent alone. I looked down at the door handle. I slowly raised my hand inch by inch 'til it was parallel to the latch. I laid my hand hesitantly on it, almost expecting it to bite me, saying, "Hands off." And I pulled. It opened. I froze. A weird, wonky awareness settled in. I was unchained. Unshackled. Unencumbered by locked doors. I was free as a feathered friend to fly. Say goodbye to guards and bars and prison garb.

In the side mirror, I saw a couple heading to the motel entrance. I panicked as I realized they would be walking right next to Wally's car, close enough to see inside. I jerked my hand away from the handle as if caught in the cookie jar. Instead, it was just a car door ajar.

What if they looked closely at me? Would they see an ex-con jailbird goosie trying to get loosie? *Okay, now I've lost it. Dang it!* Why in the world did it matter?

I glanced at my sweats, my shirt, and my shoes. No slammer stench, just stinky thoughts. My mind was still locked up and labeled. Exposed and ashamed.

I watched as Wally inserted the motel key in the door lock. He turned it and the door swung open. Stepping inside, he held the door while I walked in with bags in hand. I took three steps, stopped, then began to scan the room corner to corner. Two double beds neatly made up with cheap pukey-gold and mauve bedspreads took up much of the room. I stood mesmerized by the room decor. Although I knew it was cheap, it was a million bucks' worth of visual stimulation. Two flower-filled vase pictures were displayed above each wall-attached headboard. A large mirror hung over the left side of a four-drawer dresser with a television sitting on the right. A stiff-backed wooden chair sat in the corner of the room. I gawked and gazed. Gaped and goggled. At the window—an actual window—with pinch-pleat, pea-gold curtains. And no bars. It was a beautiful sight to behold.

"Here, I'll take those," Wally said, starting to pull the bulging bags from my hands.

The movement startled me out of my dazed demeanor. "It's okay. I can do it."

Coming out of a totally controlled environment, I wanted some sense of self-reliance. Even something so simple as to where to put my bags. This decision wasn't so simple. Wally had placed his small overnight bag on the closer bed. Nerves hit hard. We were married. What would he expect? Anything? Physical? A sense of indebtedness hit me. He's done his best to still take care of me. Were strings attached to his financial support? To his willingness to rescue me in my rapid release? Everything had a price.

My Curly-coerced marriage had come with conditions. With expectations and demands to be met. Or so I'd been told and taught. However, my mind flashed to my so-called cleansing. My purity poke. I shuddered at the memory of Curly on top of me, laughing at my uncomfortableness as he did his "divine duty," yet to me it felt like a dirty, disgusting deed. If I didn't stay "pure," what will be my punishment? I shuddered at the thought.

Fear was the influencing factor in most of my decisions. Focusing on how best to steer clear of harsh discipline or a vicious dressing down came to the forefront with the prospect of coming face-to-face with Curly. Again.

For almost thirteen months, I'd been safe serving my sentence behind bars. What would the future hold now?

Finally, we had a chance to chat, one on one. Unbeknownst to me, Wally had been in communication with Curly. I would be sharing Janice's apartment in Bismarck, North Dakota. The city where my probation officer awaited my check-in. Janice was a long-time Curly loyalist and we got along well. I was thrilled to be able to spend time with her and her two sons.

Time to hit the sack for sleep. While Wally was in the bathroom, I slipped off my sweats and crawled in the bed I'd designated as mine. The one closer to the window. He shut off the light, plopped on the bed, and soon I heard him snore. *How flippin' weird.* My brain fired on all cylinders. No cell doors locking. No guards patrolling. No lights illuminating the room. No women wards talking, yelling, laughing, singing, crying, sighing, or praying. Just cars driving, hotel habitators talking and walking, doors shutting, television late-night talk shows humming. And so much silence.

The hotel's all-you-can-eat breakfast buffet brought back vivid memories. As I sat enjoying a second donut, a hospitality staff member walked by to deliver more goodies. I unconsciously ducked. *What if she saw me? She'd know we'd snuck in to grab the goods.* The Curly-roadshow followers absent of food funds regularly raided the rolls.

Wait. Wally had paid for the room, so we weren't trespassers. We were guests. *Phew. Shake it off, you idiot*, I told myself. I forced my mind to return to the present. I began to relax and ate all I wanted with no worry.

Time to hit the road, or so I thought. Wally had a different idea.

I didn't question his driving direction. Although a brisk, nearly fall morning, my window was rolled down. The light breeze felt like feathers stroking my forehead. I sat back and enjoyed the leisurely ride.

Rimrock Mall to your right, I read, as I laughingly gave myself a heading-out-of-town sightseeing tour. Our car turned at the entrance sign then stopped at Herberger's department store. I looked questioningly at Wally.

He grinned and said, "I'm taking you shopping for a new outfit."

I was in shock at his generosity and thoughtfulness as we headed in the door.

Swarms of people passed. Moms dragging squirming little kids by the hand, teenagers giggling and playfully poking each other, guys following patiently as their wives went from rack to rack selecting try-on items. I squinted at the brightness of the ceiling lights. The overwhelming odor of strong perfume and cologne invaded my nostrils, almost making me dizzy. And the colors . . . everywhere. Fire-engine reds. Ocean-water blues. Luscious-lawn greens. Lemon-tree yellows. Spectacular-sunset oranges.

My mental capacity was exploding at the sensory overload. My brain could not process all the information my senses took in. Crisis intervention needed, stat. My nervous system froze. I couldn't move a twitch. Couldn't muster a twinge. My thumping pulse pounded, my tightly taut muscles tensed, bouncing belly butterflies almost made me regret my donut devouring. Time to beat feet and break out of this brain buster.

I burst into tears, turned, and ran. No explanation. I just ran. I didn't stop 'til I reached the car. Huffing and puffing, I put my hands on the hood to hold myself upright. I heard steps behind me. Wally had followed close behind with no clue what to do or what to say.

I looked at him with tears streaming down my face and whispered, "I'm sorry. I just can't do it."

He opened the door so that I could slide in. I took a deep breath to help reset my nerves, laid my head back, and closed my eyes. I'm not sure if it was from exhaustion or embarrassment.

We headed out of Billings in silence. Silence germinated seeds of anxiousness. Roots of worry began to spread as I feared what I might face ahead.

What kind of freedom would I find in my future?

Time will tell.

Until Death Do Us Part—1999

"Curly is dead" one of the remaining members called to tell me. Have you ever been in a situation where panic and relief take a crash course in your brain? Conflicting emotions collide like two fighting bulls, horns locked, each ready to fight to the death. Which one would live? Which one would die? The panic? The fear? The relief? The what if? The what now? My blood literally ran cold. You see it wasn't like the Munchkins in the Land of Oz who were overjoyed when the house fell on the Wicked Witch of the East. Dead. Finally free from fear. Them, not me. No. This was Curly. Self-proclaimed prophet and son of God. Dead.

Until death do us part. Oh, how I wish this were true.

Fearful flashbacks began . . . Late night. 4:30 a.m. Motel room walls. A couple of stiff chairs. Holding up the tired. Eyelids drooping. Fighting to stay open. Heads nodding. Exhaustion creeping up on the faithful followers. Fear flickering in the eyes of those struggling to remain alert. Every eye focused center stage. At the star. The stud. The heartbeat of the hub. The focal point of our fear. Curly's disciples. Sat listening. Hour after hour. Long into the early morning.

On the motel bed surrounded with books and Bibles had sat the "Holy One." No one dare touch the bed without permission, lest the wrath of his holiness spew forth. For it was holy, he had said. Because he was holy. And his holiness sat on the bed. He glanced around with an arrogant "I'm it, the reason for your existence, don't even question it" smirk. Scanned the room with his beady, piercing eyes. Person to person. His gaze reached me as I sat cross-legged on the floor. Bible open in my lap. A spiral notebook on top, taking copious notes lest I forget one word of his so-called prophetic words. I internally shrank back from his penetrating look, not daring to lower my eyes.

"I'm preparing you. What if I die? Will you still believe? You'll be tested. Will you carry on my message? Many are called. Few are chosen. And you've been chosen. Will you do what I command? I've taught you. Trained you. Will you forsake all others for me? Choose whom you'll serve. Will you risk an eternity in hell? For you and your family? You have been set apart. Are you willing to serve?" Curly had said emphatically.

After his gaze continued around the room, I had returned to my notebook, quickly scribbling every word that I could remember. I stopped. Disbelief that this immortal mission we were on would end in his death. That's like an astronaut dying enroute to Mars or beyond, wasn't it? Inconceivable. Unsettling thoughts had crossed my mind. *If he died, I'd actually get to spend time with Sunny. Get some sleep. See my family.*

Immediately, my eyes snapped to the Bible in my lap. I tightly squeezed my eyes shut, hoping that doing so would keep my thoughts from exiting my eye sockets and entering Curly's orbit.

Forgive me, Lord, for my unbelief. Fear took hold.

Please no! Please don't read my mind! At times I had sworn he did. And this was one time I was terrified he would. He'd kill me! My mind jumped to the horrifying memory of him slashing a watermelon in half with a swift blow of a sword. Intensity drove the blade through the heart of the melon, each half falling to the side.

"THIS is what I'll do to anyone who dares to leave," he had threatened. Droplets of fear beyond fear beyond fear had penetrated every cell of my body. I broke out in a cold sweat.

Attention! Pay attention or you'll pay. Big time! I had told myself. Using my diaphragm rather than my chest, I took a deep breath, knowing that any motion could alert Curly to my "evil" thoughts and lack of focus. Amazing what you learn in survival mode.

Our night had ended at 6:45 a.m. Time to get at least a couple hours of sleep before our duties to serve began. Tasks. Errands. Phone calls to be done before the dreaded summons to the holy room. Our call to report. Again.

My thoughts returned to the present. Fear was running around in my head like a pinball in a machine.

Bam! Curly's dead?
Bam! Now what?
Bam! What does this mean?
Bam! What should we do?

I hadn't seen Curly since a few days before I'd been arrested in August 1996. Almost two and a half years ago. I was given five years' parole after my release in September 1997. And I couldn't leave the state of North Dakota without permission. Curly had been traveling farther east with a few of the faithful members. Not many of his traveling crew remained. Those who had left, I'd feared for their demise. What would happen to them? In the face of the threats, weren't they afraid? I was terrified still. Even with his death. The shackles of control should have fallen to the ground. Instead, they squeezed tighter. Driven by an unseen evil gripping my soul. Entrenched from years of his influence. Ignited by a phone call. Fueled by fear. I was lost. No clue where to turn.

Arrangements had been made for his remains to be returned to Butte, Montana, to his family. A funeral Mass was planned. The date set. Special permission granted by my parole officer to attend. The Montana visiting pass tucked tightly in my wallet. Fellow followers, Loretta and Lisa, and I traveled from Bismarck to Whitehall, Montana, where we spent the night at my mom's.

With my mind still driven by Curly-controlling doctrine, it was difficult for my mom and me to communicate. She was horrified that death had not ended the vise grip of control on my mind. What mother would have thought otherwise? Heartbreaking for her. Normal for me. Terror trumps love. Fear cancels care. Not strong enough to break the bonds, the grip, the grasp of mind control.

The next morning, we drove the 25 miles to Butte, finding our way to St. Mary's Catholic Church. We parked the car. Walked to the door. It opened as funeral goers entered ahead of us. I swallowed hard, my heart in my throat. Not knowing what to expect. We walked up the center aisle and slid into a pew on the left. Other House of Restoration members sat nearby. I noticed the disloyal. The deserters who dared to attend. They stared. Family stared. Faithful followers versus family. The funeral began.

Loretta leaned over and said, "I think that's Sunny sitting a couple pews behind us."

My heart literally leapt in my chest. My baby! I could actually see my baby in the flesh. The priest's prayer forgotten, I slightly turned to see.

Yes! She's here! Sitting with a stranger. Staring expressionless as the funeral proceeded. I couldn't wait for this to end. I wanted to see my baby!

Does she see me? Will she speak to me? Acknowledge me? What should I say?

Flashbacks. To prison. Court papers in hand. Signature needed.

I, mother of Sunny Marlene Holland, hereby terminate my parental rights. No longer mine. A ward of the state of Montana.

Horror. Pain. Disbelief. I had sat on a small bench below the inmate phone hanging on the wall in the women's common area of North Dakota State Penitentiary. I reached up to hang up the receiver.

The words of the lawyer had reverberated in my head. "If you don't sign the papers, Sunny will have to testify about Curly's abusive treatment toward all of you. Do you really want her to have to go through that? In open court? Then sign the papers."

Each. Word. Stabbed. Seared. Broke. My heart. Guilt washed over me. *What have I done?* My decision to join the "ministry" had brought me here. Brought Sunny to this. A life without a mom.

Self-condemnation. Shame. Pulsed through my veins. *Why, Lord? Why?* Like a racing train, fragments of memories, snippets of scenes. Flashed. The past. Laughter. Hugs. Impish looks. Strawberry-blonde pigtails. Cool Whip fights. Punky Brewster outfits worn proudly to school. Enter Curly. Pain. Lost time. Missing out. School events minus a mom. Disappointments. Despised babysitters. Hatred of home life. A mom in fear. Constantly.

I hung my head in despair. The Whitehall High School Class of 1974 Valedictorian. Most likely to succeed. On her way to medical school. Now a former inmate. An ex-con. A common criminal. Served time for obeying a so-called messiah. Master manipulator. Brilliant brainwasher. Instilled by fear. Embedded for years to come.

I opened my eyes and returned to the present. The funeral. And

Sunny. As we all headed out, I headed to her. Tentative. Wondering. What would she say? Do?

After an awkward encounter, we agreed to meet at McDonald's for lunch. Loretta, Lisa, and I arrived first and took a seat near the door. I glanced up as the door swung open, hoping to see Sunny. Instead, in walked Curly's kids. Angry. Tormented. Spewing hate.

They stood at our table and said, looking at me, "Why didn't you call and let us know he was sick? Maybe we could have done something!"

"I didn't know," I explained. "I never knew. I haven't seen him for a few years."

They didn't understand that I had been displaced as his right-hand worker bee. Separated by jail cells. Prison bars. Parole parameters keeping us apart.

They spat back at me, "You must have at least known!"

I shook my head, no. I felt their pain. Their anguish. After all, this was their dad.

"Honestly, I didn't know or I would have called," I said. A great defense. I wouldn't have. I was loyal. To a fault. To Curly. Because of fear. Of Curly. Even now. Even dead.

Their anger put in check. They turned and left. Shaken to the core, my thoughts turned to Sunny. Watching. Waiting for my baby.

Sunny soon arrived with the woman, her counselor. Helping her with the events, the emotions of the day caused by Curly. And now, her absent mother.

We sat at a nearby table and chatted. The conversation was stiff. I asked about school. Her activities. Her life with my sister, Brenda. Living with her cousins. Little by little, she shared. Cheerleading. Boyfriends. Graduation not far off. The conversation turned to the event of the day.

"I came to make sure he's dead. I wanted to see for myself," Sunny said. Closure. Finality.

All too soon, it was time to go. After a quick hug goodbye, Sunny and her counselor walked out of the restaurant. Back to her life with my sister. Her aunt, my nieces, her cousins. A life I could only imagine.

Where did she sleep? Did she like school? Who were her best friends? What were her favorite TV shows? Was she happy? Did she miss me? Did her heart ache for me like mine ached for her? Each and every day. Each and every night.

My heart took a nosedive into a sea of conflict. Love versus fear. Child versus dead prophet. Would I see her again? Would she want me back in her life?

Bewildered, I sat down. Too troubled to chat, we walked to the car and headed back down the road to Whitehall. I shared with my mom the events of the day. My mom is not one to mince words. Anger driven by hurt. She made it plain to me that she didn't understand.

"Where is your God damned head at? What did that son-of-a-bitch *do* to you?"

Everything inside of me wanted to spill the beans. Bash the secret code of silence. Break down the wall of separation erected by Curly. The now-dead Curly. But not-gone Curly. Still haunting. Still controlling. Still driving my actions. My thoughts. The noose of fear constantly pulling, choking, gagging. Suffocating my sanity. Tightly woven. Trauma driven. Intertwined lies, twisted truths living. Breathing. Running down terror tracks embedded in my soul. Rational thoughts derailed years ago. Off the sanity track. Destroyed.

I lowered my head in shame. In pain. In guilt. Knowing my mom hurt. Knowing she didn't understand. Knowing my absence had eroded the strength of our relationship. My heart cried with unspoken words, *Mom, I hope you'll understand. Someday. It's because I love you.*

So, I sat in silence. I sealed my lips. 'Til death. To save. To secure a seat in heaven, not hell. For me. Sunny. My mom. My family. Because if I trip. Fall. Disbelieve. Betray him. At death we will part . . . for eternity. Or so he'd brainwashed me to believe . . . still now.

Joy to the Fishes—1999

"Hi Mom," I said after picking up the ringing phone. No return greeting, just her worried voice saying, "Sunny's going in for emergency surgery. It's her appendix. They're taking her back now."

My concern for my baby overwhelmed me. The Mineral County Hospital seemed thousands of miles away. Bismarck—my current town of residence—to Superior, Montana, where Sunny lived with my sister, Brenda. Eight hundred and fifteen miles. I could be at her bedside in twelve hours. But it was a place I wasn't allowed to be. Yet.

I'd had no contact with Sunny since I saw her at Curly's funeral a few months before. It was heartbreaking. Prior to that, it had been two years and five months from the day of my arrest to the day of Curly's funeral. This personal connection chasm seemed like an eternity with such limited contact with Sunny.

A few letters were all I'd received from my arrest 'til now, though I had written her constantly from prison and through the years since my release. I found out later my sister had kept most of my letters from Sunny because of my references to Curly, understandably so. My sister, who had become her guardian when I was in prison, would not allow my involvement in Sunny's life. She vowed to protect Sunny in every way she could, from any Curly influence. Even if it meant keeping me away. My mom was a bit more permissive. While visiting her Grammy, Sunny and her friend recorded a singing duet and mom shipped it to me. A treasured tape of my sweet Sunny girl's voice. I played it over and over. Each time, a waterfall of tears cascaded down my cheeks, longing for my baby girl.

My craving for mom and daughter connection consumed me. The rupture in our relationship ripped my heart to shreds. To survive the separation, I kept my wistful wants and wishes under lock and key.

Soul shutdown. 'Til the day I saw her at the funeral. Her presence was the key unlocking my longing, which invaded every cell of my being. My Sunny girl. My sunshine. My heart.

Mom called later to let me know that the surgery went well. "Sunny is doing fine and will be out of recovery soon," she shared.

"Will you please call me later after she wakes up?" I asked desperately, desiring closeness. "Please tell her that I love her!"

My mom agreed.

A few hours later the phone rang. Mom said Sunny was still a bit woozy but was doing well. I asked if I could talk with her.

I heard my mom hesitate and say, "Probably not now."

My disappointment took a nosedive. I reluctantly agreed. "I'll talk to you later, Mom," having no clue how soon "later" might be.

In about three hours, my phone rang. I saw that it was my mom again. Why was she calling? Did something happen to Sunny? I was almost terrified to answer the phone.

"Hi honey. Sunny's awake. Brenda went out to get dinner for us, so she'll be gone for a bit."

I heard a bit of *When the aunt's away, Sunny can say hello.* I understood her unexpressed intention to maneuver connection.

"*Please* let me talk to Sunny," I begged.

I heard my mom ask, "Sunny, it's your mom. She wants to talk to you. Do you want to talk to her?"

The muffled words indicated a hand held over the mouthpiece. I sucked in my breath, waiting for her response. Internally pleading—begging—God for just a sliver of my love to penetrate her scars. Her hurt. Let it unbury the broken shards of our relationship so that heart-wound rehabilitation could begin.

I heard nothing. Absolutely nothing. I wanted to scream at a decibel that would reach her ears. My pounding pulse rattled my brain. My breathing was shallow. Silently praying. And pleading.

"Hi Mom."

Two simple words and my soul danced with delight. Thrill chills skyrocketed. "Hi sweetie. Are you doing okay?" I asked with worry-filled, love-infused, nurturing words.

Drug-induced, slurred words came through the phone, "Weeell, they're givin' me some medicine so I don't hurt like I did when Auntie brought me in." She started to cry. "Mom, it hurt *really* bad!"

My motherly instinct to console her, to comfort her, to soothe away her pain kicked into overdrive. "Oh honey! I'm *so* sorry! Thank goodness Auntie got you to the hospital right away so they could find out what was wrong and fix it. You'll be up and around in no time," I reassured her. "I wish I was there to give you a big hug!"

I heard her whisper quietly, "Me too, Mom. I gotta go."

Hurriedly I replied, "Before you do, honey, can I call you again?"

"Yeah. Just call the hospital and ask for my room." I could hear her voice fading away. Pain meds numbing her brain.

"Okay honey. I'll call later to check up on you, okay? I love you!"

My heart wept for the years of tears I wasn't able to wipe from her cheeks. The countless heart hurts I couldn't hug away. *Will we ever be close again, Lord?* I silently asked. *Can the collapsed bridge between us be rebuilt?*

Mom returned to the phone and said, "I see Brenda coming down the hall with our dinner, so I better hang up so we can eat. They'll be bringing Sunny's dinner any minute, too. I'll talk with you later."

Click. The phone went dead. I looked at the phone quizzically. That was the fastest hang-up I've ever had with my mom. *What in the world?*

Clock watching. Two hours. One hundred twenty minutes. Seven thousand two hundred *tick...tick...* sounding seconds. The balance between too soon and not soon enough. To dial the phone to hear her sweet voice again. I couldn't wait any longer. I nervously picked up the phone and dialed the hospital. What if they asked who was calling? What if they wouldn't let me talk to her? What if they knew the situation of my years locked away and kept away? What if they saw me as a threat to Sunny like my sister did? The what-ifs almost caused me to hang up.

"Hello, Mineral County Hospital. May I help you?" The phone was answered. Disconnect no longer an option.

I asked for Sunny's room. Anxiety hit hard.

Brrrring. Brrrring. Brrrring. Brrrring. Panic set in when four rings resulted in nothing.

Then a sleepy voice whispered, "Hello."

My heart leapt for joy! I calmed myself so that I could act natural. Normal. Whatever that might be in our cut-off connection, strained over the years of my absence. "Hi honey. It's me. Is this a good time to talk?"

A mumbled yes continued our conversation.

"How are you feeling now? Any better?"

She poured out the fear she'd felt when the right-side pain started. About my sister rushing her to the hospital in excruciating pain. After a fifteen-minute discussion, the tiredness took over.

"I need to go, Mom. I can't keep my eyes open."

I asked if I could call her again.

"Ummm . . ." I heard her hesitation. "Mom, Auntie doesn't want me talking to you. She's afraid I'll get hurt."

My heart fell. "Do you wanna talk to me, sweetie?"

A pregnant pause, then a very quiet, "Yes." With an exasperated exhale she said, "But I don't know how I can."

My mind raced through plausible options. "A calling card! I'll get you a calling card! Then *you* can call me whenever you want." This seemed like a possible solution without sounding the aunt alarm.

My mom had told me earlier that Sunny should be heading home about noon the next day. "I'll call you about 8 o'clock and give you the number. I'm sure Auntie won't be there that early."

I knew my sister's sleep, or not sleep, habits. Her back had been injured years before when working for the phone company. So, pain often injected its "don't sleep, won't sleep, can't sleep" venom in her veins, causing a later-morning wakeup. Sunny agreed on the time.

"I love you *so* much honey. Get some rest."

She hung up and my heart soared with excitement. My Sunny girl wanted to talk to me! The salve of her acceptance soothed the scar of separation.

Even though it was after 9:00 p.m., I jumped in the car, humming happily my long-ago Sunny bedtime tune. It was her namesake song, "Sunny," or so she thought.

Overflowing with the delight of future daughter chit chatter, I headed into the closest gas station convenience store to buy a rechargeable calling card. I made sure I could add minutes so that she would always have a way to connect with me. I barely slept that night, anticipating my 8 a.m. call.

A good night's sleep did wonders for her. She sounded stronger and more alert. I gave her the calling card numbers and my home and work phone numbers. Then she had to hang up.

My work days were filled with clock watching. Anticipating the 5 p.m. work dismissal and rush-home hour. I dashed in the door, hoping and praying for a Sunny-recorded message on my answering machine. None. Staring at the phone, praying for an evening call. None came. It had been three days since I had spoken with her. Disappointment devastated my days. Invaded my dreams.

Exhaustion from waiting took its toll. The third night, I went to bed at 10:30 p.m. and fell asleep quickly.

Brrrrring. Brrrrring.

Jerking awake, my snoozing slumber hampered my ability to distinguish the rousing racket. *It's my phone!*

As I reached for the receiver, I glanced at the clock. It said 11:40 p.m. *Who in the world would be calling this late?* My fears escalated. Even though Curly was dead, late-night calls still drummed up dread.

"Hello?" I said hesitantly.

"Mom? Did I wake you up?"

I bolted out of bed. Sunny! It was Sunny. "Yes, honey, but it's okay! I told you to call me anytime and I meant it."

Apologetically she said, "I'm sorry it's so late, but Auntie just went to bed a little bit ago. I dragged the phone into my bedroom so she can't hear me. I have to be quiet so I don't wake her up."

We chatted for about forty-five minutes. She shared about cheerleading, boyfriends, senior year studies, just life in general. I lay back in my bed, phone receiver pressed to my ear. Listening and just praising Jesus. This was my miracle. I was actually talking to my Sunny girl.

Late-night phone calls became our relationship-restoration routine. If my sister stayed up past midnight, we missed our call. At times, Sunny would shush me. "Auntie's up. Shhh . . ." she'd whisper when she heard my sister in the kitchen. I'd wait in the silence, listening to her breathing. Some nights I'd hear the hang-up click. Some nights, she'd call back. Sometimes not, depending on whether or not my sister headed back to bed.

After one of our fabulous jabber sessions, some of the lyrics from "Joy to the World" by Three Dog Night went through my head. I smiled as I hung up the phone receiver and lay back in bed thinking, *Yes! FINALLY! Joy to you and me! You are definitely my joy. My sunshine. My Sunny girl.*

Each night, I thanked the Lord for the pus-filled painful pouch that brought my sweet Sunny back to me.

The Little Things—1999

The processional march began playing. We all stood to search for our Senior. I craned my neck to find Sunny. I spotted her amongst the sea of blue graduation gowns. Her strawberry-blonde bangs and shoulder-length hair were visible beneath the matching cap. Her eyes were sparkling. Her dazzling smile lit up her face. My heart leapt with joy and pride at seeing her. My sweet Sunny girl.

It had been a long road to arrive here. With her. With my mom and stepdad, Dale. With my sister, Brenda. Her husband, Bob. And my nieces, Roni and Bobbi. A place I wasn't sure I'd ever be invited.

The tug-of-war to winning this invitation had been harrowing. Brenda, the ever-protective auntie, wasn't about to let Sunny's heart be hurt by me. The Curly groupie. The corrupted criminal. The castout. The screwed-up sibling. Just a bit of arm-twisting by Sunny and coaxing by my mom helped secure the invite.

I was here! Come rebuff or rejection. I was *here*. For Sunny. Finally.

But I sank in my self-condemning contamination. My thoughts took a trip down the poor-me path, *Here I sit in this decorated high school gymnasium filled with local town some-bodies. The lowlife ex-con no-body. Beware! A beacon of badness is in your midst. Warning! Warning! Do not engage.* My self-perception was sitting in the sewer. A scarlet letter of shame branded on my brow for all the town folks to see. Unforgiven loser allowed in the door. By mistake.

I shrugged off the negative inner self-focus and allowed my sweet Sunny girl's presence to brighten the celebration day. Chosen to perform a musical selection, her angelic voice literally called down heaven, helping ease any unfavorable reception. The assumed rejection. Of me.

My made-up mind games played to stop the downward spiral

of shame as the seniors were diploma-ized and set free from high school studies. My one-day pass said, "Go." I inwardly chuckled. I'd already "Gone directly to jail." No more Monopoly game playing for me. My new pass said, "Party!" Sunny's graduation party! It was her achievement celebration, and I was invited to attend . . . at my sister's house.

A beginning. A partial patch-up began at the party. A sister relationship-repair shop, specializing in fence mending that was broken down by a fanatic. Now dead. But still alive in my head.

My travels from Bismarck to Montana were as often as my work would allow and my probation officer approved. I still had to secure permission to traverse state lines. Back and forth. Back and forth I drove. Mile after mile. Breaking down the barriers between me and my family.

Large relationship rips take time to repair. Souls ripped to shreds must be restored stitch by stitch. Delicate patchwork mandatory to mend the broken pieces. Heart-to-heart communication began the process. However, I realized that healing couldn't happen without humility. I hated the hurt I'd caused. I begged over and over for forgiveness. But the Curly conversation was untouchable. Left off my table of discussion. His deity self-designation still caused fear for my future. And my family's future. If I abandoned the belief in his holy appointment, I feared hell. If I ditched his doctrine, my eternity would exist only in hell. Or so I had been brainwashed to believe.

Month after month, family ties were reknotted. The dying embers of relationships were rekindled into flame. Acceptance from all was difficult to attain. My sister still distanced herself, allowing surface connection only.

Christmas was coming. My sister's favorite family holiday. And I was invited to attend the festivities with my mom and stepdad Dale at Brenda's house. I was thrilled to take part in the family merriment and memory-making fun. My first in so many years. It's a time of peace, joy, and love—I tried to convince myself, anyway. But my "peace on earth" was a farce, as far as I was feeling. Nerves nipped at my inner peace, stealing my joy. And I dare not even hope for love. Tolerance was more like it. I presumed I'd get a bare pittance of affection. Limited attention. But at least I was invited.

Laughter rang through the house. Shanghai card games played in the midst of cooking, baking, and gift wrapping. Accusations of cheating were said in jest. Just what we did to add to the good-humored hassling of our opponents. Jovial conversation reached deafness-causing decibels. I smiled. This was home. But I still felt like an outsider. Who had once been an insider.

Goodies galore sat everywhere. Cookies, candy, and chocolate treats sat staring at me. While others drank their wine and whiskey, I ate. Sugar, my selected remedy. My instant high. Belly butterflies beat feet running from body to brain. Busting my fit-in fantasy that didn't feel like reality. Best way to ease my apprehension. Eat. And eat some more. To suffocate the shame. To strangle the strangeness of partaking in family tradition. Again.

Christmas morning dawned early. The anticipation of gift-giving created excitement, evident in the whispers. The plotting and planning of gift-opening order. The living room was overflowing with presents and people. Of family and non-family. All invited in. I sat overwhelmed with joy, finally believing I might be included somehow, someway. Again. A bit of a chasm still seemed to exist between me and my sister. Then I realized it could just be my sense of guilt perceiving nonexistent bad vibes. And not belonging. I hoped so anyway.

I watched the thrill of gift openers as the Christmas wrap was ripped, torn, tossed, and thrown. Squeals of delight filled the air as the coveted contents were displayed.

I expected little. My gift was the gathering. Being a part of the group.

"Mom!" I heard Sunny's voice lift in excitement. Her hands were held behind her back.

"What honey?" A bit perplexed at her one-word attention grabber.

"Here. I got you this." She handed me a small, carefully wrapped box.

My heart melted at her thoughtfulness, even without knowing the contents. I was overwhelmed by the sheer presence of the present.

"Open it!" she instructed eagerly, as if it was her own gift.

I tore off the paper and lifted the lid of the wee jewelry box. A ring. An opal ring. A birthstone ring. My mouth fell open in shock. Grateful tears fell.

"Try it on! Does it fit?"

I followed each of her instructions as if in a stupor. I pulled the precious ring out of the box. Pushed it over my knuckle. Perfect fit! I knew that opals weren't inexpensive, but the extravagance wasn't just in the cost. The act of giving was worth gold. The heart of the one who selected the gift was priceless. My dear, thoughtful Sunny.

One present was left under the tree. I watched my sister bend down to retrieve the beautifully wrapped box. She turned around and held it out to me. "It's for you," she said with an impish smile on her face.

"Me?" I said, again in shock.

Another unexpected gift from an unlikely gift giver. I recognized the delightful demeanor of my long-ago best buddy, Brenda, as she held out the box. I could feel the gaze of every living room occupant fixed on me. Feeling a bit uncomfortable as the center of attraction. As a self-designated backseat sitter, I'd planned to keep the focus off my checkered past and disputed doctrines of dead deity beliefs. I didn't want to ruin my family's Christmas frolicking and fun.

In a dumbfounded daze, I stared at her eyes, perceiving for the first time her acceptance. Then I reached for the box.

I heard my mom say, "For goodness sakes, Raylynn, open the damn thing!" Her daughter directive breaking the soundlessness of the anticipated sister surprise. Everyone chuckled.

I sat down with the small box on my lap and carefully unwrapped it. Opening the cardboard box flaps, white tissue sat crinkled inside. Underneath sat a spiral-bound book of some sort, wrapped in more white tissue. Puzzled by the present, I peeled back the layers.

A handmade 8 1/2 by 11 inch laminated book titled "Raylynn's Photo Album. A Special Gift to My Sister" sat nestled in the tissue. I could hardly breathe. Page after page of pictures. From grandparents to parents, to kids and grandkids. And Sunny. So many of Sunny. While I was absent from her life. Big. Huge. Drops. Began to fall. Tears traversed the torn bridge between us. I looked up at her in little-sister awe. What an amazing time-consuming handmade gift.

She said, "I didn't want you to miss out on all of Sunny's time while she's been here."

Sobs. Huge. Sobs. Then. Oh, then. She gently turned back the pages 'til the inside cover was visible. In large, beautiful calligraphy a poem was penned:

> **The Little Things in Life**
> *Too often we don't realize*
> *What we have until it's gone*
> *Too often we wait too late to say*
> *"I'm sorry, I was wrong"*
> *Sometimes it seems we hurt the ones*
> *We hold dearest to our hearts*
> *And we allow stupid things*
> *To tear our lives apart*
> *Far too many times we let*
> *Unimportant things get in our mind*
> *And by then it's usually too late*
> *To see what made us blind*
> *So be sure that you let people know*
> *How much they mean to you*
> *Take the time to say the words*
> *Before your time is through*
> *Be sure that you appreciate*
> *Everything you've got*
> *And be thankful for the little things*
> *In life that mean a lot*
>
> *Unknown Author*

Merry Christmas, Raylynn. From your sister, Brenda.

Torrents of tears poured forth on deeply dug wounds. A big sister's arms wrapped around a little sister's hurts like a baby being swaddled in safety and security.

"I'm so sorry, Raylynn. I love you."

I could barely breathe but I mumbled the same in her ear. Hugs. Healed. Hurts. A present patched up the past. Preserved and secured the two sisters' future. The little that was left, that is.

It's the little things in life. That matter. The most.

God's a String Bean—2001

The words of the hit song, "The Sound of Silence," sung by Simon and Garfunkel, thundered through my head. Right now, darkness didn't quite seem like a friend. It was dark. It permeated my soul as I watched my beautiful sister take her last breath.

"Raylynn! Make her breathe," screamed my mom, her heart breaking as she watched in horror as her older daughter was dying.

In only three months, cancer stalked and stole her life. It was darkness all right. It was swirling around us. It was drawing us down to the depths of grief. The depths of despair. The depths of pain losing a daughter, a sister, a mother, a wife, a cousin, a friend. *Oh, my sister. Darkness and death took you today.* Or did it?

Those were the last words my sister whispered to me. I sat next to her hospital bed, gripping her hand in mine. My head lay beside hers on the pillow. I stared at her pale, drawn face, willing life to be different. Wishing for additional days filled with her joyous laughter, dirty jokes, and "Pay up, I won" when she beat us in cards. I'd even take the stubborn way she'd continue an argument. But I knew in my heart, it was almost over.

I had said, "Brenda, let's sing our song one last time."

I lifted my head and began to sing. I squeezed my eyes shut as I concentrated on remembering the words from our high school talent show performance. Then I heard it. A faint voice singing harmony.

My eyes flew open. My sister was staring at me, her mouth uttering the words of our song. She remembered the words better than I did. I choked up. It was difficult to get the words out, but I continued, following her lead as I had so many times in the past. It was our "sister" dance. She led. I followed. One last time.

Earlier in the week, I sat in the same chair, holding the same weak hand. My head next to hers.

"Can you hear it?" she asked.

"Hear what?" I said puzzled.

"The music. It's so beautiful."

I lifted my head and stared at her face. Her eyes bright and, well, you know the look. A teenager swooning over her first crush. Much the same look. Pure ecstasy is what I saw.

Then the goosebump sensation hit. A God-causing tingle. I asked her, "Brenda, do you see heaven?"

She slowly turned her head and stared back into my questioning eyes. "Yes," she said. "But you can't go with me. It's not your time."

She was going. I wasn't. The pain of separation began to tear at my heart. My sister's eyes closed and she rested.

A movement caught my eye. I glanced up at the hospital room door as Brenda's oncologist walked in and approached the bed. Dr. Judy wasn't your typical doctor type. No white coat. Just ordinary casual clothes. A Harley-Davidson motorcycle rider, wearing wire-rimmed glasses with long hair pulled back in a ponytail at the nape of her neck. My first impression was not "doctor." She introduced herself as Judy. A biker who organized annual bike runs as fundraisers for her nonprofit Guardian Angels Cancer Fund. Money raised helped defray the cost of cancer drugs for people who couldn't afford them. What compassion she had. She looked tough, but her heart was soft as a marshmallow. My sister's concern about facing unbearable pain was laid to rest when Dr. Judy assured her, "Brenda, I'll give you whatever you need. I won't let you hurt." And she didn't.

From previous conversations, I knew Dr. Judy would understand the holy happenings, so I shared my conversation. Simply, heaven's door stood slightly ajar, allowing Brenda a peek at her eternal home. Paradise had been present. One foot in heaven, one foot still on earth.

The realization hit harder and harder. My sister was going to leave me. It was her end. Or was it her beginning?

I spent night after night awake. Praying. I lay in the room's vacant bed beside Brenda, listening for her continued breathing as she slept. I'd promised the day I arrived from Bismarck I would not leave her side. Community Medical Center had been kind enough to allow me to stay. They'd even pulled back the curtains, opening up a larger section of the room for a slumber party. Brenda wanted a party, so we obliged. Me and the kids, Roni, Bobbi, and Sunny. Card playing. Movie watching. Sleeping side by side on the floor. Giggling, goofing, gabbing. Masking their misery with merriment. Avoiding the runaway grief train heading our way. Chug. Chug. Had to give her more drugs. For the ever-increasing cancer, killing pain.

The next evening was quiet. The party had worn her out. Brenda was sleeping more and more. The gradual loss of conscious connection with my sister apparent. After midnight, in the quietness, the sweet night nurse arrived. Seeing me awake, she tiptoed in so as not to disturb Brenda. We talked of prayed-for hope and belief in heaven. I shared of a God who loved, who saved, who sees each of us.

She sat quietly, then whispered, "My son died not long ago. He was only seven. Will you ask Brenda to give him a hug for me when she gets there?"

The pain of her admission and the hope of a heavenly connection through my sister tore my insides to shreds. I jumped to my feet and enveloped her in my arms. Her sobs were deep. Her grief unbearable. Yet, the Lord saw her pain and sent her a promise of eternal hope in heaven. With her son. And the Son of God.

Days ran into night. Nights ran into day. And memories. Oh, the memories that bubbled up this final week of her life.

****

"MOM! Tell Raylynn to quit calling God a string bean," wailed my sister Brenda, as she tattled on me.

I laughed, running through the house as fast as my two-year-old legs would carry me, proudly reciting the Catechism verse she had taught me.

"God is great. God is good. God is a Supreme Being." My enunciation of "Supreme Being" kept coming out "string bean." These big words were certainly not part of a two-year-old's vocabulary. Four years older, Brenda was the expert. She had to smarten up this underling-of-a-sister, who needed some schooling. She was horrified that I could be so "sinful" as to call God a name.

For hours we played school. She, the prim and proper teacher. Me, the eager-to-please student. "Say Bur..ren..da! B-R-E-N-D-A." Back to the enunciation lessons as she attempted to have me say her name correctly.

"Buuu…dotta," I'd say with an attitude of, "I know!"

Off she stamped again, "Auugghh. MOM! She can't even say my name!"

She was my best friend. She was my hero. Where she went, I wanted to go.

School, for example. Only living a few blocks from the elementary school, walking was our mode of transportation. Although it wasn't far, the crossing of a busy San Diego street was not something my mom wanted Brenda to do alone. I gladly skipped along, anxious to be with her. I hated being home without her. So, each day to and fro we went.

One sunny morning after returning from escorting Brenda to school, I played alone out in the yard. My mom was busy with chores. And as only a two-year-old can do, I got a harebrained idea.

School! I want to be in school, too, I thought.

So, I headed down the route I knew so well. I trotted across the busy street, with cars screeching their brakes to keep from hitting me. What a sight I must have been, wearing only my little pink panties. No socks. No shoes. No shirt. I reached the school, opened the door, and headed to my sister's classroom. After all, I knew exactly where she'd be.

The teacher looked up in shock as I entered the room. "Can I help you?" she said in her typical teacher voice meaning, "What in the heck are you doing here?"

"I want to play with Buuu-dotta," I said matter of factly.

She pulled up a chair alongside my sister and I plopped down. I belonged here. Next to her.

The teacher rushed to the office to call my mom, knowing she'd be worried sick. Hearing the panic in her voice from frantically searching for me, the teacher reassured her I was fine. All in one piece. Happy as a clam sitting beside my obviously annoyed big sister.

Mom raced to the school, charging into the classroom. Grabbing me by the hand, she jerked me out of the room as I screamed, "I want to stay with Buuu-dotta!"

The door to the school hadn't even slammed shut when she started paddling my butt. "NEVER leave the yard by yourself! You could have been killed!"

This meant nothing to me. "You *mean!*" I sobbed. "I want Buuu-dotta!!!!"

****

Anything Brenda said to do, I did. Not wanting to disappoint my hero.

Out the door we went to enjoy the beautiful San Diego day to "get the stink off," as my mom often told us as she shooed us outside. Showing off her strong muscles, Brenda hoisted me up to stand on the hood of the car.

"Wheee," I yelled in excitement as I jumped off at her command.

SPLAT!

My forehead hit the sidewalk and split open, blood running everywhere. Our screams brought my mom running.

"What in the world were you thinking?" Mom said, scolding me while scooping me up to check out the damage.

"Brenda told me to jump and said she'd catch me!! But she *didn't!*" I was more heartbroken over her betrayal and letting me fall rather than the six stitches my wound required.

She led. I followed. 'Til death did us part.

Home Bittersweet Home—2001

I stood staring out the large picture window of my office, a remodeled warehouse located on the outskirts of Bismarck, North Dakota. Praying, "Lord, what should I do? Do I move back to Montana to be with my mom now that Brenda's gone?" I begged Him, "Please show me, Lord. My heart says go, but is it Your will? I don't know what I'm supposed to do."

Since August 25, 2001, the day my sister died, my mom had been in a state of soul shock. Torrential torment. Dazed with internal deadness, barely recognizing day from night. Light from dark. The anguish of witnessing her elder daughter take her last breath delivered a painful punch like no other.

Although the devastation of grief was no stranger to my mom, nothing had prepared her for this. How could it? It wasn't the order of life, at least as we anticipated it to be. Kids were supposed to bury their parents. Not the other way around. Consigning a child to a grave had to be the most painful grief of all. I watched my mom go from vitality and vibrancy to limpness and lifelessness. Her body had breath. But her brain could not perceive the earthly departure of her beloved daughter, Brenda.

I hurt deeply for the loss of my only sister. My Buu-dotta. My childhood hero. My Sunny girl's protector. But the depth of my pain was drowned by the black abyss of agony my mom was experiencing. I'd never seen her so hopeless. So hurt. So heartsick. So depressed and despondent. It worried me. I was the only one left. The defecting daughter who had been absent for more than ten years. Breaking my mom's heart in a different way. Still alive but estranged by bars and beliefs. In recent years, somewhat restored to the family's good graces, gradually gaining their trust.

From Brenda's burial to her daughter Bobbi's wedding, it was twenty-one days. I'd promised my sister I'd stay to help my niece. Brenda had worried that Bobbi would postpone her wedding.

"Don't let her cancel it. Please!" she begged me, her mothering eyes filled with worry. She didn't want her death to interfere with Bobbi's happiness. It was just who she was.

My mom barely remembered her granddaughter's delightful, but difficult, day. The absence of the mother of the bride dimmed the joy of witnessing Bobbi and Marc's I-do's. The processional and pictures, the toasts and the tributes, all taunted us with *Brenda's dead. Lifeless. Not among the living. Any longer.*

In many ways, my mom followed suit. Physically alive. Emotionally dead. How did you console a walking corpse? My mom's heart died when Brenda's stopped beating. With her declining mental state, I decided to stay for a couple more weeks.

But I had a job. I had to return. I had to leave my mom grappling with grief and head home.

The remainder of the year, I traveled back and forth from Bismarck to Whitehall as often as possible. The nine-hour trek was sometimes difficult in harsh winter weather. Blowing snow creating limited-visibility whiteouts. Black ice causing dangerous slipping and sliding. Snow drifts blocking the interstate highway. But I let nothing stop me. No matter how difficult the travel, I spent Thanksgiving and Christmas with my mom. I hoped my appearance would drag her out of her dungeon of despair. Help ease the absence of a daughter, a sister, a mother whose death left a hole. A huge hole in our family. And a massive hole in my mom's heart.

And that hole, I felt, was my responsibility to help fill. After all, it had been created by a deceased daughter who departed this life. Therefore, the only available hole filler was me. The alive daughter.

My caretaker role ran deep from early on. Over the years, I sensed the rift that ruptured the relationship between my mom and Jeff. I had no way to repair it other than to love my mom deeper. Hug her harder. Dab salve on her sorrow. Douse water on the flames of her woes. Even though part of her pain was produced by me. I owed her. For my desertion. And lack of family allegiance. Time for repayment might be now.

After spending my Christmas holiday with her, I was concerned for my mom's heart and health. I longed to be with her. To comfort her. To hold her. To take care of her. Every single day.

I stood facing the office window and gripped the back of a conference table chair, my fingernails creating indentations in its leather-like material. Praying. Should I pack up and head to my hometown of Whitehall? Or should I stay? The agony of the decision played ping-pong in my chest. Pounding. *Lord, what is your will? I beg you for an answer!* In spite of my desire to be with my mom, my greatest desire was to obey the Lord. The long ago "Just Be Obedient" command still resonated in my soul.

I was the executive director of a statewide organization of people with disabilities, who I loved dearly. A position of importance. Of status. *Not bad for an ex-con*, I'd thought. Always needing the validation that I mattered. In leaving, would I still matter? *God help me!* I wanted my decision to matter to Him and to my mom.

As I stared at the leafless branches covered with snow outside my office window, something caught my eye. A car. A single gray car sitting on the far side of the parking lot. Strange. We get very few visitors located on this outlying district of town. My eyes were drawn to the license plate. The number started with a 5. Recognition slapped me in the face. Montana. A Helena, Montana, license plate. The state's 56 counties are each assigned a number, one through 56. A 5 signified Helena, the capital city.

A shocker knocker. Brain blaster. A divinely placed sign. At the very moment of prayer. Montana or not. To stay or to go. And a Montana car sits outside my window. Here. Now. At exactly the same time as my heavenly request. *Is this really you, God?* Goosebumps bit my arms. Prickly pimples. Hair follicles contracted. Standing erect. Saluting the Spirit-induced reaction to an answered prayer.

A sign to go, but to where? It said Helena, Montana. But my mom lived in Whitehall. Perplexing. Confusing. Believing I over-spiritualized the divinely sent message. He must have just meant Montana. *Or did He?* With no more clarity, I moved to Whitehall to be with my mom.

God doesn't make mistakes. His will doesn't always follow a straight path to a place. Pit stops happen for a purpose. The purpose was my mom. But His ultimate will: Helena. A year and a half later. A job opportunity took me to the place God had said I'd be. Helena, Montana.

What God speaks. Happens. It will come to pass. Just wait. Be patient. And see.

The Check's in the Mail—2004

It was a typical Montana winter. A December, almost-Christmas blizzard hit as my friend and I started our trek home to Helena after a short mom visit in Whitehall. My dimmed headlights gave little visibility as the wind-propelled, white fluffy flakes bulleted straight at the windshield. I leaned forward over the steering wheel as if six inches closer to the window would give me a better sightline through the swirling snow. I glanced down at the speedometer. Thirty-five miles an hour. Even at this slow speed, it was a white-knuckler driving experience common in Montana winters. I'd grown up driving in these slippy, slidey conditions. But experience didn't equal calm. Tenseness and nervousness permeated my body. Now, the life of a horse was in my hands.

The dark sorrel stood broadside in the middle of the road. A ghostlike mirage standing in the white swirling mist with not a care in the world. Or so he thought. He turned his head to look at us as we approached, but didn't move an inch.

Oh God! Please don't let me break his legs! I knew that a severely broken leg could spell death to a working ranch horse. No staying still for bone-healing time, since hoof movement creates healthy circulation. I aimed the nose of the car between his front and back legs. With no stopping ability, it was the best I could do.

"Jesus HELP! Jesus! Jesus! Jesus!" I repeated over and over as the horse got closer and closer, hoping that Jesus would use a supernatural spur to giddy up his canter. The brakes of my white Chevy Malibu were useless on the skating rink frozen on the black top of Highway 69 between Whitehall and Boulder.

Closer and closer. I braced for impact. *Baammm!* Square between his legs. Impact-causing horse hoist rolled him up like a rug. Crash landing on the hood shattered the windshield. Tiny glass bits blasted their way to the backseat. The mesh of safety glass left intact sat less than a foot from our faces. The non-stopping somersault momentum flipped him to the roof, crushing it within inches of our glass-speckled hair. A final flip off the back of the car looked like a gymnast's dismount as he landed on his feet.

I squeezed out my hard-to-open door, leaving my shaken-but-not-hurt friend in the car. Her door wouldn't budge. Having been raised on a ranch, the welfare of the horse was of utmost importance. I gingerly ran down the road, ice skating all the way to assure myself he was alive with no broken legs.

Bright headlights blinded me, so I stopped. A woman scrambled out of her vehicle to ensure we weren't badly hurt after having witnessed the horse-flipping accident. He belonged to her family's ranch. Surprisingly still alive with minimal injuries. She caught him and put him back in the pasture.

Still shivering and shaking, we walked the short distance to my dilapidated car. A snowplow emerged over the crest of the hill. The driver came to a standstill, seeing our vehicles blocking the northbound lane. He jumped out to assist.

With my car sitting demolished in the middle of the road, he asked if it was drivable. I wasn't sure I wanted to attempt to drive. A bit of accident aftermath had me intimidated. However, I saw the potential car chain-reaction risk, so I slid back in and started the injured engine. The driver plowed a path to the nearest intersection turnout after instructing me to follow. With no front visibility through the windshield web, I stuck my head out the window and followed his red taillights. Not far ahead, he veered to the right, clearing a spot in the intersecting dirt road turnoff. After parking, we helped my friend exit through the driver's-side door.

With the ranch house close by, the horse owner offered her hospitality. We hitched a ride to the house to call the Highway Patrol. We waited snug as bugs in blankets, sipping hot tea to dispel the bone-chilling temperatures. Awaiting a road-patrolling officer in the warmth and comfort of her home.

And it was a long wait. The huge winter storm had impacted

the highways from Bozeman to Helena, with numerous accidents being investigated. In the meantime, our kind hosts offered us drinks and snacks. And wonderful conversation. Come to find out, they were well acquainted with our family, having known my Grandpa Lauderdale well. Ranchers knew ranchers. They lived a similar life. They loved and cared for the cattle herds, the hay fields, and all the assorted animals associated with a working ranch. Including escaping horses.

A knock on the door a couple hours later indicated the end to our conversation. The patrolman asked me to climb into his car to chat. He apologized for the long wait but explained the unbelievable number of accidents in the last few hours from the quick-hitting snowstorm.

I described the details of the accident while he scribbled notes on a pad. "Do you need to see the car?" I asked.

He smiled and shook his head. "I drove by it and can clearly see the damage. You're lucky it wasn't worse."

As I started to open the car door he said, "Just a bit of advice. Montana has an open range law, but for cattle only. Not horses." He smiled, nodded, and put his car in gear and headed off to his next accident assignment.

A bit perplexed, I had no clue what that meant. I would find out soon enough the importance of his statement.

In the meantime, my nephew, Marc, had arrived in his Ford pickup to escort us back to Whitehall. He expertly navigated any slipping and sliding. Not trusting his driving, I hung on tight. As we rounded a dark curve, in the truck headlights I saw a huge buck standing in the road. I almost lost it. Marc easily maneuvered around him, chuckling a bit at my overreaction. I could have sworn I was going to die at the hands of road-wandering critters.

As we arrived at her house, my mom flung open the door. Worry apparent in her voice when she asked, "Are you okay?"

I rotated my neck and shrugged my shoulders. "I am pretty sore, but I'm okay."

My stepdad Dale interrupted and said, "Gayle is waiting for you at the clinic. He'll check you out just to make sure."

I grinned. His brother, Gayle, was the local town doctor, so he'd called in a favor. Although as a small-town doctor, Gayle was accustomed to responding to after-hour emergencies.

After an examination, we were given samples of muscle relaxers and pain meds to tide us over 'til the pharmacy was open. He diagnosed us with whiplash and encouraged us to rest.

The following week an insurance adjuster came to do his damage duty. Discussing the details of the accident, he shook his head in amazement, "This is the first car/horse accident I've investigated where both the driver and horse survived. You're mighty lucky, young lady."

After examining the remains of the car, no question about it. The auto was toast. A total junkyard junker. Time to shop for new wheels. My recent prayer penetrated my thoughts. *Lord, I'd really like a new car.* A funny way to get one, Lord. Why couldn't a new one just show up on my doorstep? Or the money rain down from heaven to purchase it? But this? *Real funny, Lord.*

I thought whiplash was no big deal. Rest a bit. Ice a bit. Relax a bit. Stretch a bit. But the negative effects started gradually. Tight muscles. Even tighter muscles. Neck pain. Even more intense pain. A low-grade headache. Even more blow-your-top-off headaches. By three months, the headaches were so severe I could hardly work. Doctors and specialists. Medicine, MRIs, and massage. And Botox.

I found a neurologist who was cutting-edge treatment minded. Botox was the new miracle muscle-spasm stopper. The saving grace for honkin' headaches, not just for old forehead folds, a frown fixer, or wrinkle relaxer. The doctor explained that Botox came from a toxin produced by some bad-ass bacteria.

"What if I get too much? Will I die?"

His amused grin and negative nod assured me I'd be fine.

I reluctantly agreed.

I was terrified, to say the least. Needles are not my friend, especially when they're stabbing me repeatedly. But, I set a date with a needle.

Breathing deeply, I kept telling myself, *It's just a few little pokes. No biggee.*

My scalp, my neck, my back, my face. Punctured by the pin pointer. I left his office with blood droplets from the pricks. Time will tell. Within a week, my nerves no longer barked orders at my muscles to move, giving them a restful reprieve. On the slow road to an almost-recovery. At least to what the insurance company would call "Maximum Medical Improvement." After thousands of dollars in medical bills, the insurance company offered me a settlement. Time to put this horse business behind me. The paperwork was in progress with final negotiations made.

After years of living in the basement of ministry members' homes, prison cells, small trailers, and apartments, I longed for my own abode. I'd worked hard building my credit from below bad to an acceptable loan-approval level, after years of paying off restitution for all the bad checks written and credit card charges at the direction of Curly. And I'd done it. I could now qualify for a home loan. With the realization that the settlement offer would provide a down payment, I went house hunting.

My budget wasn't big. Every house I saw came with a too-high sticker price. Without the cash-down money in the bank, my hands were tied. A bit discouraged, I drove from my Helena Westside apartment to pick up my friend Carol to shop the Herberger's department store yellow-dot sale as our Saturday fun. Half a block from her house, I saw a sign. "For Sale by Owner." Still lugging around the disappointment doldrums, I called the number with little hope of a home-buying opportunity. Invited to stop, Carol and I walked up the front porch steps and knocked.

A sweet couple answered the door. Touring the home from main floor to basement, back yard to garage. Although a small house with a hand-dug basement, there was plenty of room for me and my cat, Sadie. Sitting down to chat, they explained they were buying a condo on the south side of town where they'd originally planned to live. They had retired and moved to Helena to be close to their daughter. With nothing available at the time, they bought this little house. Now that their perfect place had been found, they were eager to sell.

Their asking price was within my budget. I explained my circumstances. Laughingly, I quoted the classic phony payment excuse,

"The check's in the mail." But without knowing when my settlement check would show up, I reluctantly told them I couldn't consider a home-buying deal. We left. Once again discouraged for another failed opportunity.

Sunday, my phone rang. It was the man with the affordable for-sale-by-owner house. With more of a directive than request, he informed me they'd devised a plan for me to purchase the house.

"Please be at our house after work on Monday." The phone went dead.

Although a bit taken aback by his presumptive belief that I'd just show up, I was intrigued. And I did show up. A lease-to-own proposal was offered. I would pay rent 'til my check arrived. What I paid would be added as part of my down payment. I'd have up to six months to buy the house. The insurance company had already assured me I'd have it in less than 90 days.

I sat in total disbelief. God had made a way. And he'd used this couple to show me the path to a purchase. The house became mine. Standing in the doorway between kitchen and living room, I gazed at the walls, the windows, the moved-in furnishings. And cried tears of gratitude for this beautiful blessing. I recalled the moment I walked out of prison with literally nothing to my name except my clothes and a small box of Sunny's mementos. And now this. It was mine. An answer to prayer.

As I was thanking Jesus for my new house, I almost burst out laughing. I thought, *I prayed for a new car and a house, and hit a horse.* Quite the answer, wouldn't you say? I realized that the answer to our prayers came in many modes. He can even use car accidents. I shook my head in amazement as I thought, *Be careful what you pray for. You just might get it.*

You've Got a Friend—2009

"Raylynn and I are not getting married," Daryl announced solemnly to the entire church body. He was the church treasurer giving the finance report, or so I thought.

"What in the *WORLD*?!" my mind screamed, as I sat with my mouth open and my mind racing through the last week together. *What did I do? And why would he announce this to the whole church and humiliate me like THIS? If he wanted to call it off, then FINE you ASSHOLE! But do it to my face with a bit of dignity, Mr. Van Oort! How dare you!* I went from shock to fear to rejection to anger in five seconds flat.

Just enough time for Daryl to take a deep breath and say with a mischievous chuckle, ". . . in Hawaii!"

I jumped to my feet, half relieved and half pissed. "Now tell them the truth, Mr. Van Oort! The reason is you're too cheap to pay for two hotel rooms in Seattle before we fly out."

Gales of laughter rang out. Laughing first at Daryl and his sly, devious sense of humor. Then at my descriptive response. In my outburst, I realized I'd been had. *Oh buddy, you're going to pay for this one*, I thought. *You got me good, but revenge is sweet. What an ass!*

You see, I wanted to do it right this time. This marriage. Without an I-do, no hanky panky. No shared hotel rooms until I was officially Mrs. Van Oort. I'd just announced our no-sex-before-marriage agreement to the entire church body. Oh my! A typical occurrence in the mating game of Daryl and Raylynn. What a bizarre relationship saga it had been. What a journey from the beginning.

The beginning started with an ending. Daryl's first wife, Valerie, passed away from breast cancer. I knew them both and their son, Nicholas, from the church we all attended. It was heartbreaking to watch as Daryl held her arm, supporting her trek to the restroom during each Sunday church service. She was weak. She was tired. But she still attended. Nicholas was a member of the worship team, and she loved watching her son blossom as a musician.

After ten years of fighting this horrible disease, she passed away. My heart broke knowing Nicholas was without a mom, Daryl without a wife. I had watched my nieces mourn the loss of their mother years before when my sister died, so I was focused on Nicholas. I made it a point to care. To show him love and nurturing, never dreaming at the time he would one day become my stepson.

Nicholas shared his life with me. By a fluke happenstance, he met a girl online. It was immediate infatuation. We attended a conference in the tiny town of Lincoln, Montana. Summer, his new-online-found love, was to meet him there. I was so anxious to meet her. And meet her I did. Face to face. An unknown young woman coming out of the shower with a towel wrapped around her.

I introduced myself. A polite thing to do when you meet an almost-naked person. She responded to my greeting, "Hi. I'm Summer."

My eyes opened wide when I realized she was Nicholas' Summer. "Oh, *you're* Summer! How exciting to meet you! Nicholas told me *all* about you."

A bit of embarrassment was apparent as redness flushed her cheeks. She glanced down at her towel-covered, dripping-wet body and grinned at our obvious awkward introduction. We both laughed. I adored her immediately.

No wonder Nicholas was head over heels for her. I observed their heart-to-heart happiness throughout the weekend, beaming with the newness of a love connection. I couldn't contain my excitement for him, for her. And their love story continued with a romantic proposal and wedding date set for October 18, 2011.

Meanwhile, there was Daryl. And me. No connection really...yet. Until God showed up. On a Saturday. In my living room. Saturday mornings were my time to sit in my recliner with a cup of coffee and my Bible. And pray.

Daryl is your husband. The thought ran through my head, sending shock waves from head to toe.

"I rebuke that in the name of Jesus." I threw out the standard Christian reprimand for stinkin' thinkin' thoughts. This *couldn't* be God speaking. No way. No how. My heartbeat started thumping loudly in my ears. Buried fear surfaced. Deadened pain now perceived. A shame dart hit the bull's-eye dead center. Causing a mental explosion. My memory bank lock was picked. Buried thoughts uncontainable. Unwelcomed touches. Body violations. Devastating casual connections. Ruptured relationships. And now? A husband? No way. No how. Mr. Goody Two-Shoes meets Miss Scarlet Harlot. A relationship that's destined to be "gone with the wind."

I grabbed my phone and dialed my friend, Michele. She knew the situation. She knew Daryl. She sang worship with Nicholas. She had known Valerie. And she knew me. My past. My shit.

"You've got to keep him away from me," I pleaded intensely after relaying the unbelievable God-matchmaking proclamation. "I want nothing to do with this guy, *any* guy!"

I figured old patterns of wanting male attention had raised their ugly head and were taunting me. Codependent needs for validation by a guy being resurrected from long-buried emotional baggage. Nothing I wanted to dig up and drag around ever again. No way. No how. Michele listened while I ranted. She may have been willing to help but God had other plans. Oh Lord.

****

"Will you help me pick out a suit?"

I turned to see Daryl standing behind me as I was getting ready to exit the row where I'd been sitting during the church service.

"I have to find a suit for Nicholas and Summer's wedding, and I really need help."

Crap! Why me? I looked around for help. For Michele. For a rescuer. None to be had. No life preserver thrown my way as the ebb and flow of fear became an undertow ready to pull me under.

Get him away from me, Lord, I silently screamed, all while plastering a fake smile on my face.

His kind eyes searched mine, waiting for an answer.

Crap! Just crap! What do I do? My racing thoughts searched for a way out. None to be had. So, I reluctantly agreed. As long as we met at Macy's department store. I wasn't going anywhere alone with him. No way. No how. Let a public place be my safety net.

We agreed to meet the next weekend. I swear I sweated blood 'til then. And I was a bit perturbed with God because He hadn't kept him away. After all, I'd prayed enough. Setting up boundaries was my own "keep him away from me" action, since God didn't see fit to do my bidding. I just had to do it myself. Yep. Puff myself up as my own personal protector. Boundaries builder.

I got this, God. No thanks to you! Oh, boy, was I wrong.

The following Saturday, we met in the parking lot of Macy's. I attempted a nervous small-talk conversation as we headed in the door and made our way back to the men's section. Daryl said he'd asked me to be his fashion consultant since I was a professional businesswoman who knew how to dress well. Little did he know I was less of an expert in men's suits than he was, so what in the heck was I doing there? When someone thinks you're smart, you have excellent taste, you've got it together you don't say no. I didn't, anyway. It was a deep-seated need in me. To feel important, intelligent, and worth consulting. Many might say "stroke my ego," but I had very little self-worth. It just made me feel I mattered. And seen as having value, not lesser than. So, with a facade of fashion knowledge, I accompanied him.

He found a couple suits and headed to the dressing room. Out he came wearing a nicely tailored, black suit. However, the pants were a bit too long.

He grinned impishly and said, "What do you think?" as he twirled around, letting me get a full 360-degree view. I could tell he liked it.

So, I smiled back and said, "I think it's perfect, except you'll need to get the pants hemmed a bit."

He nodded in agreement then reached down and turned the price tag around. As the price registered, he looked up a bit shocked and said, "Boy! Paying that much, I better wear it more than once. Maybe I should get married or something!"

Holy shit! Did he just say that? I couldn't even breathe. I felt the blood drain from my face. *Get it together, Raylynn! Don't react at all.*

I plastered my fake smile on and giggled a bit hysterically. It's all I could do. I hoped he didn't notice. But he was too busy with his perfect-suit find to notice how squeamish I was acting.

He waltzed back into the dressing room and returned with the tried-on suit draped over his arm and headed to the cash register with me trailing behind. As he handed over his credit card, he questioned the clerk about seamstress services to hem the now-purchased pants.

"I'm sorry sir, we don't have any at Macy's," she said.

My heart went out to him when I saw the dejected look replace the smile on his face. "I can hem the pants for you."

Crap! What did I just say?? Crap! Crap!! Crap!!!

"Really? You can?" he said looking hopeful and relieved.

And me feeling panic and stressed. What in the world had I done?

"I'll take you to dinner as thanks for hemming them for me," he offered.

The keep-away-from-me guy was planning to take me to dinner? Oh my God! What did I get myself into? Lord! My keep-us-apart plans were going out the window.

Where are You, Lord? I'm in desperate need of an escape route. Now!

The newly hemmed pants fit well. Dinner payback at Macaroni Grill. Hours of comfortable conversation. Friend-to-friend chitchat. Soon after, Nicholas and his soon-to-be bride planned friendly foursome get-togethers. A bit of secret matchmaking, unbeknownst to both of us. I was slowly being pulled and pushed into the Van Oort family fold.

How could I say no to helping Nicholas prep his trailer house for the upcoming sale? Paintbrush in hand, I plastered on paint. Outside. Front door done. With rag in hand, I scrubbed the floors inside 'til dinner time. At their insistence on me sharing their meal, I sat down with the almost married couple.

And Daryl.

Summer and I drove to my house to pick up house-staging props and she promptly decided a next-day barbecue at my house would be fun. With Nicholas. And Daryl.

Twelve-step classes, movie outings, game nights with church friends. And Daryl.

He seemed to be everywhere. Cordial connection of house calls and phone calls became a non-dating development. Friends only.

Time for the hitching happening. Nicholas and Summer's vow-exchange day. One hundred and eighty miles away. The groom-dad Daryl headed to Bigfork, Montana, with his first wife's parents. And me.

Of course, Daryl was oblivious to the awkwardness of the ride-share situation. Silence and driving concentration were his ditch-the-dialogue card, leaving me to chatter and jabber. With the beautiful parents of a beloved daughter lost to them from cancer. And here I sit. Traveling with their son-in-law. Easing my uneasiness with their overflowing kindness. My heart ached for them, for their loss.

After the night-before-nuptials family festivities, Daryl picked up his three hotel-staying passengers and headed to Bigfork Chapel. Nicholas asked me to take charge of his toddler niece if entertainment outside the chapel was necessary. Halfway through the ceremony, I headed to the nursery. A bit of fun and frolicking relief for both me and little Anne. Far from the inquiring minds that just want to know. About me.

And Daryl.

At the reception table reserved for the Van Oorts sat Daryl, his family. And me. Glances and grins. Stares and smiles. My insides churning. *What must they think?*

Daryl's mom pulled him aside, unbeknownst to me. "Daryl, you have a friend."

He nodded his head in agreement. "Yes, Raylynn and I are friends."

Again, a bit stronger in tone, "Daryl, you have a *friend*!"

Again, totally clueless he said, "Yes, mom, we are friends."

"*Daryl*, you're not hearing me," she scolded him with a slight grin. "You. Have. A. FRIEND!!"

Light bulb finally lit. Wattage ramped up. Revelation revealed.

All he could say was "Oh." He furrowed his brow and thought, *So, she's saying Raylynn might be MORE than just a friend? Hmmm . . . interesting idea.*

A not-communicated conversation to me. His thinking mode versus his talking mode was the chosen matchmaking method. According to Daryl, anyway. But not according to God. It was time to push rather than just slightly nudge to set His plan in motion. And I was the one He used to push. The "just be obedient" one. He knew my desire to do His will.

Call Daryl and tell him you're falling in love with him.

"WHAT?? That *can't* be you, God." I shook my head, hoping the cringe-causing brain cell intruders would vamoose. Vaporize. Scram.

I purposely busied myself preparing for the class I was teaching at church the following night. STEP was a Christian twelve-step class meaning "Striving to Experience Peace." Well, I certainly wasn't experiencing much peace right now.

After a fitful night of rest, I headed to work at Disability Rights Montana, where I worked as the Outreach Coordinator. I sat proofreading articles for our soon-to-be-printed newsletter.

Call Daryl and tell him you're falling in love with him.

Crap! Not *again*!! Lord, wasn't this going a bit too far? I couldn't do it! What if he rejected me? What if he took a flying leap off the lover's ledge to get away? What if he believed I've got belfry bats? Tuned to the looney channel? We've never talked about "us." We were just friends spending time together. Well, a *lot* of time together . . . like, almost every night.

The long-ago, Saturday-morning divine decree came back to bug me.

Daryl is your husband, I'd heard.

Yeah, right, Jesus. Did he know that? Had He clued him in? My rant of rejection-fueled thoughts ran unbridled in my brain.

"Lord, PLEASE don't ask me to do this," I begged. Ugh. Silence. I heard nothing more.

I swear, my little celly-telly had mental telepathy powers. *Pick me up! Dial his number! Tell him! Tell him!*

Okay. FINE!! Resigned to the rotten task of drawing sure-fired rejection, I picked up my phone and dialed. Nerves knocking my noggin'. Fainting from fear was sure to follow. At least he was at work and probably wouldn't pick up.

"You have reached Daryl Van Oort. I'm not available right now. Please leave a message," said his voice mail. *Beep.* It was recording a message. Oh God.

"Ummm, this is Raylynn. I'm supposed to call and tell you, if you keep this up, I won't be able to resist you."

WHAT? Oh my God! What did I just say? I disconnected the call, totally horrified as to what came out of my mouth. I could almost hear Jesus just busting a gut at my stumbling, mumbling, suggestive words.

I stared straight ahead at my computer monitor, unable to focus on any words. Oh GOD! Boy, did I mess *that* up.

Call him back and tell him what I told you to say. The voice again.

"What? You've got to be kidding me, Lord! Again? Humiliate myself? AGAIN?"

I let out the breath I didn't realize I'd been holding. This was the worst *ever*.

I picked up the phone. A finger poke punched the redial, indicating a bit of irritation at God's insistence. Same voice mail. *Beep.*

"Ugh, this is Raylynn. Again. I'm calling back to tell you what I was supposed to tell you the first time. I think I'm falling in love with you." *Click.*

"Okay, Lord, I did it. Are you satisfied at my total humiliation?" I literally threw down the phone on my desk with a bit of hope it would break so he couldn't call me back.

I waited. And I waited. No response. I kept glancing at my phone, staring at the clock. He would be there in thirty minutes to pick me up for STEP. I was going to puke my guts out. Maybe I could just go home and say I was sick . . . sick in the head, that is. Ugh. I guess I would have to face him sooner or later.

The phone rang. Caller ID said, "Daryl Van Oort."

Mechanically, I hit the answer button and heard, "I'm here."

I hit the disconnect without responding. My heart was thumping. Sweat was pouring. Embarrassment was intensifying. I headed out of the building. I pulled the handle and opened the car door. Without looking at him, I slid in and sat as close to the door as possible. A barrier to boost my bravery as I busied myself with purse placing and feet arranging on the car floor.

"Hi," he said and put the car in reverse.

Hi? I thought. That's ALL??? You shithead! Now what?

A little chatter that didn't really matter. To me anyway. Mostly silence. Daryl's favorite pastime. And I hated silence. It felt like . . . an emotional F5 hurricane hit my head. Catastrophic heart damage occurring. Rejection. Humiliation. Anger. Fear. So, my counter blast was calling him names in my head.

You asshole! You're just a TOTAL ASSHOLE!! I don't want anything to do with you so forget it. Falling in love with you? Ha! No freakin' way!! You're just a total ASSHOLE!!

This internal diatribe continued from car to church. I plastered on a phony smile greeting the STEP participants as they arrived, all the while sneaking sideways glances at Mr. Silent Asshole.

He was clueless. Absolutely. Clueless.

Teaching time. As I walked to the front of the church sanctuary, I opened up my trauma trunk and dumped Daryl's rebuffed behavior inside. Feelings locked down and secured. Fake-it-till-I-make-it time. I'm great at playing the part, even when I'm totally falling apart. Curly taught me very well.

The evening sped by quickly. The women in my small group engaged in painful discussion. Facilitating wasn't always easy when the pain of the past was exposed. Heavy heart work was hard. We ended with the usual reciting of the Serenity Prayer.

"God, grant me the serenity to accept the things I cannot change, the courage to change the things I can, and the wisdom to know the difference. Amen."

After hugs and a bit of lighthearted laughter, we bade goodnight to our groups. I picked up my teaching binder and purse and headed for the door, determined to not speak a word to Asshole.

I opened the door and climbed in the car, staring straight ahead. We drove in silence back to pick up my car. No need to waste words on this asshole. He liked silence better than me, anyway. My emotions had taken a foothold and I refused to let them rule me. No crying. No yelling. No nothing.

As he parked the car next to mine, I pulled the door latch.

"Wait," he said. "I want to talk to you."

My heart skipped a beat with a minuscule bit of hope attached.

"My mom talked to me at Nicholas' wedding. She made me realize that maybe we're more than just friends. So maybe we should see where things go from here."

My mouth fell open. I stared at him. "So, you *did* get my message?"

The twinkle in his eye was noticeable, but looked unsure if he should laugh or not, knowing my on-the-edge-of-exploding emotional state.

"You're just an asshole, Daryl Van Oort!" I reached over and punched him kinda playfully. Kinda not. "You could have said something earlier!"

We both burst out laughing at the same time. I'm sure Jesus was laughing right alongside us, knowing He'd been instrumental in causing the chaos. And the beginning of the final matchmaking hookup.

Passion advancement and soulmate attachment. The romance thermostat had been turned up. Progression of intention became apparent.

"Michele and Dave are going to the movie tonight and asked if we want to go, too. Want to go with them?" I asked Daryl on an early Saturday morning phone call. He'd called to let me know he was heading to church to help Stan, his friend and our pastor, with ongoing remodeling projects.

"Sounds good. What time?" he asked. And then made arrangements to pick me up.

We parked in the lot of the Cinemark Theatre and sat waiting for a text from Michele telling us they'd arrived. I asked Daryl about his workday at church.

"We got quite a bit done but there's still a lot to do. I told Stan I'll try to find a night this week to come back out to help."

After sharing about my stay-at-home Saturday, the conversation ended. If Daryl had nothing else to say, silence was his gold standard. Not to me. Silence initiates a brain-wracking word search. Convert thoughts to words. Pronto. It was necessary to fill the void. But today I couldn't dig the dialogue out of my brain.

"So . . . " Daryl started, stammered and stopped.

I turned and looked at him a bit quizzically. He was acting a bit odd.

He took a deep breath and started again, "So, do you want to get married?"

When you're dying, they say your life flashes before you. When you're facing a life-changing decision where your pukey past can impact your future, the flash can happen, too. The ticker tape announced the headlines: *Mr. Goody Two-Shoes Marries Miss Scarlet Harlot. What if Mr. Goody can't handle the tarnished Harlot?*

The only response that seemed appropriate after my flashback attack, "Are you sure?"

No wonder God informed me of His will before this Daryl dating, mating game started. Daryl smiled and shook his head affirmatively, "Yes, I'm sure."

This man of few words just rocked my world. He truly wanted to marry me, not reject me.

"Then, YES!" I answered with enthusiastic acceptance of this amazing man who wanted me in his life forever. He grinned and leaned over to give me a sideways hug as best you can in a car.

Bzzzzzz went my phone, signaling a text from Michele. They arrived. We unlocked our embrace and rushed in the theatre to find our film-watching friends.

The place was packed. Ticket buyers, excited kids, snack-line standers waiting to purchase their popcorn.

"Hey Michele, want to go to the bathroom?" I was bursting at the seams to tell someone my soon-to-be nuptial news.

She looked at the long line ahead and said, "No, I'm going to stand in line so I can get through before it starts. I think Dave went to the bathroom." I saw her strain her neck trying to locate him.

"Are you sure? We can come right back," I said trying to lure her to the lavatory.

"No. You go. I don't really have to go yet."

Dang! I'll text Sunny! What better place than a bathroom stall? I latched the door and rapidly typed, "Sunny! Guess what? Daryl just asked me to marry him!" I hit the send. *Whoosh.* It had been delivered.

I stared at the screen. No response. *Dang!*

I opened the stall door and saw Michele. "I thought I better go, too." I waited 'til she went. Then pounced with my proposal proclamation.

"He *what*? Congratulations!" she said, giving me a huge hug. We gibbered and jabbered then realized the guys were probably wondering what the heck we were doing. With full-dentured grins plastered on our faces, we headed out the bathroom door.

We settled in our seats, staring at the big screen.

Bzzzz. Bzzz. Bzzz. I felt the slight vibration and heard the muted sound of a phone call coming in. I looked at the Caller ID. It was Sunny! I would call her when the movie was over.

Ping. A voice mail left. I settled back in to watch the action.

Bzzz. Bzzz. Bzzz. Again! *Ping.* Another one.

The third time, I decided I'd better call. I knew my Sunny girl. She wouldn't give up. She was persistent. I left the theatre and headed back to the bathroom. After locking the stall latch, I hit redial.

Before hello could pass my lips, she began scolding me. "MOM! Don't you *ever* send me a text like that and then don't answer your phone!"

I burst out laughing at her animation. I loved sharing the depth of my joy with her. She'd been through hell and back with me. Her delight at my news overflowed my heart with happiness.

"Call me later, Mom!" she said as she disconnected our call.

Saying "I do" in Hawaii sounded so romantic. But staying in a hotel room before marriage was like squirting lighter fluid on hot coals. Hugs and kisses left us breathless and wanting more. However, I'd vowed to the Lord I would do this one right. Daryl was my God-given gift sent direct from heaven. After my previous promiscuous life and unwanted sexual assaults, I wanted my love with Daryl to be pure and holy.

So, we decided not to get married . . . in Hawaii.

Instead, our friends and pastors, Stan and Debbie, officiated an intimate ceremony at the beautiful home of Wayne and Sue Ann, friends who witnessed our marriage vows. On March 27, 2009, I officially became Mrs. Daryl Van Oort. A month later, we invited our family and friends to celebrate our joy at a wedding blessing ceremony.

After our honeymoon in Hawaii. Only one room needed.

Ministry Mask—2010

"Mom, you'll never guess who friended me on Facebook!" Sunny excitedly shared on a typical mother–daughter phone call. "Jill! Remember her?"

My thoughts flew to my defender at the House of Restoration more than twenty years ago. Abdomen innards started agitating, swirling around like a high-spin washing cycle. Gurgling, almost hurling, guts. But I shoved it down. Put a plug in the upchucking fountain of fear. Zone-out mode.

I listened, but I didn't listen. Anytime the past ministry was mentioned, my brainwaves silently screamed. Don't speak! Don't touch that deeply scarred part of my soul. I finished the conversation as quickly as possible. Detach. Disengage.

"Talk to you later, Mom!" Sunny's conversation-ending phrase penetrated my brain fog.

"Okay, honey. Have a good night." I hit the red disconnect button ending the call.

Daryl was still at work. Time to get it together. Collect my wits. No better way than marshmallow crème fudge. I'd learned to make a small batch to satisfy my craving, but not enough to have leftovers for Daryl. I took out the small saucepan, quickly measured the mouthwatering ingredients. And stirred. And stirred. 'Til boiling started. A teaspoon of the chocolate mixture formed a small glob in cold water, indicating the fudge was perfect. Scooping up the soft-ball tester, I licked the spoon clean. No sense in pouring the mixture into a pan. It was all heading to my mouth momentarily.

I sat the still-hot pot on a pad. Tipped it sideways. And started eating. Spoonful by delectable spoonful, soothing the raging emotions burning in the pit of my stomach. I scraped every chocolate spot off the pan and licked the spoon 'til it was clean. Emotions eased by endorphins. Calmed by candy. I hurriedly washed away the evidence. Fudge-making remediation. Crime-scene cleanup. A self-controlled wife hugged her off-work and home husband. Another day of pain prodded. Memories managed. Safely locked away. Again.

Another excited call came from Sunny a couple days later.

"Wow, Mom! I just spent two and a half hours talking to Jill. It's unbelievable how she was able to escape! I think she had angels helping her."

Goosebumps began their hair-raising event. Each hair stood erect. On my neck. My arms. My legs. Breath no longer seemed available. I couldn't remember whether to inhale or exhale. Finally, a need for oxygen induced an unconscious gasp. My goose-bumped, plucked-bird-looking arms felt like bricks.

Sunny went on to elaborate, "She left on an errand for Curly, but instead called her parents from a pay phone."

I was mesmerized by Jill's story . . .

Her tender heart had been terrified as she witnessed Curly brandishing his sword, slicing a watermelon in two while he laughingly said, "THIS is what I'll do to anyone who dares to leave me." Fear drove her desire to go home. The nearest Western Union was a city transit bus ride away. A woman who befriended her paid her fare.

After collecting her cash, a bedraggled beggarman appointed himself her guardian, accompanying her to the Greyhound bus depot. She purchased her ticket and sat down to wait. She felt a firm tug on her arm as the disheveled man approached.

"Come on!!" He escorted her out the depot door and pointed to a large refrigerator cardboard box sitting empty next to the depot wall. It was one of many used by those without shelter. He motioned for her to crawl in. Confused, she hesitated and half shook her head negating his direction.

Insistently, he half pushed her forward, "You've got to get in!" His eyes were gentle yet tinged with trepidation. He worriedly looked around and gestured more intently to the box opening.

Reluctantly she crawled in, turned, sat down, ducked her head, and leaned forward to fit. He pushed the cardboard box flaps together, concealing the human contents. The unfastened flaps gave a slit-eye view of the depot door. People coming in and going out. All carrying suitcases, backpacks, or purses flung over their shoulders. Some pulling unwilling, fit-throwing, crying toddlers. Suddenly, her blood ran cold. Fear found its way to every cell in her body.

It was Amy. Sent by Curly to bring her back.

Amy continued forward. Walking. Looking. Searching. Her defector-seeking stare stopped on the protector-appointed beggarman standing next to the box. Jill sucked in her breath. Amy's eyes glanced down at the box. Jill pulled back. Amy continued her search and "seize-her" mission and entered through the depot door. Jill stayed safe and secure. In seclusion. Amy finally departed the depot.

Her befriended bodyguard. Kept watch. She pushed on the flap to get out. He pushed back. "Stay. It's not safe." She'd come to trust this stranger. So she stayed. And watched out the slit.

A short time later, Amy returned with Rachel. Two searchers better than one. How had he known they'd be back? Bewildered by his insight, she thought he was definitely her heaven-sent angel.

Jill's seekers had left to search elsewhere. Her guardian opened the flaps and motioned her to come out. He pointed to a bus parked fifteen feet away. "Hurry. It's time to go." Not wanting to miss the bus, Jill went dashing forward. Before her foot touched the bottom step, she turned to say thank you. And goodbye.

He was gone. Not a trace. She boarded the bus and continued to look. He had vanished into thin air. She slunk down in the seat and rested her head.

Smiling she whispered, "He was my guardian angel."

Although there were more details of Jill's safe return home, my heart heard little. Instead, I was remembering a word spoken by many. Sunny. My mom. My sister. All the previous deserters.

CULT.

It's a CULT.

Like Paul in the Bible on the road to Damascus. He'd imprisoned and killed those who called themselves Christians and believed in this man, Jesus. The truth was revealed in just one instant when God saw fit to open his eyes allowing him to see. Truth. Nothing but the truth. Helped by God.

This was my "Paul" moment. The "ministry" mask was ripped from my soul. Nothing holy about Curly. It was the *Cult* of Curly.

The pain rose up in my throat and gagged me. Its intensity ascended to new heights. Survival systems engaged. Built a brain barricade to deflect emotional bomb explosion shrapnel. Commence zombie zone. I could no longer feel. Paralysis penetrated my entire being.

"Mom?" I heard Sunny's voice pierce the haze of horror that had derailed my conversation capability.

I whispered in horror of my revelation, "Oh my God, Sunny! It was A CULT."

My mind screamed . . . and screamed . . . and screamed. A flat-out, FUCKING CULT!

Making Sense of Insanity—2010

"I have something to tell you when you get home. Please make sure I tell you and don't chicken out. Love you." I hurriedly typed as fast as possible on my small BlackBerry cell phone after disconnecting my phone call with Sunny. I hesitated with my finger over the Send button. Then punched it hard before I *did* chicken out in sending my exposé text to Daryl.

With my misbelief unmasking of Curly's Cult, Sunny encouraged me to tell Daryl the truth. "Be open. Be honest. That's where the healing begins, Mom," she'd said.

Her compassion and understanding soothed the shame, the guilt, and the anger that ignited the gut-wrenching pain deep in my soul when everything came flooding back.

"Mom, here's a word for you." She read Isaiah 43 from the Message Bible. "Don't be afraid, I've redeemed you. I've called you by name. You are mine. When you're in over your head, I'll be there. . . . I paid a huge price for you. . . . That's how much you mean to me. That's how much I love you! I'd sell the whole world to get you back, trade the creation for you. So don't be afraid. I'm with you. I'll round up all your scattered children. . . . I want them back, every last one who bears my name, every man, woman, and child whom I created for my glory, yes, personally formed and made each one."

By this point, I was sobbing uncontrollably. My entire world just turned inside out. Like a hand shoved down my throat, reaching the raw buried torment, grabbing the churning guts. And jerking hard. Retching. Puking pain. Of the past.

After I hung up, a scripture I'd read a few weeks previously came to mind.

What benefit did you reap at that time from the things you are now ashamed of? Those things result in death. Romans 6:21.

I sat sobbing. I reaped ABSOLUTELY NOTHING! And my soul was wrapped in shame. For my gullibility. For believing in the high heavenly rewards promised for unquestioning loyalty. For fearing the extreme hellish punishments promised for unbelief and lack of allegiance. Dumb and duped.

In that instance, I believed it was just my own dang stupidity. After all, I'd been told all my life how stupid I was. Well, if the "stupid" shoe fits, keep wearing stupid. You didn't get rid of shoes you've worn forever, even if they constantly hurt your feet. You couldn't just take off your "stupid" shoe. Or so I thought. A sole-covering, soul-destroying "stupid" shoe.

The screen door squeaked. A key turned in the backdoor lock. The door opened. The door shut. Daryl was home. My blood-pumping nerves resurrected. I froze. Maybe he'll forget. Why did I send him that *stupid* text. Yep. Stupid is as stupid does. And I seemed to do stupid. Really well.

At least I'm good at something, I thought sarcastically, deflecting my fear of rejection. My husband of ten months might just start packing. The truth might definitely set him free. Of me. Panic penetrated my pulmonary parts, paralyzing my respiration. Was passing out a possible escape? I was in need of lung jumper cables to spark my breathing battery.

His concerned face was the first thing I noticed. Stopping in the doorway between the kitchen and living room, Daryl hesitated. The sight of his compassionate expression triggered my tear ducts. Sobs erupted from deep in my soul. Quickly he moved from the doorway to kneel in front of the recliner where I sat. And hugged me. I fell forward in his arms, absorbing every drop of endearing love he dished out. In case his love left. When I confessed. About the cult.

We sat side by side on the couch. With no clue what tale I had to tell, he held my hand for support, realizing this was going to be a difficult conversation. He sat attentive and silently waiting. His reassurance gave me the guts to reveal my revelation. To relay my conversation with Sunny. To divulge the devastation imposed by a deity masquerader.

My confession ended with scar-ripped soul sobs. Dug-up despair. Finally exposed. In that moment, no greater love had I ever felt than the acceptance of a man who'd been kept in the dark. Who could have felt deceived. Instead, Daryl opened his heart to console my grief. A man sent from the one true God. To love me. In spite of my monsters, my past, my pain. Unconditional love exhibited by selfless action.

Another call from Sunny. "Mom, I know this couple who have a ministry called Restoring the Foundations. I think it would really help you."

Having firsthand knowledge, I knew she understood. So I had confidence in her recommendation. RTF counselors were spiritual freedom fighters. Helping people dig out the darkness. Divulge the devilish refuse heaps of crud. Expose the bad beliefs in your brain.

Although booked far in advance, an opening came available over the three-day Presidents Day weekend in February. Perfect timing. God pulled the scheduling strings and I headed to Carson City, Nevada.

Fifteen full hours of kicking the crap out of my crap. Intense prayer restoring my foundation of truth in the real Jesus. The true creator of life. The Savior who saved my soul. And my sanity.

Sunny came to pick me up at RTF and took me home. She told me to read Psalm 18:16.

He reached down from on high and took hold of me; he drew me out of deep waters. He rescued me from my powerful enemy, from my foes, who were too strong for me. They confronted me in the day of my disaster, but the Lord was my support. He brought me out into a spacious place; he rescued me because he delighted in me.

After the intensity of deception nodule extraction, this scripture was like healing salve for my hurts.

"Mom, I think you need to throw away your Bible," Sunny softly suggested.

I stood open mouthed, staring at her in shock. "What? Throw away my Bible?" It's as if she suggested I throw away my faith. "Why in the world should I do that?"

I turned to glance at the book laying open on the table. It was a *New*

International Version Study Bible I'd used for years. The pages were dog eared. Special words highlighted. And notes written throughout. Many of the passages marked with jotted-down interpretations.

"Look at the notes you've written, Mom. Why did you write them?"

Still puzzled, I stared at her.

She continued her questions, "Didn't most of them come from Curly? When you read it, do you see his deception?"

I thought of his masterful manipulation. I was barely scraping the surface to untangle the mess of his misleading messages. With the years of indoctrination, my mind was struggling to distinguish deceit from truth. But I trusted the wisdom in her. She was right.

"You can use one of my Bibles until you can buy another one," she offered.

For some reason, this step was hard. It felt as if I was erasing years of my relationship with Jesus, but the truth was I was letting go of him. Of Curly. And the twisted words of a self-proclaimed god. Ironically, a sense of release enveloped me as I took off the Bible cover, gathered my pens from the side pocket. I looked at the naked Bible in my hands. To totally let it go felt like prying open the crushing claws of the predator, forcing it to release its imprisoned prey. Puncture wounds seeped. But the beginning of freedom was at hand. I dropped it in the garbage.

I returned home wiped and wrung out. Drained and empty. Bewildered and unsettled. Like sections of my life had been severed and slung into a thousand-piece-puzzle box. Shaken to and fro then strewn on a table called "Make Sense of Insanity." I couldn't. I didn't. I had no coping tools for this. Thought bubbles ran unbridled in my brain. Torturing. Taunting. Shaming me. Assailing my senses. It was nonsense for no sense. A recipe for senseless stupidity.

Baffled by my blindness and lack of bravery, I prayed for understanding. Why did it take me so long to understand? To un-cement the cult connection in my brain. The name Bob Crane came to mind. I recalled this pastor who had been a guest speaker at our church on a cold Sunday last November. He had given me a word. I went searching for my Sunday service note-taking spiral. I flipped back page after page until I saw his name. And the word he'd spoken to me.

You have something hidden deep in your heart from a long time ago. You've wondered whether it will ever come to pass. The time is soon. You weren't ready before. You're almost ready now.

I sank into the office chair by the desk where I'd been searching. The words massaged the ache on my mangled soul. God knew. He really knew. He was preparing me for this eye-opening episode. The unveiling. The exposing. Of the truth. And a heart soon to be restored. Putting the pieces of my life in place. The God who truly loves. Rescued me. From a CULT.

Pocketbook Ploy—2012

Hang the nonsense noose. For the hogwash baloney I bit. Thoughts are scattered loosey-goosey in my head. Realization hit head-on, 110 miles an hour. Full force. Crashed. Mangled. And tangled. My memory bank has filed recollection bankruptcy. Chapter Seven or Eleven. Just a crapshoot to determine the truth. A marching band of memories are clanging brain-cell cymbals. Pounding, drumming, beating my brain. I was duped by a conman from the very beginning. And I didn't even know it. But my mom did. My family did. And they were absolutely right. Yesterday, I found the proof.

On Friday, November 13, 1987, I had met Curly Thornton at McDonald's, the day he announced his run for governor at a press conference in Helena, Montana. He and his crew stopped for a cheap, fast-food dinner on their trip home to Billings. Just six days later, the Montana Supreme Court ruled in my favor to receive a lump-sum workers' compensation settlement. On November 24, the *Billings Gazette* printed this news. An article announced the ruling that upheld the district court decision in my favor. All these years, I was on a must-be-a-coincidence kick. Couldn't be a connection. How could he have known? About the bucks soon to be deposited in my bank?

But he did.

A relationship that began with targeted-money manipulation. My money was dirtied while he laundered it through his pocket. His bank. His cult. His campaigns. Spent for his every. Stinkin.' Desire. With my denarius. His wishes granted by my wilting wallet.

A self-proclaimed man of justice. Did he solemnly swear to tell the truth, the whole truth, and nothing but the truth so help him God? He didn't. Never did. Even when he professed to be God. How ironic.

It still hurts. After all these years. It still hurts. A deeper recognition of my naivety. My vulnerability. My ever-seeking yearning. To matter. To have worth. To be special. Why should I let a discovery of this initial violation affect me? Because I truly had wanted to believe, still. That I was chosen to be his campaign manager and his ministry executive director because of my worth. I wanted to be seen as exceptional. And special. And that's why I had been chosen, even by a brute.

Today, I found out differently. It truly was money. A desire to fund his fantasy. A ploy to pad the pocketbook of the politician. All the races he ran. Using my money.

But this is what truly brought me to my knees: I realized that my worth lies 100 percent in Jesus. I don't need a pat on the back. I don't need special treatment. I don't *need* anything that another human being on this earth has to give. I just need Jesus. I wanted to stand in front of Jesus one day and have him say, "Well done, good and faithful servant."

He's the approval master. The confidence created. The worth builder. Brick by brick he built our foundation. The bricks of our garbage held together by his miracle-molding mortar. He fills every crevice of our crap. And turns it to gold. For. His. Glory.

Debunk the Bullsh*t—2012

"Write Dr. Phil," my mom suggested.

I gut-belly laughed then glanced up at her face. She was serious. "Are you kidding?" I asked.

"No!" she said emphatically. "I watch his show all the time and he tries to help people. Maybe he'd help you."

I silently dismissed her thinking. *Mom, what a joke. You're just grasping at straws*, I thought. Instead, I said, "Why would he help me? Look at the kind of people he has on his show. Cheated-on wives. Drug-abusing junkies. Deadbeat dads. Suicidal teens. I don't fit in any of those categories, so why would he help me?"

My mom's jaw was firmly set. Her Polack stubbornness was evident. Through gritted teeth she said, "Just do it. You never know."

It had been more than two years since I realized that Curly Thornton was a cult leader, not a prophet. What we had experienced was not the "discipline of the Lord" or "the army of God boot camp." Nope. It was brainwashing and abuse at the hands of an egotistical, psychotic monster. I continued to be plagued with torturous flashbacks, haunting nightmares, all-consuming guilt, self-condemnation and hatred, and the inability to internally cope with everyday life. I withdrew. Mentally. Physically.

Pain became my constant companion. Dormant brainwaves of trauma erupted like hot burning lava taking control of every nerve pathway. Head to toe. Rebelling against the ever-present fear. Mindset mutiny opposing the mental anguish. Pain assaulted every cell of my body from years of trauma and psychological torture. Unable to cope, I became isolated at home, alone with my fears, my inadequacies, my past. A self-imposed prison. All feelings—good or bad, positive or negative—were held captive to maintain control. Of me.

Even though Daryl and I were newlyweds and loved each other deeply, his love sat outside the door to my locked-down heart. A fortress of pain and distrust guarded the entrance. The final curtain fell on the fall-in-love, happily-ever-after fairytale production. The dark drape of fear drawn closed for protection. Self-preservation. Never to be opened again. Or so I thought.

For more than twenty years, I'd played the part of a devoted ministry member and an avid Jesus follower—all to find out I had been living a lie. Curly's lie. I'd been a card-carrying contributor to the Curly-the-con-artist show. I'd been hoodwinked. Deceived. Misled. All in the name of Jesus. Evil had led me around by a nose ring. Pulling. Pushing. Prodding. Good failed me. Even God failed me, I had believed. If He failed me, so would Daryl. With this new husband, I wasn't going all in. No way. No how. Decision made. Keep a bit of myself, my heart for preservation. Just in case. I was weary, wary, and worried. He'd fail me, too. No doubt. No fairytale life destined for me. Yet I longed to escape this self-protected soul prison. But how?

Unconditional love heals. But healing hurts. My husband. My daughter. My mother. My family. My friends. Their never-give-up love sliced through the thick scars. The walls. My gut-level emotions began to surface. Raw. Reactive. Out of control. When my pain was poked, I came out swinging. Pain causes more pain. Hurt people hurt others. This cycle must stop. Somehow.

A deep-seated longing to live a normal, healthy life. Happy, carefree thoughts. Intense love for life. That was my dream. My daily unspoken desire. My mom sensed it. She knew. She was like Casper the ghost who walked through walls. She ignored the guard standing at attention protecting the door to my heart and walked right on in. She was a mom. And moms are like that. No regard for boundaries that kept them from life-saving measures for their kids. And my life needed saving. She stood watching the undertow of pain suck me under as I gasped for air. But she had no life preserver to throw. Except one. And it was a long shot.

Dr. Phil.

Mom knew my frustration in finding a therapist. I'd called so

Irritated and cranky. Dejected and rejected. Still a reject. Sitting in a pit. An awful pit. A painful pit. An I-want-to-lay-down-and-die pit.

What do you want from me, Lord? I can't hear you, feel you. It felt void. Nothingness. Shut in. Trapped. I was ugly inside and out. Totally screwed up. A nothing. A nobody. *Why am I here, Lord? What do you want from me?* I silently screamed. Help me.

On December 2, 2012, the Friday before my surgery, we traveled on our bimonthly bus trip to the Coeur d'Alene Casino Resort in Worley, Idaho. After reaching the casino, an email arrived from Adrienne with Dr. Phil. "Go ahead with your surgery. Nothing is scheduled at this time."

Just as I had always suspected. Rejected again. And again. And again.

As we headed home on Sunday, a text from Sunny dinged my phone. "They want us in California to tape the show."

What? My body went totally numb. As I stared at my phone, it began to ring. I lifted it to my ear. "Hello?"

"This is Adrienne, with the *Dr. Phil* show."

At this point, all I knew: we were picked. Chosen. The hidden would now be revealed. And surgery would be postponed.

Sent pictures of me. Sunny. Daryl. Mom. Emailed information about Curly. News articles. Campaign press releases. Obituary. List of cult members. Curly's family members. Phone numbers. Addresses. A whirlwind of their wants. Demands. Directions. A producer and cameraman would be at our house on Saturday to tape answers to our questions. A major inquisition. Investigation. Thirteen pages filled with personally invasive questions. The most the producer had ever been given to ask a show participant. Lights. Camera. Action. From morning 'til night, I answered her probing questions. Sitting on the couch. In the recliner. The living room. The kitchen. With Daryl. Without Daryl. Daryl alone. Answered again with more detail. Less detail. More emotion. More emphasis. It was exhausting. Emotionally draining. The exposing had begun.

When people describe an event or a circumstance as surreal, I always wondered why. What made it strange, bizarre, unusual? Sitting on the stage staring at the audience, the cameras, the production staff, I understood. This was surreal.

D-day. December 19. The emotional roller coaster was unpredictable. Adrenalin-boosting fear. Sharp curves of shame flinging me from side to side. Steep inclines of pain peaking at the top. Gravity of guilt pulled me to the bottom. Breathing slowed down. Heart rate sped up. Faster and faster. A second of hesitation at the crest. Emotions suspended for a brief moment followed by a soul-ripping eruption as the velocity increased. Mind blowing. Hair blowing. Earsplitting. Stomach lurching. Dropping. Hang-on-for-dear-life momentum. The end. It was over. Taping done.

On the limousine ride back to the airport, the realization that millions upon millions would witness my undoing. What I did. What I chose. What I believed. The pain inflicted on Sunny horrified me. Haunted me. Humiliated me. All of this to find a therapist to help me heal my brainwashed head.

"Kathryn Kelley. She's the therapist we recommend for you," said Dr. Phil's public relations rep. His email included her phone number and address. First appointment set. January 16. Let the healing games begin.

Sh*tty Shellac—2013

"What is it you want from therapy?" my Dr. Phil–recommended therapist, Kathryn Kelley, asked.

I was seated in a comfortable, cushy chair positioned directly across the small room from her. No way out of the face-to-face meeting, that was for sure. Her office was located in the back of a dance studio in downtown Helena, Montana. It had a private back entrance for clients to allow them to maintain anonymity and privacy.

When I had arrived at the alley entrance, apprehension arose in my throat like bile from the belly. *It's a secret rendezvous for the unstable. Yep. That's me. Quite unbalanced*, I thought, poking playfully at myself. I took a deep breath, opened the door, and walked in.

After a brief introduction, she motioned me to sit in the corner chair. Although I had gone to great lengths to be there with this kind, beautiful, soft-spoken professional, it was unnerving. With one straightforward question, I could feel the deeply buried shellac-covered pain abscess ready to erupt. Shellac all right. A substance made of Lac bug shit. Ironic. *My past pain is covered in bug poop . . .* inwardly, I nervously laughed. Oh boy, did I crack myself up.

The uncomfortable silence I perceived clued me into her expectation of my answer. *Patiently waiting for her patient to pop the pain pus. Yuck, what a thought. Okay, I better quit the wonky word self-amusement and focus.*

"I want to understand why a halfway-intelligent person like me would allow someone like Curly to control me." To defend labeling myself with a semblance of intelligence, I said, "For goodness sakes, I was valedictorian of my high school class. Why would I do this?"

At the time I had no clue that this one simple question would lead to five years of ripping open every scar, pulling out every sliver, facing every painful piece of my past. From the very moments of my much-too-early beginning, trudging through the rocky recollections of my life, landing in the here and now. It was time to shed the shitty shellac.

Hocus-Pocus—2013

It's got to be hocus-pocus! I thought as Kathryn asked me to watch her fingers as she moved them back and forth.

How in the world was this going to help me get rid of the horrible memories and fears? I feared that coming here might have been a mistake. She explained it was Eye Movement Desensitization and Reprocessing, or EMDR for short. Used on veterans with PTSD. All these acronyms to make it easier for us unlearned, not-so-smart patients who are non-psychology-type people. EMDR for PTSD. I had PTSD? I hadn't been in any war, so what in the heck was she talking about? I guess what I had been through might have been thought of as a war. A fight with a fanatic. A battle with a bully. But mostly a beat-myself-up boxing match. And I was a loser in more ways than one. The knockout punch was always my mama guilt. Any time I'd stand up to my inner monster mama stamp of disapproval, the gut punch would come. *How could you? Why did you? How awful are you?*

These thoughts tipped the trauma scale. Weighed down with an emotionally damaged seeping wound that continually flowed through my scarred soul day after day. Its smolders sparked an intensely heated negative inner dialogue. Kathryn explained that these wounds could cause intense suffering, blocking the brain's natural ability to move toward mental health. In other words, the information system was blocked by the impact of traumatic events. EMDR helped activate the natural healing process the brain strived to achieve. Interesting that it wasn't her words that would help heal. It would be my brain learning how to reprocess the memory so that I could heal. A powerful way of not closing off the wound but transforming it through bravery-building, difficulty-demolishing, confidence-constructing, shame-squelching, and best of all . . . love-lavishing.

Let me back up to where the healing adventures began . . .

A safe place? Really? I inwardly scoffed at her question. That was definitely a quaint white-picket-fence concept that was not particularly familiar to me. Was there such a thing?

Kathryn had asked me to describe a safe place. After my smart-aleck, smirking inner comeback, a simple picture of our nightly ritual flashed in my mind. Each night, Daryl read a daily devotional while we lay in bed side by side. When he was done, I would lay my head on his shoulder, snuggled in the crook of his arm. He would wrap me tightly in his arms, then pray. I felt safer, more secure, and loved in that very place than any other time.

"Describe it to me," Kathryn said.

Describe it? Didn't I just do that? I thought, furrowing my forehead. But the vision in my head had not been expressed in words. Seeing my perplexed facial expression, she began prompting me.

"What color do you see?"

I recalled the white T-shirt he wore as pajamas.

"What do you smell?"

I thought of his after-shave scented deodorant.

"What temperature is it?"

I began to feel a sense of warmth on my skin as I thought of our heated electric blanket against my body. I felt the coolness of the room caress my face.

"What sounds do you hear?"

I heard words prayerfully offered to the Lord by Daryl's soothing voice. I heard the inhale and exhale of our elderly cat's breathing as she lay curled up in a ball behind my knees. I heard the hot water filling the baseboard heater as the boiler kicked on and off. With each sense, the depth of my remembrance of the physical perception went deeper and deeper until I literally could perceive the tranquility of that every-night treasured moment shared with Daryl. It truly was my safe place. I sat relishing the feeling of safety that I hadn't realized existed there. In that place. Every night. Security in snuggles. And I would need to return there mentally. Time after time. As I descended to dig out the depths of trauma buried in the recesses of my brain. Session after intense session.

Phase one of first counseling session. Over. Commence phase two.

"Who do you admire?" A deliberate question, fishing again.

I searched inwardly for a similar string of purpose. After my first round, I knew she'd hook my answers and reel them in. I'd battle the bait that I'd swallowed, hook, line, and sinker. Sink her, all right. I felt like I couldn't sink or swim. A line was embedded in my heart. Hurting and tugging. By a second simple question. Where would this one lead? I swallowed hard, trying to suppress the anticipation of wide crevices of pain being ripped open in my heart. Maybe this head analysis hocus-pocus wasn't for me!

Again, further explanation. "Who are your heroes? From past, present, fictional?"

"That's easy. Jesus is number one."

"Who else?" she prompted.

Of course, Daryl, my mom, and Sunny.

"How about historically?" she continued the hero heralding. *Sigh. A history lesson now? Ugh.*

The movie of *Schindler's List*, about a man who saved 1,100 Jews from the Holocaust, popped into my brain.

Kathryn asked, "Don't you think he had to take care of himself so he could help others?" Now this was digging a bit deeper than just establishing my hero list. "Do you take care of you?" she wanted to know.

I thought about my caretaking personality. Believing that taking care of others was more important than me.

"How does this make you feel?"

Here we go again. Deeper and deeper into the doo-doo. "Devalued" popped out of my mouth.

"I want you to visualize how it feels."

Now the hocus-pocus watch-my-hand-stuff again. My eyes followed her fingers as she moved them. Slow, methodical, back-and-forth, up-and-down motions. "Now I want you to relax and close your eyes."

I saw me. A little girl in a clean pink dress and white anklet socks, sitting in the middle of a garbage pile. As I stared at the mass of refuse, I could see bodies mixed in. The stench was repulsive. I clamored to climb off but couldn't. I cried for help, but no one came.

Kathryn asked me to work to get out. My visualization continued ...

I lifted my feet and slid down the slick side of the heap. As I started to stand, a lone, filthy hand grabbed my ankle. I was stuck in the stink. And the stinking fear paralyzed every nerve in my body. Somehow, I was able to jerk my foot away. Off flew my shoe. My foot was free. Anger erupted inside at the violation. Little-girl-me self-kicked the hand hard. *I'll show you!* Defiance erupted inside. I walked away step by step. The further the distance from the garbage pile, the older and more grown up I became. The heap of bodies began melting into a putrid puddle of sewage water. Fear left, but I felt totally alone.

Once again, I sat scared and sobbing on the re-erected heap. Daryl scooped me up in his arms and gently sat me down a distance away. He was my safety. My shield. He jumped on a huge bulldozer and scooped up the gobs of body parts. I felt an overwhelming sense of peace. I glanced around. Jesus. He was here. In one swoop of His hand, He opened up the earth. All garbage fell from the bulldozer into the Jesus-created crater and was swallowed up. An empty space remained where the garbage had been removed. I filled it with a happy, scrumptious bowl of my favorite DQ Blizzard. Laughing and playing and enjoying life. Again.

My happy place always had been food. Food. Food.

"How did you hold onto your belief in Jesus when Curly was brainwashing and warping your mind?" she casually asked. Another session.

I hesitated. I worried she'd realize the depth of my delusion. The craziness of my thought separation. I shrugged my shoulders and dove into my deliberation. "I guess you'd say I've got a couple different personalities." I winced at my off-my-rocker admission. She nodded as an indication to continue.

"I created two compartments in my heart. One with me and Curly.

And one with just me. No Curly." A nervous titter escaped my lips. "A Curly-less compartment."

She didn't join in the mocking merriment. She just nodded again to continue.

Nervous now at my ridiculous admission, I blurted out, "That's how I was able to keep such a strong relationship with Jesus. I hid it when I was with Curly. Then let it out when he wasn't around. It happened more often when I went to jail and finally got out of the cult." I exhaled deeply, wondering what she'd say about her kookie patient.

"Raylynn, it's called dissociating. It's a survival technique. You disconnected from the world around you. And even from yourself. It's the same thing you've done with your pain. As you described your 'zoning-out mode.' You're disassociating your body and mind from it. To cope."

This revelation of my out-of-reality coping hit me hard. I felt like a freak. A mental patient loose as a goose. Chasing the gander. A psychiatric dipstick. So, what did I want to do? Eat! Eat! Eat! The feelings of shame brought out my eating compulsion something awful. A Dairy Queen Blizzard on the way home every session did wonders for my sanity . . . but kicked the crap out of my self-worth.

Week after week. Heart hurts yanked and jerked. Brain cells bounced up and down. And today I was stuck. Yep. Stuck in my shit. But after you continued to sink deeper and deeper, was there a bottom? A stop gap? It felt more like quicksand. The more I wiggled and wobbled, the further I sank. But quicksand isn't quick. It's just sucky. It sucks you down. The harder you fight, the further you sink 'til you fall face-first in your shit. And that's how it felt those first weeks in therapy.

When you begin to drown in the mounds of dung, where do you begin? You begin at the ladder leading out of the dung, but it's difficult to see. Which rung could I reach when starting at the bottom of the barrel?

In my first sessions, Kathryn could see the bottom of one stinky barrel. Grief. Unfelt. Unallowed. Grief. For my dad, Raymond. It's where I was stuck. A two-year-old toddler's heartache was undiscussed. Unresolved. Unfelt. Fueling my attention for a father figure. An apple-of-his-eye dad adoration. From Jeff to college hookups to Curly. Any male figure. None was found. None replaced. My dad.

She asked me to visualize sitting on my dad's lap. Holding me. Hugging me. Loving me. I saw myself sitting snuggled up, holding a tan teddy bear. My dad's love enveloped me. Then I began to cry. A huge cord was connected to my heart. Tendrils ran from it through my entire body like the dark, snarly roots of a tree. It smelled rotten. Really rotten. Years of rot smell rose to my nostrils. I could hardly breathe.

Kathryn instructed me, "Now visualize cutting it out. Bring whoever you need to help you. Superman! Lumberjacks, whatever!"

I saw myself standing in our kitchen holding onto the table. Mom sat at the table to my right, crying. Daryl stood behind me, supporting me. In a spitting, angry rage, Sunny swung an ax, hitting the cord over and over 'til it was almost severed in two. I jerked the cord, ripping the rest out. Pain shot like a knife piercing my flesh.

Kathryn's soft voice interrupted my thoughts. I opened my eyes and stared at her. "When you have a wound that deep, it must be cleaned and stitched to completely heal it. Make sure you cleanse it thoroughly."

I nodded my head in understanding and closed my eyes. Jesus! He was standing directly in front of me. A pitcher labeled "Living Water" was in his right hand. He began pouring its contents into my heart. As the water flowed, He lifted His left hand. I saw the blood. Blood flowing from a hole in the palm of His hand. The nail hole where He'd been pierced. Blood and water mixed together. As it flowed into my heart, the force of the water began pulling tendrils of the deeply embedded roots one by one from each part of my body. Worms and maggots flowed out in the bloody water, squirming as they were expelled from my body. I visualized every part of my body, one by one . . . my head, my chest, my arms, my stomach, my legs, my feet. Every part was cleansed by the bloody water. The remainder, He poured directly into my heart.

He said, "Now your heart is filled only with Me." I felt the warmth of liquid trickling in the empty channels created by the pulled-up roots, just like blood flows through your veins and arteries. Pure ecstasy. Peace. No more pain.

Softly Kathryn asked, "What feeling are you experiencing?"

Love. Being cared for. Valued. I had to remember this moment and tell myself, *I am loved, I am valued. Forever.*

Over the next five years of therapy, I would need to remember these words to help me heal. My head. My heart. My hurt.

Lick My Buttery Bits—2015

"HEEELP ME!!" I muttered as my body began to slide down the side of the bed, heading to the floor. Rubber legs gave way. Heavy limbs felt limp. No ability to stop the progression of darkness enveloping my brain. Daryl grabbed my arms and slammed his body against mine to keep me from crashing to the floor. Not easy for someone who weighed a hundred pounds less than me. He pressed hard, not saying a word. My head drooped to his shoulder as every nerve in my body turned off. Went numb. Quit working. My body just flat-out failed me.

But the truth is I failed my body. Because of my brain. Thoughts. Emotions. Brainwaves of bashing. Beatings. Berating. I'd been a bully to my body. And today my body fought back.

Years of sugar addiction translated to scale escalation. Once loose clothes were formfitting. Fat spilled over the waist of my jeans. Love handles bulged. Bigger, sloppier shirts. Elastic waistband pants. Fatter and fatter I got.

My candy-craving enslavement to the sweets was 43 years in the making. Or baking. Or feeding the fattening frenzy…of addiction. The combination of trauma and treats at my grandma's funeral began a downward spiral into compulsion. And spiral, I did…

Jeff had emphasized over and over, "If you're fat, you're ugly." I cringed in anticipation of put-downs. I attempted to gather some guts. Practiced my who-cares attitude. If I was fat, maybe he wouldn't look at me so weird in the bathroom. My bravery lasted briefly. I had to go home for holidays. Thanksgiving. Then Christmas. Desperate circumstances dictate desperate measures. And I was beyond desperate.

Shame and fear could drive you to do things you'd never consider in a million years. Like puking. Can you imagine making yourself puke? Literally *making* yourself puke on purpose? Ugh. I hated puking. I had enough of it churning in my soul. Who would ever want to do it on purpose? Desperate dorm divas? Concerned about their despicable derrières? The first time I'd heard the gagging guts, the retching regurgitation sounds, I thought a fellow dormitory dweller was sick. Well, disease sick.

Nope. She purged to cleanse the junk eaten gluttonously. It had been a common occurrence in the dorm bathroom. To smooth the bulges. Slenderize the thighs. Tighten the tummy. Get skinny. I thought I'd try this method. Enjoy my addiction, then puke it out. Yep. Eat. Puke. Eat. Puke. Bulimia was born. Frenzied foolishness fueled by fear. Gut. Retching. Fear.

My entire world was food focused. Sugar was my best friend. It consoled me when I was sad. It comforted me in my loneliness. It soothed my stress. My confidence grew. My courage climbed. And over the years, so did the number on the scale. Tantalizing tastes. Delicious donuts. Fabulous fast food. Fantastic fudge. Oh, the fudge. My best friend of all. When life handed me lemons, I made fudge. A 9 x 12 cake pan size of solid fudge. An addict's delight. Piece after piece I'd consume once Sunny was asleep in bed. Surely kids shouldn't have candy before bed. Any good mother knew that. What I knew deep inside, though, was a different truth. I'd have to share with her. Nope. Won't share my dope. My dopamine. My drug. In delight I'd eat. And eat. And eat.

Eventually disgust would rise up and stuff a cork in my mouth, putting an end to my frenzied eating. I looked down. Half a pan left. In revulsion, I would resolve to throw it away. *Never again. I can't do this ever again.* I scooped up the mass of chocolate and shoved it in a plastic bag. Twirled the top shut and tossed it in the garbage. Carefully.

I'd slink guiltily down the hall to my bedroom. Lay down in bed and cry. Knowing the scale would not be kind now. Fear. Fat and ugly, just like Jeff had said. He was right. Always right. A big fat loser. Who never lost. Only gained. Pounds and more pounds. Inches and more inches.

Fitful sleep from my full stomach resulted in a morning sugar hangover. *Ugh. Why did I do it?* After getting Sunny off to school, I sat and cried. Again. Just a big fat, ugly loser. My eyes went to the cupboard door under the sink that hid the garbage can. The fudge. Who cares? I resolved to the fact that I would never be free. I slowly got up. Opened the small door. Pulled out the garbage can. My heart started pounding in anticipation, forgetting the extra pounds the scale had reflected that morning. A half pan of fudge carefully preserved in plastic. On purpose. Just in case a hit was needed. A chocolate snort would suffice. My drug. The fudge. As I took the first bite, my taste buds shouted with glee. My brain exploded with joy for that brief moment.

So sick. Mentally. Emotionally. Physically. But I could no longer do the puking purge. Instead, a diet queen was born. On. Off. On again. Off again. Lose some. Gain some. Lose again. Gain even more. Pills. Cabbage soup. High protein. Low fat. No carb. HCG drops. Hypnosis. Supplements. Weight Watchers. Diet Center. You name it. I could recite them all backwards in my sleep.

Addiction is a relentless foe bent on destruction, regardless of the substance used. It runs deep and, if not addressed, continues to pursue you. At times you stop running away and wait for it to catch you. Embrace you. Again. Like a lover pursues the object of desire. The addiction pursues you. Or you pursue the addiction. It's the never-ending merry-go-round. Or game of tag. You're it!

Well, shit! Err . . . shoot. A more tactful word. If I could "shoot up" sugar, I'd have done it. Happy "shit" for the brain. Depressed? Cookies would help. Had pain? Donuts would deaden it. Felt ugly and fat? Giant-sized candy bars would certainly chase away the misery. The mental gymnastics of self-deprecation performed on the slippery slope leading to insanity. With denial driving. Self-preservation steering. My rational brain was out of commission. Out of control. Like my eating. It didn't matter anyway. Because I didn't matter anyway. Just shit. Anyway.

Enter Daryl. Now it *did* matter. I wanted to feel confident, sexy, attractive, desirable for this man God had delivered to my door. Enter diet. Deprivation. Starvation. From supersize to midsize. For a time.

Ding dong. Addiction calling. Mocking. At the door. With cookies. And candy. And caramel popcorn. Oh, yes. The caramel popcorn.

I had introduced Daryl to one of my best foody friends: my mom's special recipe of caramel popcorn. *So* much fun to make. *So* much fun to eat. And eat. And eat. Now, granted, Daryl liked sweets, but he didn't crave them. He just liked them. No overpowering desire for a fructose fix. An endorphin injection. He was an ice cream fanatic, having moved from the dairy state of Wisconsin. But he wasn't obsessed with eating it each and every day. Not like his new wife and her need for sweets. Like ooey gooey caramel popcorn.

"Let's just have 'our' popcorn for dinner," I'd say, hoping he'd agree. It was a concession I made to not overeat. Rationale of reduction I told myself. If I skipped dinner, then the hundreds and hundreds of calories I'd consume with our popcorn delight wouldn't be quite as devastating to the derrière. Oh, such denial. But such delight for the druggie. The drunk. The sugar-holic. I can still sense the anticipation as I'd stir the mixture of butter, brown sugar, and corn syrup 'til it was cooked to perfection. My mouth would water when I saw bubbles build, pop, and swirl. The calorie-rich combination began to boil. Slowly. A teaspoonful tested. Softball stage reached. Perfect.

Now pour over the heaping mound of air-popper popped popcorn in the four-quart bowl. I would drizzle the thick, creamy candy concoction over the gobs of popcorn and stir. My taste buds salivating after having tasted the tester teaspoonful. Once stirred, the bowl sat enticingly between the two of us sitting side by side on the couch. As we watched a weekly recorded television show, we'd eat handful after handful. Daryl sat mindlessly eating as he concentrated on the show.

Me? Carefully watching Daryl. *Was he eating faster than me? Oh no! He'd get more than half. No fair.* Faster. Fist filled with fattening flavor. Operation chew . . . fast. Swallow . . . faster. Eat . . . fastest. To get the most-est. The addict won. Always. Scraping the last remnants out of the bottom, off the sides of bowl. Finger-lickin' good. Down to the last tempting, tongue-enticing, teensy-weensy blob. Of blubber-building buttery, caramelly popcorn. Endorphins reign and rule. Well, kiss my grits. Or better yet, lick my buttery bits. Yep I did. Over and over.

Then I bit the dust. My body said no more. I failed it. It failed me. And it commanded my attention. Demanded my devotion. That day in our bedroom as Daryl held me up. After a three-day hospital stay, I came home. No answers. Just guesses. No fixes. Just temporary life-breathing measures. A tank. A hose up my nose. And fear of mortality measured in days, not years.

I'm in the market for a miracle, Lord. Shopping for a simple twig from the Tree of Life. A bitty branch would do me. Could heal me. *Do you hear me? Lord? Are you there?*

Silence is not golden.

Two-Ton Tub—2016

"Help! I've fallen and I can't get up!" The slogan for the LifeCall medical alarm ran through my mind as I faded into total unconsciousness. Ten minutes before, I'd carefully maneuvered the red electric scooter into our hotel room at the Coeur d'Alene Casino Resort. I parked it near the window next to the ten tall tanks of oxygen standing neatly in the corner, delivered by the oxygen service. Ten small. Ten large. Oxygen concentrator and plenty of tubing. All these worn, refilled green tanks standing. Towering. Leering. Mocking my need. Waiting their turn to be sucked empty by the five-foot tube and three-foot cannula inserted in my nose. Just so I could breathe. Just so my lungs would continue to dump necessary oxygen in my veins. Making sure my brain functioned. My heart beat. My body lived. All this from little green tanks standing at rapt attention in the corner.

Daryl and I had spent the evening in the casino bingo hall. B10. O74. The caller enunciated each number carefully 'til a gleeful winner hollered, "BINGO!" Game after game we sat hoping. I concentrated on my bingo cards, daubing each number as it was called. Daryl concentrated on my oxygen tank regulator. Full or empty. In the red. Time to change. On alert. Always. Knowing the consequences if it ran out.

Bingo ended without a win. With a bingo bag full of daubers in one hand and an empty oxygen tank in the other, Daryl headed back to our room. I drove my scooter down the wide walkway between the gaming machines, looking for one that might be calling my name, ready to give me a bit of luck. I stopped. Daryl continued on his way to the room, soon to return with a full oxygen tank. Just in case. I wandered from machine to machine with Daryl always close by. His ever-watchful eye making sure of my safety. We played and roamed the casino for a couple of hours, soon tiring after our long day.

We headed to the elevator and made our way down the narrow hall to our room. After parking my scooter, exhaustion hit hard. Daryl helped get my cannula hooked to the oxygen concentrator. The portable tank regulator was turned to off to save what was left for our next day out-of-room adventures.

I sank down on the bed. My always-attentive husband knelt on the floor and carefully removed my shoes and socks, knowing my difficulty in leaning down. From past experience, he knew bending my obese body increased pressure on my lungs. Doing so might decrease my oxygen flow. Then out I'd go. Out for the count. He'd seen it happen way too many times to take the chance. Easier to help.

I stood and slipped off my jeans. Daryl stood close to assist. One clothing article gone. The process took time. Took energy. Always took my dignity. I could hardly undress myself. A catch-22 of emotion at our nightly routine. Appreciation for this knight in shining armor who was ready to jump in and help. My appointed caregiver. Humiliation at my inability to help myself. Independence down the tubes. Because of the tubes. Literally.

I pulled the cannula out of my nose and off my ears and handed it to Daryl. The oxygen keeper. The cannula cop. Off it came for a brief moment so I could slip my shirt over my head and replace it with my 2XL nightgown. As it slid down over my body, my head emerged through the neck of the gown. The cannula. In my face. The cannula cop's hand holding tight to the tube. An indication to shove it back up my nose immediately. Up the nose. Over the right ear. Over the left. A ritual I knew well. Time for bed.

As I pulled the tube leash out of the way of my feet, Daryl fell backward on the bed, exhausted, letting me finish my nighttime prep first. I headed around the wall enclosure to use the sink. I unpacked the needed face-cleaning toiletries from my bag. Eye-makeup remover. Face-cleansing wipes. Nighttime lotion. All ready for use. I stood at the sink and lifted the cannula from my nose and propped it on the top of my forehead so I could wash my face unencumbered by the tube. I carefully cleansed my face of the morning-applied makeup. The soft lotion, the finishing step. Suddenly, I needed to pee. I turned and took the few steps into the small bathroom. A toilet and tub. I shut the door.

I relieved myself, stood up, and turned around to flush the toilet. As I reached for the flusher, I felt the weird sensation of lightheadedness. My body began to go limp. *Oh no! Not again!*

As my body began to fall, I tried to grab the bathtub faucet, the only protruding object I could dimly see. It slipped through my fingers. I continued my downward projection and hit hard. The back of my head bounced painfully against the side wall. My butt hit the tub bottom. My legs flung over the side. At the exact moment my body came to rest in this painful position, the fleeting thought of my cannula still sitting on my forehead crossed my mind. *I need my oxygen!* This thought screamed through my brain. I could think it. Know it. But couldn't get it.

You see, these passing-out episodes were familiar to me. The Mayo Clinic called them syncope episodes. When my body or brain got stressed, a shutdown valve was turned. No stopping it. Uncontrollable. Halfway unconscious. No movement. No talking. Only hearing existed in this fading-to-black world. Frozen. But listening. Praying.

God, please wake Daryl! The longer I lay there, the further my oxygen dropped. Finally, my ability to hear was gone, too. Totally unconscious. Sideways in a tub. For how long. No clue.

Daryl's panicked voice broke through my foggy brain. "Oh my God! I'm so sorry! I fell asleep!" The oxygen keeper realized my cannula was not in the proper place. I had not put it back in my nose. My oxygen level had fallen drastically. His fear was apparent as he shoved it in my nose, hoping it would revive me. Within a short time, I began moving. My head hurt horribly. I began moaning and groaning, trying to get up. Daryl grabbed my hands and pulled. Time after time. Pull. And pull again. When you're 280 pounds, it's a bit difficult for a 185-pound man to hoist you up.

He stared at me in total despair. Hopelessness written all over his face. "Raylynn, I've got to call security. I can't get you out."

Fear. Shame. Coursed through my body. Through every cell of my brain. Fat woman fear. "No!" I screamed, begging him not to call.

In a moment of total catastrophe, have you ever had that out-of-body, out-of-mind experience? Weird thoughts racing through your brain? Gilbert Grape's mom. That's who I was like. The sad movie of a young man caring for his sister and brother with a disability. And his morbidly obese mom. To spare her embarrassment after her death, he torched their house. No crane to hoist her needed this way. Neighbors would have gawked. Kids would have laughed. At the sight of their fat mama.

Yep. That's me. The fat, two-ton tub of lard who couldn't get up. Horrifying! I couldn't let the security guys laugh at me. I had to get up. Fear of embarrassment was an adrenaline producer. Shame created a force of sheer determination to find my way out. *I WILL!* And will is what it took. Inch by inch. Turn by turn. Finally. On my hands and knees in the tub. The two-ton tub of lard would conquer the tub.

I will climb out. I will rise out of my shame. I will. Rise. I will not let this defeat me. Not now. Not again. One step closer. To victory. To freedom. Out of the ashes of shame. I rise.

Fight And Flight—2017

I lay in bed, contemplating the horrific events of the day. I squeezed my eyes tightly shut, hoping this would block out the sickening memory. Feeling totally mortified at what had taken place hours before, tears began slowly seeping from my clenched eyes, wetting my pillow. Trying to get off these awful meds was almost worse than anything. Why is it they dish them out like great-tasting candy but don't tell you how difficult it is to kick the habit? Especially without anyone telling you which one to quit first. How much and when? What would happen when you do?

I recall one of the doctors reading my med list, shaking his head saying, "You're taking a lot of medications that could be depressing your lungs and laboring your breathing."

Yep, that's for sure. Depressing. Distressing. Defeating. Just flat-out frustrating. However, since the prescriptions had been given to me by different specialists—neurologists, pulmonologists, general practitioners, among a few—none were willing to stick their neck out to tell me not to take another doctor's pharmaceutical concoction. Their so-called curative cocktail. A mai tai mix of meds; its recipe consisting of 3200 mg Gabapentin, four to six Hydrocodone, 80 mg Esomeprazole, 1 mg Ativan, 100 mg Topiramate, 350 mg Soma, Albuterol inhaler, 300 mg Ranitidine, 250 mg Azithromycin, 20 mg Lasix . . . all downed in a day. Down for the count. A knockout punch of prescriptions. Some days it was easy to sink into a bit of mental oblivion. Let the wooziness take me away like a Calgon bubble bath. But a drug dilemma existed. Did I dare ditch the dope? I feared the potential pain escalation. The inability to cope without dope. Addicted? No doubt.

The conflict between desiring to be free and the fear of possible, but most likely probable, pain created a war in my head. What in the crap should I do?

I started with the non-narcotic, the drowsy-less ones. Easy peasy. No problemo. No ill effects. That left five sedating ones to go.

Decreasing one by one. Little by little, or so I thought. 'Til the too-low, too-fast threshold of wicked withdrawal kicked in. And it literally kicked my butt. The mental beating I took began slowly. Like hot lava oozing from an erupting volcano knocking over, burying, and igniting everything in its path. The destructive, delirious, trauma-triggered thoughts seized my brain.

And seize they did, long into the night. Vivid, torturous nightmares invaded my REM sleep. And not just a scary monster disturbing my dreams. I was barely able to breathe when the tormenting terror would awaken me hour after hour.

Visions of my dad Raymond being violently murdered. My adoptive dad Jeff dying a horrifying death. And Curly, although dead, still mocking me. Taunting me. His murderous, evil laugh I'd hear in my dreams haunted me for days. The vision of him cackling wickedly as his sword impaled escaping members was a brain burner. Awakening me in a cold sweat of fear. I was locked in aloneness in the night terrors.

With my tossing and turning and dread-filled night, I dragged myself out of bed later than usual the next morning. All day long the devilish dreams clutched my consciousness. Fear clouded my ability to perceive truth from trauma apparitions. False fabrications. I paced. I panicked. I prayed. All day.

After the darkness had descended that evening, I walked into the living room where Daryl sat. I swore I heard a noise outside. Fear flowed head to toe. It had to be Curly. The paranoia was the springboard to a demented delusion. Deadly mental images detonated like dynamite. A brain bomb blowing every rational brain cell to bits. I froze.

I screamed at the fear-producing vision of Curly clawing his way in the front door. Illogical to Daryl. Totally tangible to me. Inquisitively, Daryl looked at the door. Nothing. No sound. No movement. No shadow. Just nothing.

"Ray, there's no one there," he said softly.

I screamed louder, "YES THERE IS! He's getting in! He's going to kill me!" I was sobbing. Screaming. Unable to breathe.

Heavy heart palpitations pounded. Irregular beats. Irrational thoughts. Fright was bolted in my brain, inhibiting rational reasoning and thinking. Uncontrolled delusional thoughts threatened my sanity, my safety.

I fell into a chair, sitting against the wall facing the door. The potency of the fear flat-out dropped me. Like hot melting wax, the fear burned slowly and deep. No strength to stand. No ability to fight. I was in total fright mode. All I could do was scream. My wide-eyed expression a picture of pure panic. Daryl dropped to his knees beside me, grabbed my shoulders, and shook me gently, hoping to awake me from this day terror.

He tried to reassure me again, "There's no one at the door, Ray. I promise!"

I just sat staring at the door. Saneness went sideways. I started to rise and screamed in uncontrollable panic, "He's coming through the keyhole! Can't you see him?" I hissed at him through fear-clenched teeth, my eyes locked on the latch. "Stop him, Daryl! PLEASE!!!"

He held me in the chair. Firmly but gently, shaking me again. "Ray, I promise there's no one there."

The armor of my saving knight fell to the ground. My confidence plummeted just like his shield. My protector was a failure. He didn't see or understand the danger. I sat defeated, ready to be ravaged by evil. By Curly, the evil one. Out to destroy me.

Daryl began to pray.

My eyes fell from the terror-taunting keyhole to the brown, fuzzy-soft teddy bear with a bright red ribbon tie. It sat atop its cardboard container near the front door. It had arrived in the mail the previous day. Carilyn, a dear friend of my mom's, had sent it to me. It wasn't just any bear. It was a prayed-over bear. Her church congregation had collected numerous bears of all shapes, sizes, and colors. And prayed over them. Healing for whomever received each one. The pastor had encouraged his parishioners to distribute them to those whose hearts needed healing. Carilyn thought of me. It was boxed up, mailed, and delivered the day before my insanity incident. My brain breakdown.

There it sat by the penetrable door. "My bear. Give me my bear," I whimpered to Daryl.

Perplexed by my request, he swept it up in one hand and sat it on my lap. My trembling arms wrapped around the soft, furry stuffed animal, crushing it in my grasp. My breathing slowed. My thoughts cleared. The fear lifted. The evil left. A teddy bear had become my armor bearer. Breaking perceived danger from my brain.

Carilyn did as divinely directed. She had no clue the dreadful day on the horizon for me. But God did. And the directive came from heaven. The prayer-carrying teddy bear of a caring congregation came to me through her. Used by a holy God for unholy me. An earthy occupant, heaven sent.

Just. For. Me.

The escalation of my tripped triggers continued. And Daryl was great at tripping them. Unintentionally.

The need to stop the insanity, fanned by the flame of supposed abandonment by Daryl, resulted in downing a half bottle of Ativan. That would stop it dead in its tracks. He literally dug them out of my mouth as I attempted to pull away. To push him aside. To no avail. He won. Only a few were ingested, which led to a long night of drug-induced sleep. The morning dawn brought embarrassment and horror at what I'd done. Beyond-belief out-of-control behavior.

It didn't end there. Many times, Daryl's slow-to-speak nature was perceived by me as the silent treatment. *For goodness sakes, he's had five seconds to respond!* I'd think, as my rejection trigger was tripped. The talkative, never-shut-up Polack versus the think-for-eternity-before-answering Dutchman. When he sensed my own shutdown or heard my blasting rebuke, he'd apologize. However, once I was triggered, my emotional berating became brutal. The boiling pot got tipped and I'd rip him a new one. The intensity of my mouth was driven by the depth of my pain. Rejection. Abandonment. Fear. All colliding, crushing my sensitive heart. To deflect the pain, I'd come out swinging. It was difficult for me to just forget about what happened and let it go. My heart was swimming in pain, sadness, and rejection. I'd fight and try to run away.

After one such incident, I spewed my nastiness, screaming, "I can't take you rejecting me anymore! I don't matter to you at all! I don't care if I kill myself or drive off a cliff. I just fucking don't care because *you* don't care! You fucking asshole!"

My eyes burned with fury fueled by fear of the intensity of my emotions. Out of control. Plunging off the edge of sanity. I snatched my keys from the hook near the back door. In my extreme emotional frenzy, Daryl knew my ability to drive was severely impaired. He feared the results of this road rampage. He roughly grabbed my wrist and reached to yank the keys from my other hand, but I was on the fight—ready for flight. I wrestled frantically, twisting my arm free. He blocked the path to my getaway car. I shoved him as hard as I could and sprinted for the garage.

I heard Daryl running behind me, "Please stop, Ray! You're going to hurt yourself. PLEASE stop!!"

The intensity of my rage propelled me faster. I jerked the car door open and catapulted in the seat. Just as I tugged the door handle to close, Daryl grabbed the top edge of the door with both hands and hung on.

"I won't let you drive like this!"

"The hell you won't," I sneered sinisterly. I tugged and tugged but he wouldn't let go. *I'll show you!* I thought contemptuously. *You can't control me, you asshole!*

I let go of the door and shoved the car in reverse and floored the gas pedal. Daryl had no choice but to let go or the door would have pushed him under the car. I had no concern for his safety. Only my ability to flee. As the car headed backward out the garage door, I flung the door shut. I was free! Finally!

The back of the car started out of the garage and into the alley. It stopped. The tires started spinning. Unshoveled snow brought the car to a standstill. The harder I pushed on the gas, the deeper the tires sank in the snow.

Are you freakin' kidding me? I couldn't even leave when I wanted? Oh God! Why? I couldn't take this pain anymore.

A gentle whisper flooded my heart. *The snow was sent to stop you.*

This is where you belong.

As the ocean tide recedes in the aftermath of its height, so did my anger. My rage. I collapsed in the seat with my head on the steering wheel. Tears of frustration, of humiliation, slid down my cheeks. I raised my head slightly and saw Daryl standing helpless, a look of horror etched in his expression. Fear flashed in his eyes. This is the face of the man I love. The man who has literally gone through my hell. Walked beside me. Loved me. Not condemning me. What have I done to him? To us? Would he hate me? I had nowhere else to go.

I set the gear in drive and rolled forward slowly into the garage. Parked and opened the door. Daryl reached in his hand and helped me out of the car. Even now, after my maniac display of rage-fueled emotions and total disregard for him, he showed compassion. Gentleness. Kindness. Love. I stood up and collapsed in his arms. He's my place of safety. My security. My sanctuary.

Have you ever experienced a total inability to connect with reality? I did. My triggers were tripped. My screws became loose. My brain blew a gasket. My thoughts became toxic. Disordered. Deadly. Dangerous. Devious. Full-blown psychotic episode ensued. And a raving maniac had emerged. The narrative inside my head brought thoughts contrary to actual evidence of reality.

I was out of control. Mentally. Emotionally. Physically. Screaming in a frenzied fury. Hell-bent on escape. Breaking free of the here. The now. The fear. The terror. The have-to-flee. The must-take-flight. And the only way to do that was fight. It truly was for me. Fight and flight. From fear.

Total psychosis. The result.

Pick Up Your Mat—2017

I'd been half dozing when I heard my cell phone ring. Caller ID told me it was Sunny. A smile crossed my face as I hit the answer button and put the phone to my ear. "Hi sweetie. Whatcha doing?"

Her call was always a highlight to my boring day. I was sitting in my usual place. A dark-brown leather recliner. A prison of sorts, without bars. A place I sat much of the day watching television. Napping. Reading. Eating. My own little place of protection from falling. Hard. No soft and easy way to fall at 280 pounds. Daryl feared I would fall if I ventured too far from my chair. Bathroom needs got me up. Fifteen steps there. Fifteen steps back. Eating needs got me up. Twenty steps there. Twenty steps back. With each step, the green 50-foot hose from the oxygen concentrator to my nose rudely followed me everywhere. Nowhere was sacred. Not even sitting on the toilet.

These last few years had stripped my dignity. My self-worth. My independence. And at this rate, it would flat-out end my life. I could picture the facial expression of the doctor at the National Jewish Hospital as he gently explained my condition. They'd had such difficulty diagnosing me. After a painful lung biopsy, my medical team believed they had a diagnosis.

And it had a life expectancy of 3–5 years.

His look . . . sympathetic. My look. Shock. Terror. Jaw-dropping unbelief. Die? Me? There must have been a mistake. According to God's plan, there was. Unbeknownst to me. Then.

My three-day hospital stint after I first passed out was only the beginning of a medical nightmare. No answers. Unknowns. Passing out. Many times, over and over. Have you ever seen a fainting goat? When they're startled or surprised, their muscles go stiff and down they go. It doesn't affect their nervous or cardiovascular systems. Just their muscles. Well, picture me like a fainting goat. Oxygen dropped. Passed out. Stressed. Passed out. PTSD triggered. Passed out. Time after time, Daryl caught me and kept me from falling. If not, floor and face met. I could hear. But not move. Not talk. The not-talking part was probably a respite for Daryl.

Many times these episodes happened when I was out of control, mentally and emotionally. Screaming. Crying. Yelling. Then down I'd go. A quiet reprieve for the man who waited on me hand and foot. Never complaining. Never stopping. Holding me gently but firmly against the bathroom door. The hall wall. The door jamb. My head on his shoulder. Knees locked. Arms hanging loose. No movement. No talking. Only breathing and hearing. Daryl's gentle reassurance kept me from panicking internally.

Fear raged through me. What was wrong with me? Sometimes thirty seconds. Three minutes. Twenty minutes or an hour. He'd hold me. In whatever position I ended up after my brain shut down my ability to move, to talk.

"You'll be okay, Ray. We'll get through this." His love pouring out in eight words. Spoken time after time. Episode after episode. Reassuring. Loving. Showing me he truly meant what he vowed on our wedding day. In sickness and in health. 'Til death do us part. I was sick, desperately needing health. Hoping death was not knocking at my door.

Daryl had to return to work at the lab, a limited amount of sick leave left. Commence Babysitters Club all gathering at the Van Oort Lodge. My mom, cousins, and friends took turns on duty for a daytime shift. Following me to the bathroom. Waiting outside the door. No noise heard. "Are you okay?" My mom or cousin would say.

For goodness sakes, can't I have even a minute alone in the bathroom to poop? I'd think.

Frustration. Fear. Then falling. Thud. Cousin Marlene, the day-shift monitor, tried to open the door to the tiny bathroom but my body blocked the way.

"Oh shit! What do we do now?" I heard my mom ask, her words dripping with fear. Marlene did her best to squeeze through the door, being careful not to step on my legs sprawled limply on the floor. My upper body was leaning twisted against the side of the tub. Marlene scrambled over me as gently as possible and crawled into our high-sided jacuzzi tub. The gradual loss of muscle control was causing my head to slide sideways into the small crevice between the tub and toilet. Grabbing my head, she stopped its downward progression. Arms oddly bent. Legs twisted. All hurting from the crash to the floor.

Unable to move, my mind screamed silently, *Please help me. I hurt so bad! I can't move! I can't get up. Oh, God, why? Why does this keep happening?* Helplessness turned to hopelessness.

A twitch. A slight hand movement indicated I was coming around. How in the world would they get me up? Marlene struggled to prop me upright, eventually pulling me to a sitting position with my back against the tub. Tears streaked my cheeks as I heard my mom ask anxiously, "Honey, are you okay?"

I nodded slightly. Shame at worrying her hit hard. "I'm sorry, Mom," I whispered.

With Marlene's help I was able to finally sit up. Eventually stand up. Friday arrived. Daryl was home for the weekend. Mom and Marlene headed home.

I awoke Monday morning to greet our friend, Marilyn, who had driven from Butte for her morning babysitting shift. Daryl had headed to work at 5:30 a.m. while I still slept. Marlene had a morning appointment in Missoula so Marilyn was the substitute scheduled to take care of the passing-out patient. I sat eating breakfast at our small kitchen table dressed in my extra, extra large nightgown and fuzzy pink belted bathrobe.

Marlene arrived. Now a trio sitting, chitchatting. A patient. A cousin. A friend. Then it started. First the heat.

"It's so hot in here," I complained as I stood to disrobe.

Marlene watching me closely, her brow furrowed in concern. She knew the signs. She'd seen enough soon-to-pass-out indicators. So she watched. On guard. I walked wobbly out of the kitchen hanging onto the door jamb as I headed through the living room. The diligent duo followed like Mutt and Jeff. Tall and short. Cousin and friend.

Caring. Concerned. Catastrophe wannabe stoppers. The muscles in my legs lost the command from my brain to stay standing. At least it was a cushy couch my butt encountered rather than the hard floor.

But this time felt different. Weird sensations. I could hardly breathe, even with the oxygen hose up my nose. *Breathe, Raylynn. Take a deep breath. Breath in. Breath out. Breath in. Breath out.* My mind couldn't keep up. Couldn't really comprehend what to do. Muscles went limp. Gradually. Arms fell to my side. Slowly. My head fell forward. Inch by inch. Marlene held me upright. Marilyn grabbed the blood pressure cuff and tried to slide it up my limp arm. She got a reading as best she could.

I felt the oximeter clamp onto my index finger. Marilyn said, "It's dropped to 85." She ran to turn up the concentrator. Back to check oxygen. Back and forth she went 'til it was at maximum flow. Not enough. Oxygen dropped lower. I heard her say, "We need to call 911."

Marlene had seen this before, she thought. All outward signs looked the same. Heated up. Passed out. Oxygen dropped. Body drooped. But to Marilyn, this looked different. She was the vital signs monitor and concerned at what she saw. She repeated, "We need to call 911." Unsure, Marlene frantically called Daryl hurriedly explaining the situation. He agreed.

"Call 911. I'm on my way."

I stirred a bit, trying to shake my head no. *Abort! Abort! This maniac mission. I'm fine,* I thought. I kept myself entertained in my loose, limp state. The only thing I could control. Bebopping in my brain. Aimlessly wandering thoughts. To derail the fear. The shame. The helplessness.

Daryl arrived home just ahead of the paramedics. I began to stir. Groggy. Hardly able to talk. I felt a blood pressure cuff wrap around my arm. I heard "It's 200 over . . . I can't get the number. We've got to get her to the hospital. Mrs. Van Oort, we need to transport you to the hospital."

I shook my head no.

The paramedic spokesman looked worriedly at Daryl and said, "Since she's conscious, we have to have her permission to transport her." My continual head-shaking refusal brought protests from the Babysitting Brigade. But my simple "no" won the debate. One point Raylynn. Zero points Brigade.

It was finally Daryl who scored. "I can't take care of you like this. Your oxygen's way too low and your blood pressure is way too high. You've got to get it checked out to figure out why," he pleaded.

As my ability to comprehend increased, the gravity of the situation slapped me hard. I glanced around. Two serious-looking firemen stood staring at me. One paramedic sat beside me on the couch, periodically checking my blood pressure. Another knelt in front of me, monitoring my way-too-low oxygen saturation. Medical bags sat open on the floor. Blood pressure cuff. Oximeter. Stethoscope. Fear took root.

Anxiously, I looked up at Daryl. The look of concern on his face was the final clincher. Debate over. I hung my head in resignation. "Okay, I'll go," I mumbled meekly.

The two firemen retrieved a stair chair to deliver me safely to the ambulance. Our beautifully landscaped flat-rock twisting stairway allowing visitors to ascend from the road to our porch was a hindrance to carrying me on a flat gurney. My morbidly obese body didn't make it an easy jaunt down the stairs, even in the carefully designed descend-the-stairs chair. Emergency room, here we come.

Emergency room personnel sprang into action as the ambulance crew wheeled me in. I lay listening to the update about my afternoon adventures. It didn't feel real. *What's wrong with me?* Fear began to play pinball in my brain. Twenty-two days ago, I'd been released from this very place.

My thoughts were interrupted as they pushed my gurney into the room indicated by the charge nurse and hoisted me from gurney to ER bed. Blood pressure cuff attached. Oximeter attached. Heart leads attached. EKG performed. Normal. A serious-looking nurse wrapped a tourniquet a bit above my elbow. An IV needle was inserted in a well-defined vein in my right forearm. A laboratory technician soon arrived with his tray of tubes.

"Are you going to take it all?" I joked as I watched him fill tube after tube. *I vant to suck your blood*, I thought, chuckling to myself.

When in stressful situations, I made up ridiculous thoughts, trying to derail my fearful ones. A bit of a sanity stabilizer. He finished. Finally. He nodded his thanks for my cooperation and left with my blood. *I've met the ER vampire of Castle Dracula and lived to tell about it!* A momentary diversion of foolishness.

I laid my head back on the pillow, my mind jumping from thought bubble to thought bubble. Ridiculous to fearful. I grew weary trying to dispel the fear and finally gave in. Let it take over. Consume me. Drown me. Drive me lower and lower into despair. Depression. I was done trying. I closed my eyes and silently wept.

Another round of tests came back . . . no definitive answers. With blood pressure and oxygen stabilized, I was sent home. Discharge paperwork in hand. A Great Falls pulmonologist's name written down. A referral had been made. I was instructed to call the next day and set an appointment. God had a different plan.

"A friend of mine went to Dr. Bekemeyer, a pulmonologist in Missoula," cousin Marlene told me when she returned the next day. "You'd have to get a referral. And I'm not sure if he's taking new patients. But he's really good."

I called the emergency room receptionist, asking to switch the referral. No go. Can't do. The ER doc has spoken. I called Dr. Bekemeyer's office in hopes that he'd make an exception. No go. Can't do. Referrals only. A denial wall erected. "No" brick by "no" brick. Layer upon layer. Higher and higher. Desperation kicked in. I called the hospital back and pleaded with a lady in Medical Records to at least fax the notes from my three-day stay and my ER visit to Dr. Bekemeyer's office. She finally relented and did as I'd asked.

Another call to his office. "The hospital is faxing my information later today. How soon can I see the doctor?" I neglected to mention that no referral would be included. Just medical reports.

The pulmonologist's nurse I'd been able to reach explained, "He has a stack of referrals on his desk. And it's strictly up to him which cases he takes. No guarantee he'll take yours. If by some chance he does, it'll probably be at least two months before he can see you."

My heart dropped. Hope faded. I hung up the phone. Dejected. Defeated. Hopeless. I closed my eyes and prayed silently, *Lord,*

PLEASE help. Pleading prayers for a holy healing assuredly unheard. I thought.

Time passed. Trust in a heavenly intervention fell. Along with each tear. In silence. Night fell. Deafening silence. I lay in bed. Discouraged. Angry. Hurt. Scared. Enter sarcasm defense, *Even a silent partner invests something in the relationship.* Not *my* silent partner. He was totally absentee. Absconded with my heart. My faith. My belief. Just a thief. A one-way dialogue of deity discussions. I was just done.

Morning dawned. I didn't want to get out of bed. Disappointment in finding myself still alive set in. *Ugh. Another crappy day. Another nothing day. Another same-old-shit day.* And my attitude was just that: the shits.

Depressed, I swung my legs over the side of my bed, catching my foot in the oxygen hose connected to my CPAP.

"Shit! Shit! Shit!" I hated my life! I hated my fat body that required this hose up my nose. Twenty-four freakin' hours a day.

What if I just ripped it off? What would happen? Would I die? How long would it take? Would it hurt? Would I feel it? Or would I just go to sleep? My thoughts scared me. Did I really want to die? I thought of Daryl. Mom. Sunny. What a horrible thing to do to them. Resigned to the fact that this was the shitty hand of life dealt to me, I slid down the side of our tall bed and walked to the bathroom. My hose stalking me. Harassing me. Everywhere I went...there it was. Even in the bathroom. Laying in a heap on the floor staring up at me as I sat on the toilet. Mocking me. Depressing me. Shaming me. Pulling me. My nose. My ears. Caught on a chair leg. The couch corner. A table leg. Bossing me around. My world was limited by its length. My life dependent on its ability to blow, to puff, to deliver air. "Up your nose with a rubber hose." John Travolta's quote when he played Vinnie on *Welcome Back, Kotter* came to mind. Meaning shove it, losers. *Well, it's shoved up this loser's nose*, I thought dismally. That's all I was. A loser.

God felt it was time to intervene. His involvement usually turns your world upside down. Turns your innards outward. Hangs your weepy feelings out to dry. Time to belly up to the bravery bar and take a swig of humility. And doggone, quit the whining. I felt like a bawled-out brat. *Put on your big girl panties and call the doctor. Again.* Well, as we know, I couldn't put on anything but big girl panties to cover my blubber butt. Ass whacked. Face slapped. It was time to take charge.

I took a deep breath and dialed the number. Asking for the call to be transferred.

"This is Dr. Bekemeyer's nurse. May I help you?"

I froze. After a silence, I managed, "This is Raylynn Van Oort. Did you get my medical records from the hospital?"

"Let me check," she replied in her business-like manner. Annoying elevator music hit my ears. I started counting the beats to keep myself occupied. *1 and-a 2 and-a 3.* Repeat. I waited. And waited. And waited. *Click.*

"Yes, Mrs. Van Oort. They're here. I'll put them on his desk, but you must understand that at least twenty-five referrals are ahead of you. And there's no assurance that he'll even take your case. It's going to take him some time to review the records and make a decision as to which patients he'll see."

My heart fell. Desperation entered in. Pleading. Begging. "*Please* understand my situation. I keep passing out over and over and the doctors don't know why. I don't know where else to turn."

Internally, I was on my knees. Pleading my case before this nurse. God heard. And in his mercy, He intervened. A double dose of Holy Spirit power transmitted through the phone line. *Zap!* Silence. On the other end. I held my breath. She hadn't responded yet.

"I'll tell you what I can do. I'll put your chart on top of the pile. Yours will be the one he sees first."

My mouth fell open in total shock. "You will? You have no idea how much that means to me! You're a Godsend! I can't thank you enough." Holy Spirit touchdown. A perfect 100-yard return. GOD-SCORED! That was Monday.

The phone rang Tuesday. "Dr. Bekemeyer would like to see you Wednesday, October 14. Can you make it then?" Barely two weeks away.

My mouth fell open. I closed my eyes. "Of course. Thank you so very much. I'll be there." As I hung up the phone, I was overwhelmed with emotion.

Jesus, You saw me. You intervened. You haven't left me. I hung my head in submission to the amazing God who once again showed up for me. Showed His power. His will. His love. His mercy. His grace. For a mess. Missing faith. Mastering in misery. Needing a miracle. Never ever. Give up.

The following week, I met Dr. Bekemeyer in the emergency room of St. Patrick's Hospital in Missoula, Montana. No ambulance this time. Just a gurney ride escorted by the emergency response team from the pulmonary lab to the ER. This time I passed out in the plexiglass booth during pulmonary function tests. Lung power performance . . . not. Not functioning well, that is.

"Deep breath in. Hold it. Breath out," they said a couple of times. I guess I had gotten it wrong. Breath out. Pass out. I began sliding sideways down the backside of the booth. No longer able to choose to move or respond. The door swung open and I heard Daryl's voice, "We need to get her out of there!" He leaned in to keep me upright.

Over the intercom system I heard, "Code 66 to the Pulmonary Lab. Stat."

I thought, *That's crazy. I wonder what happened? I hope the person's okay.* A bit perplexed, though, because I hadn't seen anyone else in the lab but me. Voices discussing how best to get me out of this enclosed 3-foot by 3-foot booth penetrated my thoughts. *Oh crap! They're here for me! Yep. It's a problem.* Getting the tub out of the tube. The 280 pound Two-Ton Tony and my tonnage wasn't muscle like Tony the fighter guy. Pure blubber. Fat cells galore. Didn't fat float? *Maybe they should just run water in here and I could float out.* No backs would be hurt in the making of this tidal wave movie. *Showcase this Fat Lady floating down the river and I ain't gonna be singing.* My attempt at fear-calming humor faded.

When will this end? Dear Lord, PLEASE, I begged in humiliation. All the while, the wonderful responders carefully pushed, pulled, and tugged 'til the flabby tubby was on the gurney heading to the ER. Dr. Bekemeyer had been summoned and met us at the ER. What a first impression on the prayer-answered doctor.

That day began another journey. From St. Patrick's Hospital in Missoula. To National Jewish Hospital in Denver. Back to more poking and prodding and testing. In Helena. Scanning my brain. In Missoula. Lung Biopsy. Back to Denver. Dire diagnosis. To Rochester, Minnesota. The famous Mayo Clinic. Testing. More testing. More and more testing. Probes up the nose. Down the throat. Into the lungs. Pulmonologist. Cardiologist. Neurologist. They thought I needed a psychologist . . . and a surgeon. For a gastric bypass.

"I *can't* have another surgery," I cried to Daryl in horror and shame. "How could the doctor say I was morbidly obese? I *know* I'm a bit overweight, but morbidly obese? Really? That's for all those really super fat people." Tears of shame. Words of denial. Yet down deep, fearful of my future. My fat future. Afraid of my fate. My fat and ugly fate. Just like Jeff had said. A predictor of poundage. 280 pounds of fat. Fat-fueled fear of fatality. Not vanity any longer.

Home again, home again. Jiggity Jig. Went the fat pig. Home again, home again. Jiggity Jog. Hopeless and helpless. Was the fat hog. Me. The will to live lies deep in the core of your soul. Life tragedies. Loss. Traumas. Pain. Disease. Despair. Desperation. Bury it even deeper to the point it begins to suffocate. No essential air. Absence of oxygen. Barely a breath can reach it. It begins to choke. Struggle slightly. Then give in. Give up. Lie dormant. Surrender to the pain. Accept defeat. A slow descent into a lifeless existence. Who really cared if I live or die? Not me. Yet, the innate desperation to remain alive played ping-pong with the dread of my daily existence. *I have no fight left, Lord. I am nothing but a burden. Nothing but a blob of blubber. Existing.* Just woe is me. The victim was victorious in staying a victim. Oh, woe is me.

"You hate me, Lord!" I'd cry out in anger. "You have the power to heal, so why won't you? You love everyone else but not me! You could heal me in a billionth of a second! Don't you see me? See my crappy life? My pain? Don't you even care?"

Boy, my pity pot was stinking to high heaven. Yep. To heaven, all right. And He had no plans for a divine healing intervention. No passport out of my pain prison. No spiritual-salve shortcut to stop suffering. No admittance to the almighty ailment alleviation. Nope.

Not my way, anyway. When Jesus is involved, expect the unexpected. Expect His intervention. His way. Enter stage right. From behind the curtain. Hiding His holiness 'til your ears are willing to hear His words. His will. His way to heal. That day came.

"Pick up your mat and walk," said my daughter Sunny, explaining her upcoming teaching. Her words weren't loud. But Jesus increased the decibels. Emphasized. Underscored. Blasted through the blubber. The cover. The crust. Encasing my heart. I hung up the phone. These words ran unrestrained through every electrified wire in my brain. Every neurotransmitter.

I sat in silence. Listening. My mind screaming, *What Lord?! What are you wanting me to do?*

"If you want your miracle, pick up your mat and walk." These weren't just words. They were a directive.

Holy thunderbolt. Holy lightning strike. Bull's-eye! Direct hit to the heart. Doubt. *Snip. Snip.* Fear. *Snip. Snip.* Failure. *Snip. Snip.* Holy Spirit wire cutters at work. And it hurt.

Are you kidding me? Dumbfounded, I looked down at my broken body. Felt the hose up my nose. My life limitations. *I can hardly even walk, so how, Lord?* I grabbed my Bible and read the scripture looking for answers.

As soon as the paralytic did as directed. Stood, reached down, picked up his mat, and walked. He was instantly healed. Since he hadn't moved a leg muscle in thirty-eight years, I'm sure his legs were pretty darned weak. But he did it anyway. He stood up and walked at Jesus' command. I knew that Jesus was speaking figuratively to me. If I wanted healing, I had to be an active participant. Just do the dang work. One step at a time. My thoughts turned to Sunny sharing with me about her recent new "health journey." I'd scoffed at it. Another stupid diet, I'd thought.

"Mom! I only need two more clients and I'll make a $100 bonus!" Sunny had told me excitedly. My daughter, the new health coach.

Then the trap was set. I bit the bait. Helping my sweet Sunny, the hook. Reeled in turn by turn.

"One of my coaches is showing me how to do a Health Assessment. Would you get on a Zoom with us so I can learn?"

Ugh. "Of course, honey," I said with false enthusiasm.

Daryl set up a table in the living room so that we could sit side by side staring at the computer screen. I was nervous. What would she ask? My health history was overwhelming to share. Plus, all the doctors hadn't really given me hope that healing was possible. So why in the world was I wasting my time, their time? I remembered: to help Sunny learn. That was the purpose. As long as it was for Sunny, I would answer any stupid questions. My un-positive attitude was palpitating my pulse. Bubbling in my brain.

"Mom. Daryl. This is Laurie, one of my coaches." A sweet, beautiful lady began speaking, asking, digging. Deep.

"Why do you want to get healthy?"

My first impulse was to scream. I said, "I want to live!"

She continued, "Why?" This wacky why question was destroying my demeanor.

Why? Why? Why? From the depths of my soul that she'd penetrated, I sobbed, "I want to jump on the trampoline with my grandkids. I want them to remember me as a fun grandma rather than 'Watch out for grandma's oxygen hose.'" They had heard this over and over as they danced around my hose twisting around our tiny living room floor. Taunting me. Haunting me. Hampering me from the joys of gramma-hood.

Laurie must have sensed my fear. My failure fear. "I believe in you, Raylynn. And you can borrow my belief in you until you believe in yourself."

Sold to the highest bidder. Or non-quitter. "FINE!"

On June 30, 2017, I picked up my mat and began my walk. With Daryl and Sunny walking beside me. Helping me. Holding me. Encouraging me. At times carrying my mat for me. But I kept walking forward. Baby step by baby step, my healing began. I equipped myself with knowledge. I became empowered by my better choices. I began to stare in the face the destructive habits that had kept me a prisoner for so long. I chose to embrace my new way of living; not fall back into old unhealthy eating habits driven by negative emotions and pain. In less than a year, 130 pounds of blubber burned away. The oxygen hose up my nose was no longer needed. Health returned day

I was healed. By a God who saw and responded. Loved and

manifestation of my healing continues bit by bit. Still in
As I just do the dang work. Each and every day.

You Are Invited

HE. SAW. ME.

I invite you to sit at my table. The final course served is HOPE.

The sweetness of this dessert came after I'd tasted the desert. I'd swallowed the wilderness of my wantonness. My recklessness. My unrestrained sinfulness. The syrup of shame poured on my sundae of suck-duction into my own personal insanity. I would have been trapped here. But…

He. Saw. Me.

He knew me before I knew myself. He loved me before I desired love. He forgave me before I even realized I'd sinned. He invited me before I knew I wanted to attend. Before I knew…

He. Saw. Me.

As I've written a sampling of my "shit" to share with you. My desire of opening up the crap of my past is to show you God in it all. It's not because I did or didn't do anything right or wrong. It's because He invited me. In His grace. In His mercy. I'm so thankful…

He. Saw. Me.

It's not because "I accepted Jesus." It's because He accepted me. In my broken. In my dilapidated state of despair. In my begrudging obedience to His will. It's not because I attended or didn't attend church. It's not because I read or didn't read my Bible daily. It's not because I was good or bad. Wicked or wretched, virtuous, or victorious. It's simply because…

He. Saw. Me.

All my life, from the first moment I took a breath and landed in a preemie palace. 'Til now as I write my final chapter of my *Shit to Sunshine* story, I've been looking for a table to sit at. Where I'm invited without expectation of my perfection. Where I'm welcomed without questioning my pure-ness. Or judging the piles of pure-mess. Where betrayal is butt-kicked out the back entrance. And bravery is welcomed in.

And love. Oh, the love. A song dripping with sweetness sung to my soul. And no matter the intensity of pain, the depth of insanity, the "shitty" shame of my past. I'm loved. And I'm invited. To sit at God's table. Why?

He. Saw. Me. And my friend . . .

He. Sees. You.

El Roi

Epilogue

My hope is to hook. Hook people. Hook their hearts. Draw people through my story to sit at the table with me. To those who desire to come close, I'll gently guide them to the outstretched hand of the Great Shepherd. He's the giver of life, the healer of wounds. The beacon of light out of their wilderness. Out of their darkness. A lighthouse helping guide those drowning to reach shore.

I've trudged through shit so I could truly bask in the "Son shine." He walked with me each step of the way. I will continue to write as He directs. For His glory. And His name is Jesus.

For Daryl

...rue love. All my life, the fairytale fantasy I imagined lay ...side my grasp. No white knight in shining armor came to ...e. My male interactions had only brought pain. I believed ...oken pieces of my life were not fixable. Not acceptable. Not worth gluing together. I was shattered. In shreds. From scars.

Then you entered my life. You have taught me what true love and loyalty look like. What the vow of "in sickness and in health " really means. You loved me when I was just a shell of what God created me to be. You saw me despite my failures. My insecurities. The impenetrable horror chamber of guilt and shame I'd slammed and bolted shut within me. You've been the key that's unlocked my hurt heart; the best of me has emerged and flowed forth. Because of you.

Deep down, I prayed for you. I longed for you. Someone who wouldn't require me to live up to his expectations, to be perfect, to be holier than thou, because we both know that's far from reality. I lived through hell, so I created a hell for you through my hurt. My pain. My misperceptions of your motives. You saw me when I didn't see me. You demonstrated over and over that you loved me unconditionally. No matter how I treated you. No matter my explosive reactions. I didn't have a clue that someone like you truly existed on this planet. That's why I know, beyond a shadow of a doubt, that you were heaven sent.

You used softness, kindness, gentleness, and acceptance to rupture the impenetrable recesses of my heart. Scraping off the scabs, reopening the scars to help them heal and hurt less and less.

Time cannot heal wounds. But a man driven by his desire to seek God's heart can help bind up the wounds, soften their intensity. A man sent by God to embrace me and my messy life. One who entered into a triangled relationship with Jesus at the top connecting the two to become one.

To my Lord, Jesus Christ, and to the man who was sent to love me, I dedicate this book. My shit-to-sunshine story. It's a story of love. Of redemption. Of wholeness. Of completeness. Of a God-purposed life. Saved. Shined up. By the Son.

Acknowledgements

To my beautiful daughter, Sunny. You've truly been my ray of sunshine since the day you took your first breath. Your unconditional love has been an anchor in the stormy waters of life. No matter how forceful the waves crashed against us, they could not rip us apart. I will be forever grateful that God saw fit to give me such a wonderful gift in you.

To my mom, sister Brenda, and dad Raymond. You all molded my life from the beginning. Although you've each left this world at different times, the love I have for each of you will last forever. Thank you for helping to shape the person I am today.

To my daughter in-law, Summer. Your continual gentle nudges of reminders to begin writing my book were purely God using you to encourage me to do what He'd placed in my heart to do. Your reminders were a catalyst for me to overcome the fear and just write.

To my therapist and now friend, Kathryn. I will be forever grateful for the years you spent walking alongside me in my quest for healing. You facilitated the unraveling of twisted twine of my past pain. You encouraged me to tear open the scars and pour self-soothing salve on my wounds. Through your unwavering commitment, I came to believe … I matter.

To my editor and dear friend, Nadia. The meaning of your name … hope … is what you've given me from day one. You believed in me when I didn't believe in myself or my ability to write. You pushed me out of my comfort zone to accomplish much more than I ever thought possible. Most of all, you understood my desire to glorify Jesus and helped me never stray from that vision. My dream to publish this book has become a reality because of you. I'll treasure our friendship forever.

To my editor's sidekick, Lindsay. Thank you for devoting your time and energy to assist in the early stages of chapter editing and development. Your willingness to understand me and my purpose in writing this book gave me such confidence in your work. You handled the messiness of my story with utmost care. For you and your heart, I am most grateful.

About the Author

Raylynn Van Oort was born in San Diego but raised in Montana where she currently resides with her husband, Daryl, and two cats who run the household. Their blended family includes four children, their spouses, and nine grandchildren.

Disability advocacy was her passion and work for over ten years. Her life-changing health transformation sparked her desire to become a health coach. She supports others in attaining freedom from obesity and the physical and emotional mismanagement that caused it.

Now an author and motivational speaker, Raylynn's raw, redemptive story offers a rare insider perspective of survival and liberation to help others trapped in toxicity. Gold nuggets of wisdom were forged in the painful fires of her story providing hope for anyone longing to walk in wholeness after trauma.

Raylynn is known for her loud, joy-filled laughter and hugs her way into everyone's heart. So expect both when you meet her.

Book Club Discussion Questions

1. In what ways are you able to relate to Raylynn's life?

2. Did this book stir up any experiences or pain that you've hidden?

3. Of all the experiences told in this story, what will stay with you the most?

4. What was your relationship like with your mother or father?

5. Has reading *From Sh*t to Sunshine* changed you in anyway? If so, how?

6. Did you find anything inspiring about Raylynn's story?

7. Who in your life should read Raylynn's story? And why?

8. Did this book reveal anything to you about God?

9. What coincidences have you experienced that you see now may have been "God incidences"?

10. When you feel helpless or afraid, do you turn to God and pray? If not, what do you do?

Resources for Help and Support

You are not alone.

If you or someone you know is struggling or in crisis, help is available. **Call or text 988 or chat 988lifeline.org**

National Domestic Violence Hotline:
1-800-799-7233 or text LOVEIS to 22522

National Child Abuse Hotline:
1-800-4AChild (1-800-422-4453) or text 1-800-422-4453

National Sexual Assault Hotline:
1-800-656-HOPE (4673) or Online Chat

Visit **FindTreatment.gov** to help you find a provider for treating substance use disorders, addiction, and mental illness.

Visit the American Psychiatric Association Foundation (**finder.psychiatry.org**) to find a psychiatrist in your area.

Contact the American Academy of Child and Adolescent Psychiatry (**www.aacap.org**) if a child needs psychiatric help.

Visit the American Psychological Association (**locator.apa.org**) to find a psychologist in your area.

www.ingramcontent.com/pod-product-compliance
Lightning Source LLC
Chambersburg PA
CBHW010330030426
42337CB00026B/4879